Two Hearts, One Passion

DICK AND MARY CABELA'S
HUNTING CHRONICLES
with David Cabela

Dick Cabela, Mary Cabela & David Cabela

Mudhead Enterprises LLC
Cabela Publishing LLC
3020 11th Avenue
Sidney, NE 69162

Printed in the United States of America

Cabela Publishing LLC
3020 11th Avenue
Sidney, NE 69162

2005, Sidney, Nebraska

ISBN 0-97555-440-9

Library of Congress Control Number: 2004099435

Cabela, Dick, Mary & David
          Two Hearts, One Passion:
          Dick & Mary Cabela's Hunting Chronicles

1. Hunting -- Africa -- Australia -- US

Book Design and Illustration by Hughes Design LLC

First Edition

10 9 8 7 6 5 4 3 2 1

Acknowledgments

Like all books, Two Hearts, One Passion took a concerted effort from many. David Draper's skills as an editor made this book much better than it would've been otherwise. Jeff & Erin Hughes went beyond the call with the late hours and creative input. Thanks to Cari Wamsley for her hard work and dedication to ensuring our success. Once again, the love and support from Shari, my wife, kept me working hard and reminded me to keep things in perspective. You have all embraced this project and have my deepest gratitude.

- David Cabela

For all the Professional Hunters around the world who have
pushed themselves to help us create lasting memories.
We love you all.

Two Hearts, One Passion

Table of Contents

Foreward

Most outdoor enthusiasts know Dick and Mary Cabela as the founders of Cabela's, The World's Foremost Outfitter. The family, outfitters, guides, professional hunters and friends contained here know them as Mom and Dad, clients and friends. These are the people who have seen them at their finest, and sometimes as their most unguarded selves. This work comes not only from Dick and Mary, but also from those who know them best. Their insights and memories greatly helped to make this possible.

Many of the stories – the details, the successes and failures and the grand adventures contained in the following pages were written down in journals Dick and Mary began writing the first time they went to Africa. These journals were an inspiring glimpse of a married couple who have, without a doubt, lived extraordinary lives both on a professional and personal level. However, these stories are more than just journal entries; they are memories of people and places which have played a significant role in shaping a remarkable pair. Throughout the creation of this project, I had the distinct pleasure to meet some of these excellent people and visit some of those places that can change you forever.

Both their lives began humbly, but what they have done with those modest beginnings equals success by any definition of the word. Although this book deals with their lives as hunters, anglers and conservationists, it gives us an insight into the people they were, the couple they have become and the dreams we can attain, if we are only willing to reach for them. Bear in mind also that although this is my mother and father's story, it is inevitable that part of me will end up on the pages. Much of what I am, after all, is the sum of these two people.

Dick and Mary Cabela have hunted and fished all over the world, but both started young, when the extent of their adventures led them only as far as their feet would take them. Dick grew up in Chappell, Nebraska, a small rural town in the sparsely populated panhandle. Mary spent her childhood years surrounded by the peaks and valleys and the seemingly infinite horizon beyond her home in Casper, Wyoming.

Their paths would eventually cross at St. Patrick's Parochial Academy in Sidney, Nebraska. Long before that – a time which both seems like yesterday and so long ago it might never have existed, they were children, entranced by a natural world as savage and unforgiving as it was beautiful and peaceful. Where they come from and where they have been are important to who they are and where they are going. As children, the endless prairies, the unreachable mountaintops and the rivers that never stopped flowing taught them lessons a book could never teach and gave them a freedom only a child could understand. By following this lifelong passion, they have, in some small way, been able to retain a taste of that freedom they knew when they were young.

–David Cabela

Part One:
The Wild Within

Girl With a Gun: Mary

In my youth, my hometown, Casper, Wyoming, was a town where people hunted. They hunted, not only for pleasure, but for sustenance. Families depended on the animals they killed to supplement their food supply. We were never in danger of starving, but the meat my brother brought home from the field was always a huge help. Hunting was part of living. Not everybody did it, but we all knew its importance.

I understood the inseparable connection between the hunter and prey through need; yet at the same time, a set of circumstances led me to despise that fact of life. You see, I helped raise a Bambi. Its mother had been shot, leaving the fawn to fend for itself. We took it in as our pet. I fed it and loved it like any child would love a puppy or a kitten. I hated hunting; I hated hunters because of what they'd done to my deer's poor defenseless mother. How could anyone be so cruel? I didn't understand, couldn't. My young mind was led by emotion. So that's how it was – hunting and all hunters were bad.

But time and experience cause change. Our Bambi grew fast and I made other friends. It was my best friend, Mary Ann Wiesenberger, and her father, who began to change my mind. They introduced me to hunting in the only way I could truly understand – they took me. I was reluctant at first, but if Mary Ann, my best friend, did it, how could it be all bad? It took a little coaxing, but they finally convinced me to go. So there we were, two shotgun-toting girls chasing rabbits.

The North Platte River was framed by golden hills painted with sagebrush as far as we could see. Cottontails darted in and out of cover like speedy little racers. It wasn't long before I was hooked. Stew made from rabbits we'd shot filled my little heart with pride. I had put food on the table.

One afternoon, we climbed from a canyon and crossed the railroad tracks. I was bringing up the rear, concentrating hard on some nearby bushes, trying to spot a cottontail. I took one step over the first rail and stopped cold. Rattlesnake!

It coiled, threatening my advance with the *rat-a-tat* of its tail. I couldn't move. Whispers in Casper were filled with snakebite victims, but I'd never seen a snake up close before. I was too terrified to move; too scared to call out. I just stared at the deadly reptile and whimpered.

Mary Ann's father, Leroy, must've wondered what was keeping me because he came back just as boredom overcame the snake and it slithered away. He found me pale and on the brink of tears, still standing motionless in the middle of the tracks.

"What's wrong?" he asked.

"There was a huge snake. I didn't know what to do." My bottom lip quivered.

"You did the right thing by remaining calm. Just remember those snakes are as afraid of you as you are of them and you should always give them lots of room."

I nodded, but couldn't believe the snake was anywhere near as afraid as I was. It was an important lesson though. One that has stayed with me – wild animals demand and deserve respect.

I eventually lost contact with Mary Ann. Our lives drifted in different directions, as often happens, but I will always remember those days on the sage-covered hills with her and her father. They'd given me a brief and limited introduction to hunting, but that time in my youth altered how I looked at the world. It was as influential for me as the contours of the earth are to the flow of water. I will forever be grateful.

My brother, Jim, was an avid hunter and fisherman. If he wasn't hunting, he was usually fishing. I don't know how he found time for school and other less-important endeavors. Though Jim sometimes played hooky, it would never occur to the rest of us to skip school in the name of outdoor fun – at least hardly ever. But often was the weekend when my mother, sisters and I would accompany Jim to a small spread just outside of Douglas.

The Conway's lived humble lives of less than meager means. In our eyes, they were rich beyond all comparison. They lived on a parcel of

Mary has always had a passion for hunting, jumping at every chance to head into the field.

land where there was always one animal or another running around the yard – chickens, ducks, pigs, cats, dogs. It was a while before I realized some of the animals weren't pets. It was the Conways and my brother, Jim, who introduced me to the joys of hunting upland birds, in particular, prairie chickens.

"We're going to go get dinner. Want to come?"

Of course I wanted to go. They always made it sound like so much fun and, without exception, returned beaming. I had to find out for myself. Besides, any reason to go for a hike was a good reason. I loved to hike, loved being outside, and even though I acted like I didn't care if we found any birds, deep down I really wanted to shoot one.

"How long does it usually take to find a prairie chicken?" I asked.

"Sometimes it takes a while," the oldest Conway boy said.

Then he swung his shotgun and fired.

"Good shot," Jim said.

"Hey, I thought we were hunting birds. That was a rabbit."

"And a good eating rabbit too. Now we won't have to find as many birds."

"Why not?" I asked.

"Because this here rabbit will feed a couple of us tonight. We get a few birds and we'll have a feast. If we shoot all the birds today, what're we supposed to eat tomorrow?"

I guess that made sense. The Conway's had no way to preserve any extra prairie chickens, so they never shot more than they could eat any particular evening. I thought it was a heck of a way to live, almost romantic. But on the evenings the boys returned without game, dinner was lacking.

Half an hour later, we flushed our first birds. The grass exploded. Both Conway and Jim fired their shotguns, dropping one bird. I never lifted my gun. My heart was racing. The boys turned to see one wide-eyed girl.

"We got one, Mary. Let's go have a look."

We all ran over to the dead prairie chicken. I was the last to arrive. Jim showed it to me before stuffing it into a small bag strapped to his belt.

"So, what'd you think?" he asked.

"They scared me. And you guys were so fast, I wouldn't have had a chance to shoot anyway."

Jim smiled. "So you didn't like it then?"

"Yeah, I liked it. It was really neat, just more than I expected. I mean they're not like the chickens back at the house."

The boys muffled a laugh.

"No they're not anything like those chickens. Those chickens wouldn't be any fun to hunt."

"Not like prairie chickens," I said.

The muscles in my young legs burned by the time we'd scaled enough hills and covered enough ground to flush another prairie chicken. Like before, I was wholly unprepared when it took off. They yelled for me to shoot, but by the time I shouldered my gun it was too late. I shot anyway.

"I'm never going to hit one. They're too fast."

"C'mon," Jim said. "It's getting late. We'll hunt our way back. Be ready – the next bird that flies has your name on it."

The shotgun was heavy, but I held it, barrel up, with both hands. I was darn sure going to be ready the next time a prairie chicken popped up. It was only a little .410 single-shot, but I was just a little girl and my arms strained to hold it. It was almost to the point of being unbearable when another bird flushed, loud and fast. My heart skipped a beat, everything else felt natural. I don't remember shouldering the gun, aiming down the barrel or even pulling the trigger. But I sure remember the sight of my first upland bird folding in mid-air among a flurry of floating feathers.

The boys whooped and hollered. "You got one! You got one!"

I ran over to pick it up. Its body felt warm in my hands.

"It's so beautiful," I said.

"And tasty," the Conway boy said.

I never questioned whether or not he understood the beauty of it all the way I did. I know he did. He just came at hunting from a different perspective than I or many hunters today do. The Conway's hunted, because if they didn't, they didn't eat – plain and simple. I've always enjoyed the taste of wild game, but I don't hunt because I have to eat. Don't get me wrong, I have to hunt, but not because I'll starve if I don't. I have to hunt because it is part of who I am, of who I've always been. I am closely connected to the land by hunting. It is the most intimate and honest relationship a person can have with nature.

I've hunted birds and small game most of my life, but it was Dick's passion for big game that opened my eyes to another type of hunting which would take me around the world with him in search of adventure. I am thankful for that.

Back Yard Bandits: Dick

I can't specifically recall the first time I picked up a gun and headed to the field, nor can I foresee the last. It's been a part of me for as long as I can remember – as important as the air I breathe. It defines me. I've been a lot of things in my life: student, entrepreneur, husband, father. Through it all, I've always been a hunter. I embrace them all – they are me.

As far back as I can remember, it was my brother, Jim, and I, an old .22 pump-action rifle and darting cottontails on a stretch of prairie between the safety of our home at the edge of town and a haunting graveyard with a broken wooden fence. We were two brothers, filled with an awe and wonder rarely found again in a lifetime, eager to put our stamp on the prairie as adventurous hunters.

Mom made us eat breakfast. We devoured it like ravenous dogs. Our plates were flung into the sink for Mom to clean as we raced to the back door, sure to snatch up the old, wood-worn, rusty-barreled .22 on the way out. In the growing distance between our house and our ears, we could sometimes hear the faint voice of our mother hollering for us to be careful. Even if we didn't realize it then, that freedom we were allowed as boys was a freedom we would never match again. It helped to lay the foundation of two independent men.

"Let me shoot first today," Jim said.

Feeling generous, I handed the rifle to my younger brother. If he was going to shoot first, he sure as heck would carry the gun for most of the mile-long trek across wide pastures undulating with small hills that looked like mountains to a couple adventurous boys. Each giant slope was a challenge; reaching the top felt heroic.

The plains we grew up on were treeless and went on forever. Cottontail rabbits, we knew, preferred cover. The only cover we knew of was a small patch of tall grass along the way to the graveyard and the tumbleweed-catching fence of the cemetery itself. We always checked the grass first.

We crawled up the edge of a hill and lay prone overlooking the weed patch.

"If a rabbit is out feeding you take him Jim."

"I can see something moving in there," Jim said.

"What is it?"

"I don't know. It looks kind of big."

Just then something burst from our honey hole.

"Damn, a coyote. Shoot him! Shoot him!"

But it was too late. The predator was moving way too fast. He was too far gone.

"Well, we can forget about any rabbits today."

"What about the cemetery?"

It was almost a dare and came out rather cautiously. And once it was out there, we couldn't turn back.

"Okay, let's go."

We both put on a brave front. In the back of my mind, I saw visions of ghosts and ghouls. It wasn't a place we fancied, but it was chock-full of cottontails. That was more than enough temptation for two budding hunters. So we hiked to the graveyard. The closer we ventured, the slower our steps became.

The wood on the leaning fence had long since grayed. A single, leafless tree overlooking the outside edge cast a mangled shadow upon the few lonely tombstones within the cemetery gates. As always, there seemed to be a dark cloud hovering above it. When we snuck close, it was as much from trepidation as for stalking rabbits. Eventually, we'd settle in and lie in wait for a bold cottontail to scamper away from the broken corner post overgrown by weeds and grass. Sometimes we'd get a rabbit, sometimes we wouldn't, but we were relatively patient for two young brothers. We could wait all day as long as someone didn't show up and scare us away.

"Here comes one. Get ready."

The lone cottontail came out cautious. The tree was a favorite perch for birds of prey to sit waiting for their unsuspecting dinner. We liked them about as much as we liked the coyotes. They were our competitors. Every rabbit they killed for themselves was one less for us. But that doesn't mean we didn't think they were neat. A hawk pouncing on a bunny or a coyote chasing one down was an awesome sight. We may not have liked their competition, but they were the cool animals, the predators. And I guess in a way we felt a sort of kinship with them because we tried to emulate them in our own predatory endeavors.

When Jim shot the rabbit, it performed a spectacular display of back flips and aerial somersaults before giving out a single cry and falling dead.

"You got him! You got him! Great shot Jim."

We sprinted for the cemetery, giving little thought to any ghosts or goblins. We'd conquered the day, the world was ours. The beams from our smiles were surely blinding.

Mom was waiting for us inside when we opened the back door. We were breathing hard and dirty-faced, holding our prize high in the air, proud of our accomplishment – mighty hunters returned.

"Take that thing away from the house before you clean it," she said. "We don't need any more scavengers around here."

It didn't matter much to us. There was never a better tasting meal than one we brought home ourselves. More often than not, we wandered home rabbit-less, but occasionally, when we opened the back door smelling of sweat and grime with giant grins, our mother would run us off to clean it away from the house, but she always cooked it for us. They were the meals of kings. We were Princes of the Plains.

The exact number of times we opened the back door to the fresh air of the Nebraska prairie is irrelevant, but the impact those journeys played in our lives has been everlasting. Some of us are just meant to be hunters. It's impossible to explain, harder to understand. We try by using words such as instinct or atavism, but even they are inadequate. We are called by an unheard voice – a force beyond our comprehension. We follow it because that is who we are. Although unbeknownst to Jim and me at the time, those rabbits would lay a foundation to a lifetime devoted, both personally and professionally, to conservation and the freedom and struggle of the hunt. I am a hunter, plain and simple.

Part Two:
Fuel on the Fire

<u>Ducks and Deer:</u> Dick

"Would you like to go duck hunting tomorrow morning?" One of my father's employees asked one evening as we closed up shop.

Like most teenagers, interests like school, sports, and girls encompassed the greater portion of my time, but rabbits and the untouched beauty of the prairie continued to beckon. I had to make time to hunt and jumped at every opportunity that presented itself.

"Sure," I said. "What time?"

I tried to conceal my excitement by rearranging a few items on the counter that didn't need rearranging. I'd never hunted ducks before, but I often saw them along Lodgepole Creek and was intrigued by water-fowling stories I heard from friends or read about in *Sports Afield, Outdoor Life* and *Field and Stream*. There was one small problem though.

"I can't go," I said.

My head drooped as I headed for the back room to put the broom away.

"Why not?"

I turned around. "I don't have a shotgun. All I got is an old .22. All it's good for is rabbits and coyotes."

"That's okay. You can use one of mine."

My face must've lit up the room. "Really? Thanks."

I couldn't believe anyone could own more than one firearm.

"I'll pick you up at six," he said.

"But I have school at eight."

"If we don't have any ducks by eight, we most likely ain't going to get any. They've been flying pretty early the last few days. Don't worry, you'll be back in time for school."

It was a restless night. I kept turning on my flashlight to check my watch as it inched toward six. The more I checked, the slower it seemed to tick. It finally got to the point when I couldn't wait in bed any longer. By the time my new hunting companion pulled up in front of my parents' home, I was dressed, my boots were tied and I'd been sitting on the front steps waiting in the crisp morning air for well over half an hour.

We snuck along Lodgepole Creek southwest of Chappell as a thin veil of mist rose from the water's surface. The banks had started to change colors, holding just enough shades of green to remind us fall was still in its beginnings. My young eyes were wide from the blood-pumping adrenaline of a new adventure. My hands caressed the contours of the borrowed, yet strangely familiar, shotgun. We crouched down, taking a step only once every few seconds, but the ducks always flew off the water too soon and too far out for a shot.

"Up around this next bend there's usually a few ducks." My co-worker-turned-guide pointed at a low cut bank barely hiding the water's edge.

It was a cool morning, but it wasn't frigid. I wasn't wearing gloves, still my palms began sweating. I could tell we were getting close. My hunting partner's step slowed, his muscles tensed, his breathing became more forced. One slow step at a time, we closed in on the bank. I could just see the water from the creek, but no ducks. We inched closer. More and more of the water came into view. After one more footstep, half a dozen mallards exploded from the shallow creek. I can still see the droplets of water spraying from their feathers and feet.

They were so close, so impressive; I almost forgot why we were there.

I faintly heard the words, "Take 'em" from beside me. More on instinct than practice or skill, I swung the shotgun, focused on a target and fired both barrels. One of the drake's wings folded and it splashed back into the water.

I sprinted for my first duck, floating on the creek's surface.

It was beautiful. The shiny green head, yellow beak and distinctive white stripe circling the neck. The wet feathers gleamed brightly in the morning sun, like sparkling rainbows on dewed grass. I smiled when I rolled it over in my hands. It was a grand introduction to waterfowling for a budding teenage hunter whose hunting adventures had scarcely taken him more than a few miles beyond his boyhood home.

Since then, I've spent immeasurable hours sitting in waterfowl blinds. I've shot a few ducks and geese and missed a few more, but I remember that first jump-shot mallard every time I find myself near a creek or river on a cold, misty morning, waiting for the sun to rise, filled with the hope that waterfowl will soon fill the sky.

After high school, I continued my formal education at Regis College (now Regis University) in Denver, Colorado. While diligently concentrating on my studies, I met fellow student Hugh Duncan, whose family owned a ranch near Douglas, Wyoming. Our love of hunting, fishing and the outdoors laid the foundation to a close friendship that has lasted through many years and many miles. It was Hugh who introduced me to big-game hunting.

"I'm going home to hunt mule deer this weekend. You want to come?"

Did I want to come? He knew the answer before he asked the question.

"Do you have a rifle?"

Uh oh. I kept running into this same problem.

"Nothing but an old pump .22 and that's in Chappell."

"That's not a problem. You can use mine."

It was too generous.

"What will you use?"

"I'll use it when you're done. And if I don't, it's no big deal. I've shot plenty of deer."

Plenty of deer? He was my age. Both of us still wet behind the ears. How could he have shot plenty of deer? I'd never shot even one. Though Hugh was not one to stretch the truth, I had a hard time believing "plenty of deer" meant more than one or two. But I was going deer hunting, and that was something.

I've always been a heavy sleeper, but at Hugh's place the night before the hunt, like the night before my first duck hunt, rest came in short, fitful minutes. Long before first light, when Hugh came to tell me it was time to get ready, I sprung from the sleeping bag, throwing on my gear with the speed of an army recruit one week into basic training who'd overslept.

Thirty minutes later, I found myself hiking up a sage-covered hill under the orange-yellow glow of the sunrise as it slowly inched across the amber hills of Wyoming. The morning dew sparkled. I tried desperately to take it all in. I was hunting mule deer in Wyoming. Was I lucky or what?

We crept up to a large overhang and peered over the edge into a deep, open valley. Stretching my neck, I still couldn't see beneath the

Dick's first try at big-game hunting bagged him a mule deer buck. He was hooked forever.

cliff's lip. I scanned the entire area for anything resembling a deer. It didn't appear as if there were deer for miles and miles.

"There's deer under here right now," Hugh said.

"You can't even see down there."

"Yeah, but I know they're down there. If they're not out in the valley, this is where they usually are."

"You're so full of it. They could go anywhere out here. There's no way you could know if there's deer right below us."

"Gimme the gun," he said.

He chambered a shell and fired into the air. A mini stampede of mule deer followed the echo. As if straight out of the cliff beneath us, a herd of around thirty deer bolted for the tree-covered hill across the valley, disappearing into the shadows.

"How'd you..."

"Wait, here comes one back out. It looks like a buck." Hugh handed the rifle back to me.

"Should I shoot him?"

He let out a puff of air through his nose and shrugged, surely amused by this tenderfoot. "Sure, I guess."

I scooted into the prone position, steadying the rifle like I had so many times on rabbits back in Chappell with my .22. It seemed far, but this was a big target and the bullet was larger, more powerful. The buck stood just outside the tree line, looking in our direction like he was a little confused. I remembered everything the cottontails and coyotes had taught me. A slight breeze tickled my cheek, but I ignored it. I could no longer hear the birds or the trickling sound of a nearby stream. The world had compressed to just me and the deer. My concentration was so intense, I don't remember squeezing the trigger. That part had become purely natural.

The rifle bucked at my shoulder. The mountain seemed to vibrate. And the deer fell.

"Damn it!"

"What?" I was a little shocked at my friend's outburst.

"I didn't think there was any way in hell you were going to hit that deer from this far. Now we have to climb down there and pack it out." He pushed himself up off the rocky ground and slapped me on the shoulder. "Hell of a shot, by the way. Unbelievable."

He shook his head as he went to find a path down the steep mountainside. So much for the tenderfoot.

The truth is, it was more luck than anything else – but don't tell Hugh.

Cabela's, the Beginning: Dick and Mary

Within a year after we married, we moved back to Chappell. Dick went back to work for his father as manager of the family furniture store and together we worked on raising a fast-growing family that would reach nine children. How we found time to start and grow a business is beyond us. But we worked hard, struggled at times, and yes, even found a few minutes here and there for outdoor pursuits. In fact, Dick squeezed it in, even in small increments.

"Jim and Jerry and I are going to try to hunt ducks in the morning. Will you be okay with the kids?" Dick asked.

"I don't know how you have time to go hunting and then get to the furniture store to open by 7:30. But yes, I'll be fine."

"The ducks don't fly for very long anyway. Besides if I happen to get some at the last minute, I'll just put them in back and clean them over my lunch – unless you want me to drop them off here for you to clean."

"Oh, no. If you're going to have the fun hunting them, you're going to clean them too. I'll tell you what though. I'll cook them if you bring them home – after you clean them."

"Deal."

So if he was lucky, Dick got to hunt for an hour or so early in the morning sometimes before work. It was better than nothing. He cut it

Some of our fondest memories revolve around time spent together in the field.

close a few times. A. C., his father, was not a happy camper if the store opened late, but if the air was alive with ducks or a small flock was circling their blind along the South Platte River, Dick just couldn't pull himself away.

We founded Cabela's in 1961 when we started selling hand-tied fishing flies through the mail from our home. We had little in profits and success was still far from certainty. It was imperative for Dick to keep his job at the furniture store in order to provide for our growing family. Time for hunting was limited, but passions have a way of making us find time and we loved the outdoors – fishing, camping, hiking, wildlife viewing, and of course, hunting. We did what every dedicated outdoor enthusiast does – we made time.

Many autumn Sunday afternoons we would take a break from filling orders for our new company, pack dinner, load the kids in the station wagon and cruise out of town on gravel roads to fields where we had permission to hunt pheasants.

"No, you go ahead and go first this time," Mary would say. "Maybe I can get the kids to take a nap. Then you can watch them while I give it a go. I just like to watch sometimes anyway. Good luck honey."

We'd kiss and Dick would hit the field. One man, without a dog, in a huge field was tough hunting, but beggars can't be choosers. At least we were hunting. Occasionally a rooster would flush. Sometimes when everything was right, when the bird flew into a hard wind and the gun floated to the target smoothly, we'd have pheasant for dinner. We don't like to admit it, but we went home pheasant-less more often than not.

As Cabela's grew from our kitchen table, sales reps eventually considered this small mail-order outfit out on the Plains worth calling on. Most of the good salesmen knew in order to get us excited about their gear, they had to get us to use it. So the reps would call to tell us they had a great new product we really should be selling and they'd like to come show it to us. We'd say great, bring it on down, we'll give it a try. Don't forget your shotgun and if you have a good dog, bring it as well. And just like that, we started our famous field-testing program.

We were putting so much time into growing Cabela's, it was amazing we made it out hunting or fishing at all. But how could we be expected to sell outdoor equipment if we didn't go out to test it once in a while? So we went to the cornfields and the rivers and the lakes, followed dogs and blew warm breath on our fingertips in goose blinds as often as we could. Those brief excursions with sales reps created lasting relationships and friendships that helped elevate our humble company into The World's Foremost Outfitter.

We closed many business deals after the invigorating cackle of a flushed pheasant or after a dozen Canada geese circled to our calls before setting their wings to drop toward an open spot in the decoys. After all, it's much easier to conduct business when your blood is pumping from excitement as opposed to fear and the face looking back at you is wearing a smile.

We grew Cabela's by taking calculated risks, nurturing a concept we believed in and surrounding ourselves with intelligent, talented people who knew the products and shared our belief in customer service. All our great ideas have been grand in possibilities, yet simple in infancy.

In the end, Cabela's fed off an entrepreneurial spirit and a collective passion for the outdoors. What we were able to accomplish with a handful of dollars and a ton of hard work has surpassed all our expectations, but that's what it's all about – reaching for goals and attaining dreams.

A Recurve in My Hand: Dick

"I think I'm going to try bow hunting," I said to Mary one evening.
"Wouldn't a rifle be easier?"
"Maybe, but we can't afford a rifle. Besides, I know where to get a good deal on a new recurve." I winked at my wife.

It would be a few years before we'd sell rifles at Cabela's, but our archery line had been growing rapidly. The truth was, we could barely

Jim Cabela, Warren Childs, Dick and Howard Penny shared many successful days in the field. Some of the best friendships are formed in the outdoors.

afford a recurve even if we bought it from ourselves, but I'd been itching for another deer hunt for some time. There was something about big-game hunting that was utterly alluring to me. I couldn't quite put my finger on it, but I'd had a taste and I wanted more. Maybe it was the adventure of it, maybe it was the intimacy with a single creature, maybe it was the challenge, the quest – maybe. I didn't know then and can't define it to this day. I just wanted more of whatever it was.

My brothers, Jim and Jerry, had about as much experience big-game hunting as I had, but when opening morning rolled around, they were eager to join me on my first bow hunt.

"I'm going to try sitting in that tree at the end of the draw where we've seen that buck wander through. You guys will probably have the best luck if you stay just inside the tree grove. They use that trail over there quite a bit."

"Good luck," they said.

"Thanks; you too."

It was a cool morning, I could see my breath with each exhale. My fingers were starting to freeze. I told myself it was good for the hunting, suck it up. With considerable effort, I'd pulled myself into the tree. I made my way up to the thick fork and leaned against the trunk – then I waited. I couldn't see my brothers, but knew they were somewhere in the trees, just as cold as I was – and their hearts were pumping just as rapidly.

Through the pre-dawn haze a mule deer buck appeared, sneaking down a game trail. The wind was in my favor, but the buck approached slowly, cautiously, its sonar-like ears making regular rotations, listening for signs of danger. I didn't dare move. The deer jerked its head back like it heard something – maybe Jim or Jerry. I didn't know and didn't have time to care what caused the deer to move at a more brisk walk, slightly less cautious. With effortless grace, he slipped around a tree and hopped over a fallen branch, stopping broadside in easy range.

I drew back the string slow and quiet, held for a brief second and released. The arrow zipped through the air and imbedded itself in the deer's shoulder. The shot was too far forward, the shoulder bone preventing the blades from penetrating. The buck reached back with his mouth, pulled the arrow out and took off under a fence, running to another group of trees nearby.

Jim and Jerry both saw the deer crash into the trees and pinpointed the spot. The three of us, fairly new to bow hunting and big-game hunting in general, came up with a plan to find the wounded animal and put it down as quickly as possible.

"You think it will work?"

"You got any better ideas?"

In point of fact, nobody had a better idea.

"We'll go around to the other side of the tree grove and get way out in front of him, maybe make a little noise and try to hold his attention. As long as we don't move in too close and stay in sight, he should keep his eye on us. Just be careful when you try to sneak up on him."

I gave my brothers ample time to gain the deer's full attention before beginning a sneak from behind. I spotted the deer right away. Like we'd hoped, it was watching Jim and Jerry. My impatience fought each soft, slow step, but caution won out and I somehow found myself within fifteen yards without detection.

I pulled back on the bowstring again, a barely audible *ssss* whispered when the arrow's shaft slid along the shelf of the bow. The deer's ear twitched and rotated, but it didn't turn its focus from Jim and Jerry. There was little of the deer exposed above the tall weeds. I couldn't even see his back clearly. I focused all my concentration and held my breath with the string at my cheek for a split second before I let it fly. The broadhead slammed into the back of the deer's neck and he folded.

Jim and Jerry were hollering, waving their arms and rushing toward me. I believe I was smiling, but was surprised we'd actually pulled it off. It took me longer to go my fifteen yards to the downed buck than it took my brothers to sprint across the entire field.

"Great shot," Jim said. He shook my hand while Jerry slapped me on the back.

The bull elk often eludes hunters, but it's hard not to have fun in elk camp.

It was then that it hit me – I'd just successfully hunted a deer with a bow for the first time. I think I stood a little taller that day. As my brothers and I field dressed that deer and packed it back to Chappell, we knew with certainty that it had indeed been a good day.

With regular practice, I eventually became a decent bowman. For years, the bow was my weapon of choice for big game. We eventually moved to Sidney, thirty miles west of Chappell, because it offered better growth opportunities for Cabela's. As our company grew, so did our employee base. Most of our new employees were enthusiastic anglers and hunters. It was only natural that some of us would occasionally get together for a few days and step out into the field in order to test new products and confirm their quality.

On one trip, I found myself with my brother, Jim, and two of our employees, Mike Wieser and Rick Bouldin, in the Colorado mountains, clad in camouflage, sneaking through the valleys and up the peaks in search of the majestic, elusive Rocky Mountain elk.

It had been a slow first day without a glimpse of wildlife larger than a cottontail, let alone an elk. My feet were dragging on the hike back to camp. I was tired and focused on one thing– getting back to camp for a bite to eat – when I nearly had a heart attack as a small group of spruce grouse exploded from under my feet. I almost dropped my bow, but recognized the game bird immediately as they landed beneath a blue spruce.

The idea of a fresh, succulent, juicy, dark grouse breast sounded much better than the salty, dried jerky and runny canned food we packed in. I couldn't resist. They were nervously milling about and seemingly felt safe from the slow bipedal fellow slinking in the shadows. I was able to close the gap with minimal effort, surprising myself almost as much as the closest grouse when the arrow sliced straight through the bird. It dropped where it stood. His buddies took off, but like clueless dodos, didn't go far. I might've been able to take another, but I didn't want to impede the soaring confidence in my marksmanship – I could've missed. Besides, it was still a ways back to camp. I didn't want to take more than I could carry.

I ambled into camp with just enough time to light a fire and prepare my kill for the frying pan. My companions trickled in as the butter melted, looking beat – in more ways than one.

"Tough hunting today, huh?" I asked.

"Yeah, we didn't even hear a bugle. Not a peep all day."

"Maybe we'll have better luck tomorrow."

"Whatchya got there? Smells good."

"Spruce grouse. I shot him on the way in. Figured we could use some fresh meat," I said, proud of my feat.

"How you cooking it?" Rick asked.

"I just cut it up and threw it on the skillet with some butter."

"I know a better way."

"Yeah, how's that?"

"I'll go shoot one tomorrow and show you."

I shrugged. "Sounds good to me." I don't recall any complaints that night and there was nothing left of the bird after dinner.

The following evening we all stumbled into camp – skunked again. All but Rick, who had, as promised, returned holding a grouse by the legs. He plucked it while Jim, Mike and I started the fire and relaxed, pleased to have fresh food again and a self-proclaimed master chef to boot. We didn't say a word when Rick approached the fire. It soon became apparent he'd exaggerated his culinary skills. We didn't say a word, but we could hardly stifle a laugh. With a stick shoved into the bird's body, Rick smiled, held it over the fire and slowly started turning it.

"We're going to be eating good tonight. This is the only way to cook a grouse. None of them fancy pans and fatty butter. Mmm." He even licked his lips.

Soon, we were all gathered in our big, white wall tent, cautiously eager for a bite.

Rick ate most of the bird himself.

After a small taste and too tired to cook for ourselves, we opted for a few pieces of deer jerky.

"You guys don't know what you're missing. This is good."

To Rick's credit, he devoured the bird. I guess his idea of fine dining was a tad different than ours.

It had been a hard day on the mountain and, with semi-full stomachs, sleep was sure to come quickly. I'd finished my last bite of jerky and pushed myself to my feet.

"Where you going?"

"I better go water the bushes; they're looking a little peaked."

I took a final drink of water from my tin cup before slipping out the tent to relieve myself. When I returned a few minutes later the others had finished their meal and were cleaning up.

"I can't believe we haven't even heard a bugle or seen a cow," Mike said. "I've never seen it this slow up here before."

"Maybe it's the weather," I said. "It'll probably be better tomorrow."

"Yeah, maybe, but I wouldn't hold your breath."

"Shh," Rick waved his hand at us to stifle our conversation. "What was that?"

"What was what?"

"Shh, there it is again."

We all heard it that time, faintly at first, then with more force. The unmistakable, almost eerie, bugle of a bull elk off in the distance.

Their faces lit up. Hope and anticipation of tomorrow suddenly filled the tent. Nobody said anything for a few moments. Their eyes and smiles made words unnecessary. With rejuvenated energy, a serious discussion on the next day's strategy soon began. I almost felt bad – almost.

"What the hell are you laughing about, Dick?"

I stood up, didn't even try to hold back the grin, pulled the tent flap back and walked outside. Three perplexed stares followed me.

When I returned, I was holding a small black device.

"What are you doing with that?"

I pushed a button on the tape player and the sound of a bugling elk filled the tent.

I'm not sure they fully appreciated the humor of the situation; I was the only one laughing. I don't remember if any of us took an elk that year, but the camaraderie we shared around the mountain campfire is unforgettable.

Cabela's continued to expand and our family grew by the year, demanding more time and limiting the minutes in my day. Less time on my hands prevented me from dedicating the hours of practice archery requires. I couldn't give up hunting if I wanted to, but I couldn't continue to bow hunt with un-honed archery skills. The risk of missing, or worse, wounding an animal would be too great. To be proficient with a bow and arrow require more hours of target range preparation than I could commit with a growing business and a growing family competing for my attention. I bit the bullet and took up rifle hunting. Now, the rifle also involves a multitude of time to develop and refine, but to a lesser extent than more primitive hunting methods.

I remember the last deer I took with a bow. Although not a trophy buck, it had tender steaks that were complemented with a glass of red wine at the dinner table.

I was hunting in a draw south of Sidney with Dennis Highby, who, many years later, would rise to CEO of Cabela's. We'd scouted the area four consecutive afternoons before opening day. Each evening deer began to trickle from a cornfield like silent ghosts just before the sun dimmed. The deer used two points of exit, hanging along the edge of the last corn row before venturing into the open.

I positioned myself at one exit point while Dennis stood guard at the other. An hour later my eyelids were drooping and a chill breeze was working its way down my neck. Then there it was – a small flash of gray. Then nothing. Maybe I was dreaming. I waited another few minutes, staring into the corn. Just as my vision was blurring, a doe's head popped into the open, testing the air with her nose. She was twenty yards downwind, standing broadside when she stepped from the corn. I cranked back on the bow and released. The string sounded a gaudy twang, shattering the tranquility of the crisp evening air. The deer sprung in alarm, turning back for the cover of the corn as the arrow arrived. The two-bladed tip almost hit the black end of the deer's tail as it sliced into her backside. Damn.

Anyone who's hunted for any extended period has, at one time or another, wounded game. It's not an enjoyable situation, but it's a reality. One bad experience makes the hunter better understand the importance of extensive shooting practice. Sometimes, though, it's truly beyond your control. You may have shot well, but unforeseen variables can quickly turn a perfect hunt into a disaster. Any person worth squat would also fulfill his or her duty to expend all energies to find the injured creature.

I needed help. So I hollered for Dennis.

"What's going on Dick? Did you shoot a deer? I heard one crashing through the corn."

"Yeah, I think I wounded a doe. She jumped the string. The arrow hit her right in the butt. It looked like it might've gone in pretty far though. You never know." I shrugged.

The moon and stars replaced the sun as our only source of light by the time we picked up the blood trail. Fortunately, we'd packed flashlights along. We scanned the prairie for clues of the deer's condition and whereabouts and were nearly ready to call it a night. We convinced

The last deer Dick took with his recurve was a doe trying to sneak from a cornfield.

each other to go just a little further.

"There." Dennis pointed with his flashlight. It was too late – the deer bounded off. We followed the blood trail one more time only to have the deer bolt again.

"It's too dark," Dennis said.

"Yeah, if we keep pushing her, she'll be impossible to find."

"We should let her lie down. Come back at first light. Hopefully, before the coyotes get here. It sucks to leave, but if we don't, I'm afraid we'll push too hard and she'll be long gone. At least as it is, we have a pretty good idea where to look in the morning."

With reluctance and heavy hearts, we postponed the search until first light. It's like folding a monster hand in poker. You hate to do it, but sometimes it's just the right thing to do.

Sleep came hard. I couldn't get the deer out of my head. Would we beat the coyotes? Would we find it in the morning? Did I shoot too soon? I pondered these questions all night while my stomach churned. An hour before dawn, we pulled on our boots, determined to find the deer. The pre-sunrise glow shadowed clear vision. Cool air tickled our cheeks as we approached the point where we backed off the night prior.

"As long as she didn't circle back into the corn, we should be able to find her," I said. We were both scanning the horizon with our binoculars.

"I think I see something over there on the next hill." Dennis lowered his binos and pointed.

"Let's go check it out."

We hiked the few hundred yards down into the draw, maneuvering around yucca plants and cactuses. On the way, the morning brightened and the heaped form we'd seen through our optics began to take the definitive shape of a deer. We approached slowly at first, careful not to spook her. As we narrowed the gap and started up the other slope of the shallow vale, it became apparent the deer wasn't going anywhere. The arrow penetrated deep enough to hit vitals and predators hadn't caught the scent yet.

"Thank God we found her. I was worried some coyotes might get here first."

"Congratulations Dick."

Dennis shook my hand. I could see he was as relieved as I was.

"Thanks," I said.

And that was enough.

I think I still have that recurve somewhere in the storeroom. Maybe someday I'll pull it out if I'm not too old by then.

Summer Fishing: Mary

There's a funny thing about time. Whether you want it to or not, it changes things. Sometimes for the better, sometimes not. But these things are inescapable – time and change.

Dick loved hunting big game, but the needs of nine children and the demands of the company had us stretched thin. Our other passions were essentially put on hold. It wasn't easy, but we were at a point in our lives when the first thing sacrificed was free time. So how do you confront such a dilemma? We decided to integrate family time with the joyful hardships of outdoor endeavors. Summer family trips began finding us in fewer crowded, smog-infested theme parks and in more forests crowded with trees and lakes and streams loaded with fish.

Luckily, one of our favorite fishing destinations was just down Highway 30. Most people around the country have probably never heard of Lake McConaughy, but for us it's more than just a recreational destination. It's like a second home – filled with more family memories than almost any other place we know. We loved it and the kids loved it. Whenever we were there, we could count on lots of smiles.

The lake is large enough that fishing from a boat made the most sense. So our first seafaring vessel was a huge pink pontoon Dick and I built from a kit. We spent hours and hours on the weekends building that boat. In reality, it was nothing more than a few 50 gallon drums bolted and bracketed to a few wooden planks. There were benches and rails, but that's essentially all it was. It wasn't elegant, but it was practical. We could fit the whole family comfortably. We spent many enjoyable days on the water – some more enjoyable than others.

A stiff wind or an unexpected storm (both common in Nebraska) can turn the 35,000-acre lake into a churning cauldron of danger in the blink of an eye.

"That cloud's looking a little dark over there," Fred, my brother-in-law, said.

"Almost black, isn't it?" Dick said. "We better head in. We don't want to be stuck out here when it hits. Especially with all the kids." There were ten children on board, seven of ours, three of Rita and Fred's.

"Yeah, fishing's been slow today anyway."

Just then, one of the rods jerked.

"Fish on!" I grabbed the reel to set the hook. Everyone perked up from their sluggish state. "Oh, oh. That rod over there has one too."

Our son, Chuck, sprang to the rod. Before long we were both fighting big, fat walleye. They were in the five pound range – good-eating walleye.

"Think we have time for another pass?" Fred asked.

"I don't know. Wind's starting to pick up. Maybe just one more. A heavy bite might be starting," Dick said.

Enthusiasm among the passengers was at its highest level of the day. Quick action can sometimes cause fisherman to forget smart thinking.

We'd barely put the lines back in the water when the wind let us have it. We tried to keep trolling our worm-baited spinners for a few more minutes – tried to ride it out through just one more pass over the hot spot. Waves crashed against the 50-gallon barrels we used for floats, spraying water all over the wooden deck. We were all drenched. Running the motor at trolling speed, we were at the mercy of the lake. Dick couldn't keep the boat in line. We tangled the lines, tested our sea legs and held on for dear life.

"All right. That's it," Dick finally said over the wind. "Reel 'em up. We're going in."

Carolyn was a toddler at the time. She was on the floor sleeping in her life jacket before the waters started to rough us up. Then she was screaming, making sure we could hear her over the racket. Some of the other kids seemed a little nervous and Rita and I were nearing hysteria. And then there was Chuck. He was standing at the front of the boat whooping it up, laughing every time a wave crashed over the bow and slammed into him.

"Sit down, Rich-Dan-Chuck – whatever your name is. And for goodness sakes, put your life vest back on."

I had my hands full with the younger kids and it was all Dick could do to control the boat, so Chuck mostly ignored me. Teenagers. He did throw his life jacket on loosely, but he didn't sit down.

Waves crashed, splashed and thrashed against our watercraft. Somehow she held together, but it was getting rougher by the minute. I tried to hold Cari tight. One of the younger children slipped and bumped his head and started to cry. Little arms wrapped around my waist. With all the water spraying into my face, I could hardly see who it was. I peered ahead, trying to see how far we were from shore. It seemed so distant. Sometimes a big wave would pick us up so quickly and violently, I prayed we wouldn't flip over.

It was another fifteen minutes before we were almost to the beach. Everything was soaked. The tractors were busy pulling in other boats. We honked our horn and waited our turn. Most of the other boats were smaller vessels that were able to zip right up onto their respective trailers. Not so for the corpulent, flat-nosed pontoon boat loaded with passengers, ten of which were children. The wind pushed us from the trailer four times before the man on the tractor waved us off.

"This isn't going to work," he screamed over the wind and waves. "Try taking her into the cove. Shouldn't be so rough in there." He pointed to a nearby cove surrounded by trees.

Fred gave him a thumbs up. "If we can get in there, we should be able to tie up until this blows over," he said to Dick.

"We're getting off first," Rita and I said almost simultaneously.

"I'll get you as close as I can. You'll have to wade a little ways to the beach."

"I don't care how I get off this lake; we're not staying one minute longer."

The older kids jumped right off and swam into shore. Fred helped Rita and I with the younger kids, then he and Dick turned the boat around, cranking up the speed right into the waves. The wind and waves fought against their advance. They had to top her out just to make progress. This seemed to anger the wind. It blew a massive wave straight at them. They didn't back off and the wave hit them head on, immediately swallowing the front of the boat. From shore, it looked as if they'd sink. Water rushed over the floor, carrying all the gear to the back of the boat. Most of it was saved by the back railing, but a few items were lost forever. With water up to his knees, Dick backed off the throttle until they popped up to the surface. After the next wave, he made his turn and rode it toward the cove. We hurried over to meet them.

"We're not keeping this boat, Dick."

"What?"

"We're getting a different boat. This is too dangerous."

"It's fine," he said. "This was just a fluke."

"It's always like this when it's rough. I don't care. I'm not getting back on this boat."

And I never did.

We sold it and bought a deck boat. Still large enough for our growing family to fit on and more solidly built. I don't know if it would've been much more seaworthy in that kind of tempest, but it felt safer.

Then one stormy evening, a barrage of dark coal-like clouds billowed in with an impressive show of thunder, lightning and wind that would make a tornado proud. The storm's arrival forced us to speed to the beach, tie up the boat and head for cover. The following dawn opened the day with such a soothing peace and tranquility, the night's violence was hardly remembered. But the storm wouldn't be forgotten so easily. It appeared as if our deck boat had been swept away, but we soon discovered the squall had sunken the family watercraft. It was buried under three feet of sand and lake. We spent a long weekend digging it out, but found it would be more sensible to buy a new boat than repair the shipwreck.

We spent many summer weekends along the sandy shores of Lake McConaughy trolling for walleye. The water level and the boat which carried us changed every so often, but the quality family time and biting fish always kept the days refreshing. Occasionally, when the sun's heat burned the color of the skin lobster red and the fish wouldn't cooperate, the kids would become restless. Bored kids are often the main ingredient for mishap pie.

The boat had become a massive Bayliner with a small cabin and a cushion in the hollow hull that passed for a bed, although sleep was often difficult, especially in rough water. Dick and I, our three youngest, Joe, David, Cari and a couple of their friends were out on the water one slow, hot day. The kids often wanted to refresh themselves in the cool water of the lake on blistering fishless days. We had two downriggers and four lines rigged with walleye lures and bait. Dick was reluctant to stop the boat, raise the downriggers, reel in the lines and let the kids take a quick dip just to put everything back out again. The Bayliner had a step ladder which hung off the back and Dick compromised by allowing the kids to dangle their feet in the cool, glistening water.

Sometimes when Mom and Dad weren't looking, they would, one-by-one, immerse themselves, holding onto the ladder while the boat pulled them behind as we slowly trolled along. Eventually, they became more daring and loosened their tight grips on the ladder. A game of who could let go for the longest, before swimming to catch up with the boat, would soon commence. Fortunately, there was no danger from the prop, with the trolling motor way on the other side of the boat. The need to test themselves and the cockiness of youth soon caused one of them to let themselves float too far behind the boat to catch up.

Joseph swam hard for as long as his arms could endure, but fatigue seized him before he could draw near enough to grab on to the dangling ladder. Being the good siblings they were, the other kids let him drift by the fishing lines before mustering up the courage to tell their father, concentrating on holding the best course for intercepting fish, he was going to have to reel in all the lines and turn the boat around to rescue his youngest son.

"Oh my God, Dick!" I said. "Joe's in the water."

"What?" Dick glanced back. "Hurry, everyone reel in a rod," he said, lunging to raise the downriggers.

He cursed under his breath as Joe leisurely treaded water, waiting for us to turn around to pick him up. He was fine, but the ladder became off limits for the remainder of the year.

Cabela's continued to enjoy a sustained level of growth. Although responsibilities had dug deep trenches in our lives, many of the everyday duties were comfortably passed on to competent management allowing us to find a little more time for leisure. Our summer family vacations began taking us further from the plains of Nebraska. By the time only three children remained at home, our trips had found us in exotic far away places like the Alagnak River in Alaska and Mexico's Baja Coast.

The family trip for 1986 was a deep sea fishing expedition off the shores of Cabo San Lucas, Mexico. Dick and I brought along our teenagers, Joe, David and Cari, as well as our son Dan, who was attending the University of Texas in Austin. We rented a cozy villa and chartered a fishing boat with a two-man crew for the week. We specifically hoped to catch a few giant blue marlins, but soon discovered wishes don't always come true.

The heat of the thick air was oppressive and the giant swells on the open water wreaked havoc on the motion sickness sensitive. It didn't take long for some of the kids to hang their heads over the side to add their breakfast to the ocean.

"I doubt if that's a good source of chum," Dick said.

"Yeah," Dan said. "I think you guys are scaring every fish for miles."

The first day was unnervingly sluggish. Half of us were drenched in sweat, staring blankly behind the rocking boat with sporadic hopeful glances at the rod tips, while the other half were vomiting off the starboard side or passed out from medication designed to keep them from losing their meals.

Just when it seemed the sun had cooked all the energy from the entire boat, a rejuvenating *zzzzz!* signaled a fish had taken the bait and was racing away with it. The short, stocky deck hand jammed the rod into the rod holder on the chair Dan happened to occupy at the moment. He yelled at Dan with the entire three-words of English he knew motioning for Dan to crank the reel.

"Beeeg Feeesh! Beeeg Feeesh! Weeel! Weeel!"

Dan cranked on the reel handle with everything he had while the tall, heavy captain jerked his ship into reverse and encouraged Dan with the extent of his English.

"Weeel! Weeel! Beeeg Feeesh! Beeeg Feeesh!

The fish thrashed and jumped once, water splashing white all around it. Both men continued to supply Dan with their frantic words of instruction as he watched the boat back right by the marlin, the line from the end of his rod following to the bow. When the line slackened, the big fish spit out the lure with ease.

"What just happened?" Dan asked his father.

Dick shrugged. "I guess that one got by him. You can keep the chair if you want."

"No, I had my chance. Let someone else sit. Why don't you take it?"

"Maybe later, after all you kids have had a turn."

"Well, I guess since Cari's sick and David's sleeping, it's your turn Joe," Dan said, hopping from the seat.

Joe jumped in eagerly. The sudden action had revitalized him. He followed the surface lure intently for forty-five minutes before the boiling heat began to melt his expectations once again. But the chair was his. He wasn't going to miss his chance so he stayed put, occasionally pulling his bare back and legs from the sticky leather – our kids didn't need to sit on towels because they were tough.

Over an hour later, another marlin hit. It leapt, whipping itself between the sky and ocean, like a flag on a windy day. Seemingly convinced the new fisherman hadn't heard their prior instructions, the two crewmen repeated themselves, sporting huge grins the entire time the fish was hooked.

"Beeeg Feeesh! Beeeg Feeesh! Weeel! Weeel!"

Compelled to keep Joe informed of his duties and the size of the marlin, the captain backed right by the billfish once again. The great fish freed itself as soon as it was in front of the boat. Disappointed, Joe stepped down from the seat while the two crew members conversed in their native tongue.

"I knew I should've paid more attention in Spanish class," Dan said.

We all knew a little, but the truth was we only knew a few more words of Spanish than the two-man crew knew of English.

"If we knew what they were saying we might be able to figure out if we're doing something wrong," Joe said.

"I don't think the fish is supposed to get in front of the boat like that," I said.

"It's not," Dick said. "We've been deep sea fishing a few times and I don't ever recall the captain doing that intentionally. They have to back into them some and go forward sometimes too. It's tough to keep an eye on the fish and maneuver the boat at the same time. The captain's job is the most important. You may think your doing all the work in that chair, but he's working just as hard. Sometimes the fish just go where they want to. I wouldn't worry about it."

The remainder of the afternoon proved to be as fishless as the morning. We returned to shore a little discouraged, but not without hope. We weren't beat yet.

Out a little late the next morning, the captain sped toward a gathering of other fishing boats. The shoreline became nothing but a hazy brown horizon.

"Look at all those boats," David said.

"I don't see anybody catching fish. Probably just like back home where two boats in one spot turn into fifty boats in the same place and nobody's catching anything," Dick said. "Hopefully, our captain isn't just following the crowd."

Sure enough, morning went by and we not only didn't hook a fish, we never saw another boat with any action either. A several hundred-pound billfish leaping behind a nearby ship is hard to miss. One by one the boats gave up on the crowded spot and zoomed off.

The swells grew and before long they were much higher than the boat. Huge waves in the middle of a massive body of water, stuck on an all-of-the-sudden miniscule fishing boat, gave us land-lovers a lonely feeling. We could no longer see the shore's outline and the only time we saw another boat was when one happened to be at the top of a swell at the same time we were. Sickness soon set in for a couple of the kids again.

The portly captain eventually gave up on the area. Nobody could remember exactly when, but at one point the swells gave way to flat, smooth, utterly peaceful water, dancing with sparkles under the midday sun. The stout deck hand suddenly barked something in Spanish to the captain, prompting him to cut the engine and stumble to the stern of the boat. He briefly peered over the edge. Both men lunged for two rods that had been lying unused in the corner. They dropped the already tied lures in the ocean, thrust the rods into Dan and David's hands and pointed into the water.

"Beeeg Feeesh! Weeel!"

Joe stretched his neck over the stern. "Look at all those fish!"

We all crowded to the back of the boat. Twenty feet below the surface of the clear water were thousands of tuna – a seemingly endless school of fish. The two crewmen frantically changed lures on the other two rods while Dan and David fought to land their fish. When the captain and deckhand finished re-rigging the other lines, they lowered the spoons into the mass of tuna. They barely had time to hand the rods to Cari and Joe before Dan and David had their fish up to the boat. By the time they gaffed both tuna and threw the lure back into the water, Joe and Cari were bringing their fish in. Dick and I sat back smiling.

This went on for over thirty minutes before their arms began to waver. The boat was filling with fish, 10-20-30, but the two crewmen were on a tear – gaffing, unhooking, throwing fish in the boat, dropping the lure back in and, of course, constantly repeating their words of encouragement.

"Weeel! Weeel! Beeeg Feeesh! Beeeg Feeesh!"

Dick and I would take over for one of the kids when fatigue overcame them. They were relatively small for tuna, but that's ten to twenty pounds of pulling and reeling. Our arms could only take so much. We all rotated for a while until, much to the chagrin of the captain and the deck hand, the schooling fish left the area. When we caught our breath, we looked down. The floor was covered with tuna, a few of them still flopping around. The live ones were put out of their misery and all were pushed into a built-in ice chest. Within minutes the deck was washed free of fish blood and the lures were changed. The captain went back to the steering wheel and, as if we'd never stopped for the frenzy, we were once again in pursuit of the elusive marlin.

We never caught one. We hooked a few, but every time the captain backed by the marlin, the line would slacken and the fish would shake loose. Whether he was inept from lack of experience or just having a bad week, we don't know for sure, but all signs point to the former. We lucked into a few more schools of tuna and found out later the enthusiasm of our guides was directly correlated to a premium price they received at the market. We couldn't complain much. We kept one or two every day. There are few culinary delights that compare to a fresh tuna steak.

I sometimes miss those summer fishing vacations and wish the kids were young again, but then I see the men and women they've become. I am proud to have been a part of that and wouldn't give it up for all the marlin in Mexico.

Part Three:

Call to Africa

1987: August 6 - September 15

Zimbabwe

A New Adventure: Dick

"Dick, there's a call for you. I'll patch it through to your office."
"Hello."
"Mr. Cabela. How're you doing? I'm an outfitter in Zimbabwe. A friend of yours told me you were looking to book a trip to Africa."

That's how it began. A phone call from an outfitter I'd never heard of. That wasn't saying much, since I didn't know anything about Africa in the first place. But the price was good and we'd begun selling African Safaris through our travel agency, Outdoor Adventures. I thought it might be a good opportunity to check them out. Since we were going to Zimbabwe, why not book a second hunt with Ronnie Kay of Safari South in Botswana. And since we were already going to be in Africa and we figured we'd probably never get back, why not play tourist as well and book a photo safari. We'd never been away from home for so long, but if we were going to spend the money, we might as well make it worth it.

Mary and I are both big fans of Ernest Hemingway, Robert Ruark, and Peter Hathaway Capstick. We'd often envisioned one day packing our bags for the adventure of a Teddy Roosevelt-style safari. Unfortunately, circumstances didn't allow for a six month leave. However, with advancements in travel, you could enjoy a taste of what Roosevelt experienced in a fraction of the time. This new speed with which we live our modern lives has in some ways stripped away the laborious joys of such a journey, but often the destination becomes a journey in itself. We couldn't spare six months; the month we planned was too long. Mary and I talked it over, then we talked it over with the few kids still at home. We decided to go for it.

We knew little about traveling to a third-world country and even less about what an overseas hunting expedition to such a locale entailed. A few conversations with the outfitters helped us compile a list of equipment and clothing we would need. Then after months of nervous anticipation, departure day arrived. Once we got on that plane, there was no turning back. Before we knew it, we were in the air. We left the Denver airport at 10:30 a.m. on Thursday, August 6, had lengthy layovers in New York and London before finally landing in Harare, Zimbabwe, at 8:20 a.m. Saturday, August 8.

We were glad to get off the plane, but exhausted with a heavy dose of jetlag.

"What is the name of your safari camp?" The young uniformed customs agent never took his eyes off our papers.

Uh oh.

"Just a moment, we'll try to find it."

Mary and I rummaged through our luggage. After so many phone calls and so much preparation we couldn't find the name of the camp where we'd be staying.

"I can tell you who our outfitter is," I said.

"Without the name of the camp, I cannot let you through," the young man said, crossing his arms over his chest.

"What are we supposed to do honey?" Mary asked.

We'd finally made it to Africa and were stuck in a crowded airport.

I was irritated, but tried to remain calm. "Our guide was supposed to meet us here. If we can get somebody to page him, we can get this sorted out."

"I cannot call on the intercom unless it is an emergency."

"Look, if you don't page him we'll be stranded here. What's the big deal?"

Thankfully, the outfitter and his son soon pushed their way through the onrush of passengers who'd been allowed to pass through the gates. Upon their arrival, the customs agent suddenly became overly agreeable, happily helping us fill out our paperwork for the firearms and ammunition.

The drive through Harare was not the Africa we'd read about. We could've been in any city in the world, save the haze of pollution that made L.A. sparkle and the security checks every ten minutes. There were tall modern buildings, heavy traffic, billboards, and people everywhere. In the name of progress, the urban world had inevitably tightened its grip on the elephant-ear-shaped continent. It is a major part of Africa now, but not really the part two small-town Nebraska outdoor enthusiasts had come in search of.

As we left the city limits behind, we passed through a barrage of checkpoints, where teenage security guards kept nervous fingers on AK-47s pointed in our faces while they searched through all our gear. The further we traveled from Harare, the fewer checkpoints we encountered and the scenery slowly transformed. The number of vehicles on the highway slowly dissipated. When we turned onto a dirt road, traffic became virtually nonexistent. Skyscrapers gave way to scattered villages where dwellings consisted of huts made from sticks and straw. In the vast distances between villages, open savannas were covered in tall, yellow grass for as far as we could see. The few umbrella trees dotting the landscape precluded the somewhat woodland setting of the ranch near Kadoma. We thought it looked a little like Texas.

"I like to take a drive through the area when we first arrive so clients can get a feel for the ranch. Are you up for it?" Jack, our guide, asked. He was originally from Michigan, but had moved to Africa nearly 20 years ago.

"Yes, I think that'd be nice."

We were curious about this new world and probably got on Jack's nerves with all our questions. Looking back, he probably did the drive through first thing to try to get as many questions out of the way as soon as possible.

"What's that?"

"Duiker."

"Look Dick, a warthog. Is that a kudu over there?"

"Yes it is."

"Oh, wow look at that huge antelope."

"That's an eland."

"How come all these trees are knocked over?"

"A herd of elephants came through here and destroyed the place. It will take many, many years for the habitat to recover, if it ever does."

"I can't believe how much damage one herd can do."

"Yes, and this was a small herd. A big herd is devastating."

We were in Africa. You couldn't have smacked the smiles off our faces with a baseball bat. The entire trip had already been worth it – we couldn't wait to go hunting.

We didn't know it at the time, but the outfitter who introduced us to Africa wasn't all that was advertised. Zimbabwe is an exceptional hunting destination, but we were in the wrong area. His ranch was big, but the game was average at best in quantity and downright poor in quality. It was Africa though. Having never experienced a truly excellent safari, or any safari for that matter, we were impressed with what we saw. The feeling Africa gives the first time visitor can never be duplicated. That feeling's the same whether you're in a second-rate camp or traveling alongside Roosevelt himself. I already wanted to come back and we'd only just arrived.

The 6:00 a.m. chill was joined in the air by rising anticipation and mild trepidation as we prepared for our first morning afield. We piled into the Land Rover and left camp as dawn transformed the horizon from a hazy gray to a pale orange. Thirty minutes later a common waterbuck slipped into the trees. It was time for a stalk.

"There's a water hole not too far from here," Jack said. "I'll bet that's where he's headed. We can go right after him or we can try to cut him off."

"What do you think?" I asked.

"Normally, I'd say we try to cut him off, but the wind is telling us to try to stalk right from here. I think we can do it. Let's go."

I've stalked a lot of game, all over the world, and I'd like to say my first stalk in Africa on that waterbuck was tough, that we made all the right decisions, but I can't. We walked a few hundred yards to the trees, snuck in a few more yards and there he was, standing in a small opening.

"That's a good one. Shoot him quick."

I had a new Dakota 7mm I'd purchased specifically for this trip. It was the first time I'd actually aimed it at an animal. I'd practiced until I was intimately familiar with it and when the waterbuck dropped in his tracks, I wasn't disappointed with the rifle's performance. I rushed over to inspect my first African trophy. As I approached, the first thing I noticed was the antelope's horrendous stench. I tried to ignore it. I placed my hand on its gray neck, then ran my fingers up the nearly 26-inch horns. With a few modern tools, I shared an ancient ritual with the first human who'd roamed these same untamed lands eons ago. It was invigorating.

Other than the obvious desire to stalk game on one of the world's greatest hunting arena's, a specific goal of this trip was to collect quality representatives of a number of African species for display in our retail stores. We hoped to share some of our experiences with our growing customer base. Unfortunately, some of the game we took never made it to the U.S. Our outfitter, who'd claimed his operation was one of the best

Dick's first African stalk was on a waterbuck.

anywhere in Africa, never fulfilled his promise to ship all the hides and horns, robbing us of an important reminder of the first days we adventured on the Dark Continent. Live and learn.

Regardless of our guide's inadequacies or dishonesty or whatever, he couldn't take away what Africa gave us on that first visit. It consumed us with an inescapable desire to return, an indescribable sense of belonging. It was like we'd returned to a home we'd never been to, but which had somehow always been a part of us. Going back to Nebraska left us with a void that could only be filled by returning to Africa. Our memories, somewhat tainted by what we'd later discover, are of beautiful country, magnificent wildlife and wonderful people.

We hunted hard the rest of the day, spotting numerous game animals that sprinted away at the sight of the vehicle. We tried to stalk a few of them, but kept coming up short. Our main tracker was always adamant he could track the animals, but our guide mostly ignored his pleas.

It wasn't long before we spotted an ostrich cruising along in an open field. I'd told our guide I was interested in an ostrich for an authentic African diorama we hoped to recreate for our Sidney retail store. So we drove ahead and pulled into some brush we thought he might come by. And he did. Running.

"Shoot him quick before he gets away."

Without time to think about it, I steadied myself on one knee. "Shoot! Shoot!"

I couldn't remember why or when I squeezed or how far I led, but the bird crumpled like both its legs had suddenly been broken. Part of me only took the shot because I thought I'd miss. Another part took it because I wondered if I could hit it. How I did, I'll never know. As a rule, I don't take running shots. Looking back, I probably wouldn't take the shot again. But everybody has been guilty of getting caught up in a moment. It happens.

We'd never seen an ostrich up close before. Mary and I ran over to inspect the huge, gangly, warm-blooded vertebrate clad in massive black and white feathers. It had great muscular legs that provided a succulent red meat which almost rivaled our own famed Nebraska beef. Its huge toes donned rapier-like claws that compare to those of many predators and its long lanky neck was mostly featherless. Mother Nature was at her best when she created this creature.

"This is the portion of our ranch we dedicate to cattle," Jack said on the way back to camp.

"Looks like some of the other animals like it here as well. Is that a kudu?"

Mary pointed to a long spiral-horned gray antelope. It was colored with white stripes running vertically down the back half of its body. It grazed leisurely among a herd of brown and white cattle.

"Yes it is," Jack said smiling.

"I wonder what it's doing over there with the cows."

"A few years ago, when it was a baby, we put it in there as kind of a ranch pet. He grew and now we seem to have a bit of a problem. He thinks he's a cow."

"What?"

"He was raised like a cow and now that he's older, he's become very aggressive toward the bulls. He chases them away easily with his long horns. He hasn't figured out how to breed with his odd harem yet, but it's not from a lack of effort." Jack raised his eyebrows. "We've tried to get rid of him, but he keeps coming back and harassing all our other bulls. I'm not sure what we're going to do, but when he's around the regular bulls can't breed with the cows. We can't have that."

I imagine the bulls were most impressed with the strange cow's horns. I know I was. It was a big kudu.

A colorful array of tents made up the camp. No two tents were the same in color, size or style. The red, blue and military green collapsible living quarters were conspicuously out of place along the high bank of a slow-moving river. But the serene and savage surrounding had a way of absorbing our temporary quarters. The orange glow of the African sunset traced a golden pathway of sparkling ripples across the living waterway. Tender, succulent impala steaks smoked over the distinctive aroma of mopane wood provided the main course to a meal that could've made a five-star chef weep tears of delight.

After the long day in the Zimbabwe sun, we'd eaten ourselves into a heavy slumber. With little fanfare, Mary and I retired to a blue tent nestled on the shores of an ancient river snaking through a prehistoric land. The recent memory of our first full day among Africa's creatures along with the excitement of what tomorrow might bring battled with Mary's lethargic state. I was snoring when my head hit the pillow. Between my log-sawing and the many unfamiliar sounds of the African night, it was no wonder Mary enjoyed little rest.

I felt rejuvenated when 6 a.m. arrived. It was easy to see Mary was a little groggy, but her eyes were energetic and lively. It was a new day, a new adventure. We started out on the vehicle again, but just after daybreak, Jack slammed on the brakes.

"Did you see that warthog?"

"No, where?"

"He just ran into the brush over there. He looked pretty good. I think we should go after him. You've got to have a warthog for your display. It just wouldn't be authentic without it."

He had a point, but then again, the same could be said for nearly any animal we saw. We were paying him on a trophy fee by animal basis. The more animals we shot, the more he was paid. But how often do you make it to Africa? Might as well make the most of it.

"Let's do it," I said.

It turned out to be another fairly easy stalk. We circled to get the wind in our favor, then began squeezing in. The hog scampered into another brush line, but he hadn't busted us. Sometimes warthogs just like to scamper. We followed straight in after him, finding him tearing up the grass with his tusks. Once again, the Dakota performed flawlessly. The warthog made it about fifteen yards before skidding to his side.

I was feeling rather happy with myself after stumbling onto an impala on the way back to the vehicle and dropping it with one shot. Big-game hunting in Africa was quite different than hunting back home. In a few states you can carry multiple tags for multiple animals, but even in those states it's rare to shoot an animal and run into another of a different species worth shooting on the way back to camp. Sure you may have an elk tag and a pronghorn tag, but you usually have to travel to entirely different areas to find good representatives of both. In Africa, hunting five different species in the same day in the same general area is not uncommon. I could get used to this.

On the way back to camp, our tracker said something to Jack from the back, causing him to slam on the breaks. He looked at me with a huge, almost salivating smile.

A day in Zimbabwe wouldn't be complete without seeing a warthog.

"Duiker," he said. "Let's go."

To tell the truth, I wasn't even sure I knew what a duiker was. I'd looked up most of the animals on the list, but I couldn't remember what a duiker looked like. I just knew it was a small antelope.

We found the little sneaker in the shadows. Not the big shadows of a forest or jungle, but the tiny shadows. The kind of shadows you can find in your bushes. Jack pointed him out. There was a bit of urgency in his hand movements. I only saw shadows. I stared hard. The tiny flash of gray fur in the different shades of the undergrowth finally gave him away. He was looking right at us.

It was an easy shot, other than the fact I had to take it quickly. We were close, the light was good and the southern bush duiker stood still. It was a small antelope of about 20 inches in height and maybe 40 pounds. It had a sandy gray coat and tiny horns of just a few inches.

"Holy smokes Dick. This is a new record for sure. Look at those horns."

It didn't seem like much – they were only a few inches long and not much thicker than my finger, but Jack's enthusiastic reaction was almost contagious. I didn't care much about the record, but it felt good to know we'd taken a fine, mature animal.

Later that afternoon, I shot another warthog.

"These tusks are fabulous Dick. I wouldn't be surprised if this warthog doesn't compete for the new world record."

This time I didn't share the enthusiasm. At best, it was only marginally bigger than the warthog I'd taken earlier in the day. It was obvious even to us. The odds of taking two record animals in the same day were astronomical. I was suddenly suspicious of our guide's integrity, though I didn't make my doubts known. Apparently, he believed Mary and I would only be happy if we shot world records. Sure we wanted mature representatives of each species, but this was almost ridiculous. We were novice African adventurers. He played off that. We were captivated by Africa; he didn't have to lie. Perhaps his exaggerations were one of the reasons he never shipped some of our capes and horns. We'll never know.

First Times: Mary

"Grab your rifle Mary. You're going to get us a tasty treat for tonight's dinner," Jack said. "A duiker just ran into the brush over there."

We were quick to learn to avoid the tiny spikes of thorn bushes – it meant avoiding almost any bush or branch. We soon found in Africa, it either bites, stings or pokes. None of those were pleasant. I did my best to avoid them all. We tried to proceed with silence, but the dry leaves rustled under our feet. I didn't hear the small antelope bolt into the open.

"There he is." Jack pointed, whipping up the shooting sticks. A second later, the duiker stopped. "Whenever you're ready, take him."

Take him?

It was a tiny little thing. How was I going to hit him? He'd take off soon if I didn't go for it. I steadied the rifle on the shooting sticks, holding my breath for a moment. The butterflies in my stomach were fluttering their way up to my heart. There was only one way to stop them. The duiker took a step, his head jerking our way. Not a moment to spare, I squeezed. The duiker jumped straight up, kicking up a cloud of dust.

When it settled, my first African animal lay still 100 yards away.

It was slightly heavier than Dick's duiker, sporting a more brownish tint in its fur. I'm not sure I was ready for the emotional range following a first big-game kill. It was overwhelming. I didn't know if I should shout for joy or cry, so I smiled sheepishly, returning to the truck in silence as I came to terms with the conflicting thoughts.

"Wait until you taste the meat. It's delicious," Jack said.

To our pleasant surprise, he was understating the truth. It was barbecued over an open pit and served with fresh fried potatoes and peas. We asked for more though we were already stuffed. We'd eaten

Dick's impala the night before and could hardly believe any wild game could taste better. As I've discovered many times, Africa has a way of reminding you her wonders are limitless.

Hunting was tough for the next few days. We rarely saw game.

"We've been having a bit of a problem with poachers," Jack said. "The animals are skittish. They run at the slightest hint of danger."

Dick and I never saw any poachers, but the snares we continued to find were a constant reminder of their presence.

"Usually with hunters in the field, poachers will leave the area or practice their trade with more discretion. I am surprised we've found so many snares already. I must tell you, if we see them, I will pursue them. If we catch them, penalties will be harsh. It is the way we do things here."

I was glad we didn't see any.

Then, one day, animals were everywhere. There weren't any spectacular bulls or rams, but at least we were seeing game. It was on this day, shortly after Dick and I had each taken a zebra, that our hunt was cut short just before noon. We were driving along the "road" when the vehicle jolted and we veered into a bush.

"Damn," Jack said. "We blew a tire. I hope you were in the mood for a break."

We were in a nearly barren area where shade was scarce and game nonexistent. I wondered what we could do to help, but with all the trackers and spotters, I figured we'd just get in the way.

"That's a different kind of rope," I said, pointing to the cord used to tie down the spare tire.

Jack smiled politely, then said something to one of the native trackers who took off running into the bushes. A few minutes later he returned with a long branch. He handed it to Jack.

"This is where we get our rope." Jack held the branch up so I could inspect it. He peeled back the bark, leaving a rope-like strand of surprisingly strong twine.

"It can be used for a multitude of purposes," he said. "As you can see, we use it for tying up any loose equipment in the back of the Rover. Whereas you chaps in the States would use nails and screws, the local villagers can build their entire community out of nothing more than this rope, sticks and a few bundles of straw."

The village structures were sturdier than outward appearances suggested. They were built without the use of any tools, save a machete for chopping branches. The frames were erected from long branches as straight as possible and cut to relatively even lengths. The limbs were then tied together and the small spaces between them filled with straw or mud or a combination of the two. The roofs were made by tying bundles of straw to the slope of connected branches. A significant portion of the trophy licensing fees hunters pay during their safaris go to these communities. They are largely used for medical and educational supplies – necessities more difficult to come by than the building materials the land provided.

We were impressed by what little the native people needed to live. Back home we have so much, yet are rarely satisfied; in this part of Zimbabwe, the people had very little, yet were completely content with their lives. The land provided everything they needed. The hunting camp had a few modern comforts like the Land Rover, but they still found most of what they required was available for free if you knew where to look.

Even if we failed to realize it at the time, we were in one of God's grand school rooms. An education of this land we would come to love was just beginning.

The following morning after tea, toast and biscuits, we left for the day's hunt with four fully inflated tires and a patched spare in the back. The next thing we knew we were traveling down a road so rough, so bumpy, so unbearable we began to think even the light breakfast had been a bad mistake. If those fanny firmers advertised all over television could shake away the pounds, then we should've jiggled the fat right off our buns. The going was slow as well. I'd be surprised if our top speed ever surpassed 10 mph.

About the time my heart was in my stomach, my liver was in my throat and my lungs had flip-flopped, Jack stopped the Land Rover.

"Look. Over there. It's a nice sable." He pointed, but we didn't see what he was pointing at.

But a sable. Wow. I had to see it. I'd seen a picture or two and wondered if they'd be as impressive in real life.

We scanned the tree line with our compact 8x10 Zeiss binoculars. It didn't take long to locate the jet-black bull grazing.

"Oh, he's beautiful." I was awed by its wide chest, sleek coat, the distinctive white markings on its face and the long scimitar shaped horns sweeping back over his neck.

"He's so majestic. His face almost looks like it's been painted on." It was one of the most regal creatures I'd ever seen.

"He hasn't seen us yet," Jack said softly. "The wind should stay in our favor if we sneak back into those trees and try to stalk up to him from the cover."

We backed away. One of the trackers led Dick and Jack slowly on a stealthy, zigzag course through waist-high golden grass and around thorn bushes and grayish mopane trees. The tracker was a tall, thin man who always wore green coveralls, even on the hottest of days. His aged gray shoes were virtually sole-less and the holes worn into the toes revealed brown socks. He walked with feather-light steps, his tracking ability, passed down from generations of sustenance hunters before him, second to none. If he couldn't get them in range, nobody could.

The sun burned away the coolness of the night, but the air was dry and the heat barely noticeable. They rounded a wall of impenetrable acacia bushes, but stopped short. Five warthogs threw dust up from their hooves, scampering off straight for the antelope. They froze. What bad luck. The hogs were on a collision course with the sable. It appeared their chance would be spoiled. Then, without warning, the lead warthog veered right – away from their target. I could almost hear the collective sigh of relief all the way back at the truck.

Standing in the truck, I could still see them. The tracker led them another 40 yards through a dense conclave of short, slender-stemmed trees. Leaves crunched lightly under their feet. He stopped and pointed. Neither Dick nor Jack could immediately discern what the tracker was pointing at through the blurring mesh of branches. The tracker motioned for them to crouch down. On one knee, Dick steadied himself with his rifle scanning the area ahead of them. He later told me how things went down.

He tried to focus through the intermingled barrier of woody flora. Then he realized he was looking for the entire antelope. In that kind of brush, he was better off searching for a leg, an ear, or a nose. A few moments later he thought he saw something. It was nothing more than a dark solid patch less than 75-yards away. He stared hard – it moved – and then it was gone.

"He's just ahead," Jack whispered. "Come on." He waved Dick forward.

Hunkered down, the three of them began to close the distance. The sable was on the move. Any change in the wind might alert him of their presence. Changing wind was always a possibility.

Jack turned to Dick. "If you get a shot, you need to take him quick. If he sees or smells us, he'll run. We won't get a second chance at him."

Twenty minutes later, the wall of small trees gave way to an open field of short grass. They stayed inside the edge of the cover to study the field. And there he was, 125 yards on the other side, awfully close to the brush line beyond the short grass. The sable jerked its head up. Dick knew he only had a moment. He took an off-hand shot. The antelope's quick jump and the *thwack* signaled a hit. Before Dick could reload, the sable disappeared into the brush.

They scurried across the open plain to locate a blood trail. The pinkish bubbly drops indicated a lung shot.

"He probably didn't go far, but our African antelope are incredibly resilient. You can never be certain," Jack said.

After the shot, the driver and the other tracker led me to the boys, so we could help locate the sable. A few dozen yards further we heard a loud snort.

"That's him. Let's go." Jack grabbed Dick's sleeve to pull him along.

We found the antelope lying under a tree. Dick and Jack took a few cautious steps toward it. The sable lifted its sweeping horns to face them. He wasn't done yet. It struggled to get its feet under it, but Dick quickly put another bullet into its boiler room. It was finished. Still, they approached with caution.

"A sable can be an extremely dangerous animal," Jack said. "Especially when wounded or cornered. The tips of their horns are sharp and they can use them with the skill of a fencer. They've been known to inflict mortal wounds on lions. They've killed two village dogs just this year."

You rarely feel more alive than during a hunt, but when it has ended with a kill and you're standing above your prey, a confusing yet intoxicating mixture of conflicting emotions wrap themselves around your heart, penetrating your very soul. Sorrow and elation, adrenaline and fatigue, pain and joy, all become indistinguishable. It forces you to reflect upon who you are. There is truly nothing like it – a prehistoric rite into a pure and honest connection to nature, forgotten by far too many.

The morning's coolness was soon replaced by a midday heat wave. We were soothed by the melody of a slow-moving river and the harmony of two song birds during lunch. Before we knew it, we were napping in the shade. A swarm of mosquitoes was kind enough to wake us up within the hour.

"I think we'll try something a bit different this evening. There's a water hole nearby. We'll just take it easy. See what comes in."

It was different than the driving around or hiking we'd been doing, but there were similarities. For instance, there were long periods when we saw nothing and just keeping our eyes open became a struggle. These dull episodes were always followed by a fervor of excitement, rarely lasting more than a moment. Any time an animal came to drink was cause for renewed enthusiasm. More often than not, it wasn't something we intended to harvest.

Dick was lucky enough to bag a primarily nocturnal bush pig that wandered in for a sip and I shot an impala. We didn't know it at the time, but the bush pig was a highly prized and difficult animal. It seemed pretty easy to us. Sometimes luck trumps experience.

With all the racket we'd created, nothing would be joining us at this waterhole anytime soon. It was back to the vehicle. I hoped the trail wouldn't be too bumpy.

Rarely encountered during the day, the bushpig is one of Africa's more elusive game animals.

This was my first true attempt at big game. I'd be lying if I didn't admit to the occasional miss or two. I found my confidence level on a roller coaster of ups, downs and loop-de-loops. My nerves slowly began to relax as I became better acquainted with the feel of the trigger and the recoil on my shoulder. Practice was one thing we did a lot. Hunting was entirely different and exponentially more difficult. There were no perfect rests and our targets weren't endowed with bull's-eyes. On many occasions, we were shooting after a long, tiring stalk. Oh, and the targets don't tend to stand still for very long.

I thought about my last shot. Everything seemed so smooth. It was easy to get steady, the squeeze of the trigger felt natural and the impala went down quickly. I can't stand to see them suffer. Now if I could only remember everything next time.

I was running through the shooting motions in my mind when Dick nudged me.

"Look at that," he said.

Off to the left, two male ostriches appeared to be dancing.

"That's a kind of territorial display," Jack said. "The one with his feathers up is telling the other bird to stay away from his turf – in particular, his females."

Jack's attention, along with everyone else's, was focused on the gangly, almost awkward, strutting ballet when the Land Rover came to a jolting halt. We were high centered on a boulder. Fortunately, the situation wasn't too serious. A four-person shove sent us on our way again.

"I wonder if those ostriches found our predicament as comical as we thought they were," Jack said.

Probably so.

The Gray Ghost of Africa: Dick

The gray ghost. The elusive kudu, uncanny in its ability to blend in to its surroundings. So much so, that, at times, they appear to be almost transparent. He stands perfectly still, complete with his long corkscrew horns and massive cupped ears, less than fifteen yards away in a group of small trees and you can stare right at him, or better stated, right through him. He has a constant alertness, intensified by a remarkable sense of hearing and smell. You can bet he knows exactly where you are long before you even suspect he's around.

Overnight the weather brought in a wind storm. Jack decided it was a good day to attend to work he had in camp while we waited out the gale.

"We'll see if we can't find a kudu once this lets up."

"What if it doesn't let up?"

"Then there's only one thing we can do. Butt heads with it."

It seemed the wind would never stop. I wanted a shot at the greater kudu. There's just something about a kudu. It's considered by many the number one trophy antelope in all of Africa. I'd read enough literature on the subject to know why. They are cunning, difficult to hunt and those long, spiraled horns are nothing less than awesome. It was a kudu that topped the list of plains game we came for. The wind, of all things, was keeping us from that challenge.

Morning came and went and there was no relenting to the blowing fury. The tent flaps whipped. The camp staff was constantly chasing one thing or another that had been swooped up. It wasn't until after lunch that things began to die down a bit. Though there was still a stiff warm breeze, it was time to hunt.

Like every day, the afternoon air was overly dry. Few green leaves remained on only a small fraction of trees and the hard, dusty ground was topped off by clumps of dying amber grass. The sun beat down from an indigo sky void of clouds. Though the climate was arid, an occasional bead of sweat trickled down the side of my face. A single vulture circled high above, as if waiting for one of us to collapse.

Suddenly, there was a crash in the brush ahead of us. A kudu. He tilted his horns back as he charged off into the trees. We were on his trail

46

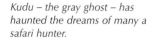

Kudu – the gray ghost – has haunted the dreams of many a safari hunter.

like hounds on a fox.

Forty minutes later, we stopped. One of the trackers pointed. The bull was standing beside an acacia tree. I saw a leg first and followed it up to the spiraled horns. I'd looked right past that same spot when we'd first stopped. The kudu's natural camouflage was impeccable. He truly was the gray ghost.

The wind had died down considerably, but we were out of position – straight upwind of our prey. We'd hunted kudu nearly everyday. We'd seen a few cows and two or three young bulls, but our time in Zimbabwe was dwindling. It looked like this might be my last chance – it was fleeting.

The bull watched us closely – he could charge off at any second. Jack thrust the shooting sticks into place and I jammed my 7mm in the crux. The kudu turned.

"Quickly Dick, before he runs."

I rushed the shot – it was too far back. My gray ghost vanished within seconds.

"You hit him, but it may have been a gut shot. We better go have a look. Just be ready."

We followed the tracker, who was on the trail instantly. Spoor was minimal, but within a few minutes the tracker pointed to the ground and spoke.

"He's starting to stagger," Jack translated. "Might have hit him better than I thought. Be ready to fire. Oh, there he is. Shoot!"

The bull fell in a heap before my finger reached the trigger.

I had my kudu. It was a long, tough day. A good day. A day worthy of celebration. And it wasn't over.

The horns were fifty inches around the curves, the spread thirty-three inches wide. A fine kudu bull.

"The record is only fifty-four inches," Jack said. "This is an outstanding trophy."

Maybe he was talking about the camp record. I don't know, but I suppose he was just trying to make us feel better. The actual record was well above the sixty-inch mark.

How were we to know? Mary and I had never hunted kudu – we'd never been to Africa. It was easily the biggest bull we'd seen so far. There was no reason to question our amiable guide. He seemed sincere and diligent. We believed him. It didn't matter; we would've been pleased with our animals regardless. He may've had experiences with clients who lost their tempers over a few inches – it's hard to tell. Not that trophy quality doesn't matter, it does. It's important to have goals, to try to meet and exceed them. Everyone knows truly superb animals are the most challenging to hunt, but people overly concerned with world records miss out on too many aspects of the African experience. An animal should never be degraded because it is lacking an inch or two in horn size.

It turned out there were very few heavy-horned antelope on the ranch – of course we didn't realize this until later. It was just managed poorly. It wasn't until we arrived in Botswana that Mary and I understood he was mostly just having us blast away at the first decent (some were far too immature) specimen we came across. Minimal extra effort was given on many aspects of the hunt – though Jack always seemed eager to please. It was our first time in Africa. His actions and lack thereof were irrelevant. Africa gave us a sense of freedom and wonder a person rarely experiences. In many ways it was like being a child again. Each new step was an exciting and unknown adventure.

"What do you say we try to find Mary a nice kudu now?"

"Sounds good to us," I said.

Her face brightened with the suggestion. She'd been enamored with mine.

"Good. We'll spend the rest of the afternoon working on it then."

On safari, as in life, well thought out plans often clash with the unexpected.

Less than twenty minutes later, we were headed down a rocky ravine and for the second time found ourselves high-centered – much worse this time. We piled out to take a look.

"I guess we should try to rock it off again." Jack shrugged.

CRACK.

"Uh oh."

Jack raised his eyebrows. Then he crawled under the Land Rover. When he finally slid back out, he stood up, wiping the dust from his hands onto his chest.

"It appears we have a broken rear axle," he said.

He sounded a little disappointed, but took it rather well. Minor setbacks are part of any safari operation. All you can do is deal with them.

The day's hunt was over.

Stuck in second gear and without four-wheel drive, we inched our way back in. The drive was slow, but it wasn't overly boring. It could've been much worse. We were among scattered woodlands and open grass fields, hiding the occasional zebra, impala, ostrich, or other animal. Our eyes were wide and alert. Anything can step out from behind a tree or from a drapery of tall grass, it was important to be ready. By the time we finally made it back to camp though, our eyes were heavy. We took overdue showers, had a bite to eat and retired to our tent. I hardly got to celebrate my kudu.

The crippled Land Rover wasn't the only vehicle in camp – there was one other. It was an old gray jeep, rusty and looking as if it might crumble from our weight. This would be our mode of transportation for the remaining three days in Zimbabwe. We crammed into the jeep the best we could first thing in the morning. Within the first half hour of leaving camp, the tracker spotted a waterbuck ducking into the bush.

"Are you ready, Mary?" Jack said as he and one of the trackers stepped away from the jeep and started for the brush.

Mary grabbed her 7mm and hurried to follow. We were hunting for eland, but apparently this waterbuck was too good to pass up. Mary was eager for a chance at him.

Waterbuck rarely venture further than a mile from a water source. Jack and the tracker used this information to deduce the waterbuck's destination – a small pond less than 400 yards through the very brush the bull sauntered into. If they could reach the water-hole before the bull, they might catch him coming in for a drink. I decided to tag along for the stalk.

We took slow, soft steps like a pride of lionesses sneaking into position, waiting for the perfect moment, barely able to contain themselves before the final ambush. Mary looked up just in time to see the unmistakable white ring around the waterbuck's rump. It slowly disappeared behind a thorn bush.

He was just moseying along. We hadn't spooked him. Nobody said a word; we just continued on our cautious stalk. The pond was close.

A fish eagle perched upon a dead limb watched over the entire scene – hunting. A saddle-billed stork worked slowly and deliberately along the weedy shoreline, its orange, black and yellow beak pointed downward, ready to strike – hunting. Excitement and trepidation snaked like a river. The fish eagle and the saddle-billed stork shared an instinctual force. Their senses were alive and only one word came to mind – freedom.

We stepped around a four-foot, bottle-necked, termite mound and positioned ourselves behind a mopane. The bull stood alert in the shadow of an acacia, the thorny limbs highlighted on his shaggy coarse hair. His sweeping horns curved forward. They sported heavy ridges from the bases up. Mary tried to use the tree to stabilize her rifle.

"Shoot him whenever you are ready." Jack's words were almost inaudible.

She was shaking and couldn't get the rifle to steady. Then the bull glanced our way – it was now or never. She chose now. She pulled herself closer to the scope in an unconscious effort to help her steady the crosshairs. She squeezed. The recoil slammed the scope into the bridge of her nose. It began bleeding immediately. It was more embarrassing than painful and she brushed it off easily. Few hunters can say they haven't been bitten.

The waterbuck was down.

"We're pretty close to camp. I think we will go back for lunch. Besides it gives us a chance to drop off the waterbuck. There's not nearly as much room in the jeep as we've been used to."

By the time we rolled in, the slight breeze had become a stiff wind. The afternoon wasn't looking as promising as the morning had, but we only had two more days. It had gone way too fast.

We ate and returned to the tent for a short nap. The sound of an approaching vehicle soon woke us up. Jack was waiting for us with two official looking natives in army green military uniforms.

"These men need to see your papers," he said.

Like many of the young men in the city, these two had AKs slung over their shoulders, so we didn't ask questions. We just retrieved our passports and other paperwork and handed them over.

One man was obviously in charge. He made a point out of making sure we knew this. He briefly glanced at each of our passports before handing them to his subordinate.

"Are you here for hunting?" he asked. His English was quite good, though heavily laden with accent.

"Yes we are."

He smiled at us. "Very good." His partner handed him back the passports and papers. "These are now officially valid," he said handing them back to us. "Please enjoy your stay in our country."

Then he pulled our guide off to the side and spent much of the afternoon asking him questions and going over all his paperwork and equipment. At one point he even crawled under the Land Rover. I guess it was to "officially" declare the validity of the axle break. Nevertheless, he was there for the rest of the day.

The afternoon had been wasted. Two days left – not nearly enough time.

The Sable and the Safety: Mary

At daybreak, in the gray hazy light before the sun turns the morning fresh as dew, we cut an eland track less than 100-yards from camp and were hot on his trail. We hiked and hiked. The spoor was always fresh, but we never seemed to close any distance. I guess that's the way of a nomad antelope – don't stop unless you have to.

The morning dragged on. All we'd seen were a few impala and a small group of warthogs that scurried into the bushes, like kids caught misbehaving. When I looked at my watch, I could hardly believe it was only 8 a.m. Around this time, we crossed paths with three blue wildebeest, all bulls. We were so tired of following an apparition, we abandoned the eland tracks without a second thought.

The three wildebeest were unaware of our presence. It should've been an easy stalk. Yeah right.

We had company. Two comedian baboons followed our every move. We paid little attention to them at first and for the most part, didn't even realize they were there. Then, just as a shooting opportunity would arise, they'd bark and bark like yapping little dogs, causing the wildebeest to run off in alarm. The first time was just a little irritating, but this incessant pestering went on for over an hour. It cost us half a dozen opportunities at the bulls. Finally, we'd reached our breaking point – I was near setting my sights on the little buggers. To continue the stalk would be futile, the wildebeest were on to us and the darn baboons, they were laughing it up. Two of the trackers eventually picked up rocks and sticks and took off after them. They screamed like banshees, scampering away. Every animal within two miles was now on the defensive. Like I said – darn baboons.

"Now that we've chased those yappy baboons away, what do you say we try to re-find the wildebeest tracks? They'll be a little spooked now, but finding the trail should be simple."

It was simple. The trackers were on it like we'd never lost it. We'd tracked for about ten minutes when we all almost dove into the brush at the unexpected appearance of the eland.

"Well bugger me," Jack said. "Didn't expect to run across them." He took his hat off and pointed with it.

There were five of them, three cows and two bulls, marching along like they had somewhere important to be. We waited for them to cross the trail in front of us so we could size them up. Both sexes displayed straight, tight twisted horns – with the female's being a bit thinner. The cows were massive, but they paled in comparison to the bulls, known to reach up to 2,000 pounds. The two bulls also had more of a gray contrast, but it was the size that made them easy to identify. They are the largest antelope in the world. Their top speed is slower than many others, but their ability to keep going and going like the Energizer Bunny can be frustrating when you're on a track.

The small herd was working their way back to the river, away from the wildebeest.

"What do you say Dick?" Jack asked. "We can keep after the wildebeest. There was a really good bull in that group. Or we can try for the eland. The bull in the back – he's a shooter."

"Let's go for the eland," Dick said. And just like that, the wildebeest were forgotten.

Because of their size, eland can cover a substantial amount of ground with each step. A person would almost have to sprint just to keep up with their walk. Half an hour later, we still hadn't closed the gap – and we couldn't walk any faster. Yet we pushed on. Maybe they'd stop to eat or drink. They were now on more of a route perpendicular to the river, so determining their destination was next to impossible. Soon the high sun was turning the air to fire. The tracker's steps slowed, he felt we were close, very close. Maybe the tracks were fresh. Maybe he heard something. Heck, he might've smelled them for all we knew. But you trust the tracker. If he believed they were close, we were probably right on top of them. It was appearing as if we may've finally caught a break when the wind pulled the old switch-a-roo on us. The hunt was over.

"We'd better head back to the jeep now," Jack said. "It's going to be a late lunch as it is."

"How far is it?"

"Oh, it'll take us over an hour."

Funny, it hadn't seemed we'd been on the trail that long. But time's correlation to fun and flying is a proven theory. It had been a good morning, even though our legs and lungs shouted insults at us.

Halfway back to the vehicle, we encountered three inconspicuous kudu cows blending in with the shrubbery. Two were browsing on vines wrapped around the stalks of a bush. The third was more alert, its big ears taking in every sound. The breeding season was in full swing, a bull could be close by. We backed into the shadows to wait.

The cows were alert. They fed closer, but their muscles were tense. They jerked their heads at every sound. We watched them feed nervously for fifteen minutes before another kudu slipped into the open.

"It's a bull. But I cannot see the horns properly. He's got them in the branches. Can you see him Mary?"

"Yes, I see him."

"Find him in your crosshairs and be ready to shoot if I tell you to. I want to get a good look at the horns first."

I didn't respond. My hands trembled. I took a few deep breaths to calm myself, but the blue-gray bull was reluctant to pull his horns from the trees. He was huge, but strangely, the size of his ears made his head look tiny. The white markings on his face and the stripes down the back half of his body were like artwork. When he finally stepped into the open, his high spiraled horns completed his look – it was regal in every way.

A kudu bull can stand motionless for an eternity if it feels danger is close and believes it is hidden. This kudu, however, was in hot pursuit. The cows were in season and his sense of self-preservation was overcome by an insatiable need to breed. Typical male.

"That's a good one Mary. Take him if he gives you a clean shot."

The bull stepped away from a small tree and turned broadside. This was it. This, I knew, would be my best chance. Still, I am not one to rush a shot. I never have been and never will be, something that sometimes frustrates my professional hunters. I held my breath, just for a second. I knew I had him even before my finger touched the trigger. It was one of those moments many athletes talk of – I was in the zone. I couldn't miss and I knew it.

The big bull ran less than twenty-five yards before he fell.

"Congratulations Mary," Jack said, slapping me on the back. "You've just taken one of the most coveted trophies in Africa, probably even the most coveted of the common game."

I thought about that for a moment – common. It's often used to describe some of the African plains game. I've used it myself. No word could be more wrong. All of Africa's unique ungulates have distinct physical characteristics and mannerisms. They offer a wide array of challenges to those who hunt them. After only a single safari, Dick and I found very little which made these magnificent creatures common.

While we took a few pictures of my kudu, one of the trackers ran ahead to retrieve the jeep. It took the strength of everyone's muscles to pull the more than 600-lb. animal into the back of the vehicle. By the time we had it loaded, it was well past lunch time.

Mary took her time and made a perfect one-shot kill on one of Africa's most coveted trophies – Kudu.

"It's so beautiful here," I said. "Peaceful and untouched."

"Yet there is a violent and unforgiving side to the country," Jack said. "Both here in the bush and even more so in the highly populated areas, where the political voice is as unpredictable as a wounded buffalo. The people are being pulled in many directions by leaders influenced by greed; turning people against each other with empty promises and impossible goals. My hope is that someday an identity everyone can be proud of will be found."

We found his genuine concern for the future of the country admirable.

"Do you think the country can ever be pulled out of its steep economic downfall?" Dick asked. "It was my understanding this used to be one of the most successful of all African countries."

"Yes it was. But I don't think we are going anywhere positive under the current leadership. The people are told to hate each other. The only profitable enterprise which has not been stolen and sucked dry is the safari industry. The little foreign currency which comes across the borders is mostly from big-game hunters. I fear it is only a matter of time before this is ruined by the corruption which has left this country staring down the barrel of bankruptcy. But enough of political problems. You've come to enjoy yourselves."

"It's okay, every country has problems."

"The United States seems to be doing fine."

"Then why do so many seem to hate us? The U.S. I mean," I asked.

"Not everyone hates the U.S. and for those who do, it is jealousy that begets hate."

"Maybe so, but it might just be an unwarranted jealousy."

"How do you mean?"

"Now, don't take this wrong. We love our country and would never want to live anywhere else. But our prosperity has given even the poorest American far more than most of your local residents, yet we are never happy with what we have. We always want more. I see so many people here with virtually nothing who are utterly content with their lives."

"Yes, but without your prosperity you wouldn't be here on safari, witnessing first-hand how others in the world live. Your freedom gives you the opportunity to become what you want. What you make of yourself is entirely up to you. It is rare for the government to strip away all that you've worked for. Here, it is an everyday occurrence. I don't wish to give the wrong impression either. I love it here and wouldn't want to be anywhere else. I only fear I may not have a choice."

"Who wouldn't love it here? This place makes you feel so alive. Almost to an overwhelming point. I can't really explain it, but it just feels right."

"Africa has a way of doing that to you. Although, I imagine the wilderness of America has the same effect."

"Yes in some places, I suppose it does. Yet, there's something I can't explain about this place. It pulls at you; frightens you and gives you comfort at the same time. I don't know how else to put it – it feels perfectly natural."

The remaining ride to camp was in relative silence, as was a light lunch of chicken and fries. It was quiet. It seemed everyone had the earlier conversation on their minds. Were we fortunate? Of course we were. Should we feel guilty? Of course we shouldn't (even if we do at times). The world is made up of differences – it makes it great. We look different. We act different. We feel different. Should the rich man feel sorry for the poor man, or should he envy him? Should the healthy man shun the ill or embrace him? Should the self-proclaimed intellectual scoff at the simple man or should he try to learn truth and humility from him? Silent rides back to camp and silent lunches aren't always so silent.

After lunch, Dick and I read awhile, then wrote in our journals.

"I'm going to try to take a nap," I said. "Dick, are you awake?"

His answer was a deep guttural snore. How could he sleep through that sound? Dear God, please don't let him call in a pride of lions. I could forget about sleep myself, so I read some more. I woke Dick when it was time to go.

"What's the plan for this afternoon?" I asked our guide.

"I thought we'd go out and give the eland or wildebeest another go."

We all piled into the jeep and were off again. Each time out was unique. You never knew what was going to happen – monotony was impossible. New species of game were seen every day of the safari. What's more, wild animals are never as predictable as we might believe. That very unpredictability can bring an endless flow of game or hours upon hours of empty landscape where wildlife has apparently disappeared. The afternoon's uncertainties were in the shadows of the latter. Sometimes when game is scarce, it may only be because you've missed it. So we took a closer look.

We looked and we looked. It wasn't until God was just about ready to bless us with the simple pleasure of an African sunset, that our tracker's trained eyes found movement one hundred yards into the bush.

"There's an eland," Jack said after the tracker tapped him on the shoulder.

It sauntered into a clearing, its sleek, light tan coat and long, thin horns were hard to miss. It was an old cow.

"Let's wait a bit, in case a bull is around," Jack said. "We're running out of time for much of anything else anyway."

Eventually, the cow went the way of the sun, melting into the twilight. Gregarious animals that they are, it was surprising no other eland made an appearance. Light was fading quicker than hope at the moment. We'd take the long way back to the vehicle, hunting as we went.

It wasn't long before we stopped – sable.

"Get ready, Mary. Use that branch for a rest." Jack pointed to a two-inch-thick twig jutting upward from the undersized tree we were trying to hide behind. I'm sure we looked like a Three Stooges bit.

The twig wasn't much of a rest, but it was the best we could do under the circumstances. The sable hadn't detected us, but he seemed aware something wasn't right. He looked ready to charge away at any hint of danger. We had the wind in our favor, but the landscape offered little cover, any movement might spook him into a sprint.

I sensed the animal's agitation. I had to move quickly. I just couldn't keep the rifle steady on the small bough. The sable jerked his head toward us. I tensed. The crosshairs finally landed on his shoulder and I squeezed. Slowly...a little more...harder...why won't it fire?

"Oh cripes!"

The sable was long gone. I was left holding a 7mm with the safety on. It's usually just an instinctive click of the thumb. I was concentrating so hard on steadying the rifle and watching the antelope I just forgot. Chances at a sable are few and far between; I'd just missed mine.

"Don't sweat it Mary," Dick said. "It happens to everyone. It's no different than a missed shot, except you've saved a bullet. We've all done it."

"He's right, Mary," Jack said. "There's no such thing as a perfect hunter."

Still, I should've checked the safety. It was a mistake I didn't plan on duplicating any time soon.

Both Dick and I were ready for a relaxing warm shower after the long day. We got more than we bargained for. The gas generator which ran the camp pump had gone kaput earlier in the day. The holding tank had water in it – hot water only – near boiling. It took us longer to enter the shower, trying to acclimate our bodies to the torrid spray than it did to clean ourselves up. Somehow we survived unscathed, though just a bit scalded, dressed and headed for dinner. The menu was a barbecue sampling of cuts from all the animals taken during the safari. The enticing aroma drifted toward us. We quickened our pace.

Our noses led us straight to a wild-game feast fit for a king. Ostrich, warthog, impala, duiker, bush pig, sable, kudu, steenbok and wildebeest were all cooked over an open fire. Overindulgence was a foregone conclusion. We couldn't resist the craving desire to taste a bite of everything. Every plate was piled way too high. Our stomachs were at full capacity in short order.

"Oh, I'm miserable." I leaned back in my chair slightly. "I couldn't eat another bite."

Two seconds later a dessert of bread pudding with strawberries and custard was placed on the table. It looked good. I just didn't have any room.

"You have to try this Mary. It's out of this world." Jack scooped a generous portion onto a small plate and handed it to me.

"Oh, I couldn't."

"No, you must, Mary. It is too good not to try."

"Okay, thank you. But I think Dick and I will just share this plate."

"It'll be a miracle if we finish it," Dick said.

We both took a bite.

"It's delicious," I said.

Jack heaped another plate full, placing it in front of Dick. "I knew you'd like it. We've got plenty. And you're on vacation."

It was good, but I didn't know how I was going to force it down. My stomach could only hold so much. Still, it appeared as if it might be rude if I didn't give it a try. It was strange though. If Jack thought it was so wonderful, why didn't he eat any himself? I never did understand that.

The cool night air was still, but crisp. The chilled touch of nature's hand stung our cheeks and fingertips as we plodded, with bulging midsections, back to our tent. It was a pleasant stroll nonetheless. The cloudless sky revealed millions of miles of open space crowded with the brightness of other worlds. In so many ways, Africa reminded us of our insignificance – the possibilities of days to come were infinite. Africa gives something to her visitors. It cannot be explained or even completely understood. You return home with an emptiness and a longing for the embrace of a place you just left. We took a moment to enjoy the starlit sky. A part of us would never leave Africa.

Everybody leaves something.

A Tear Falls: Mary

We were awake well before sunrise – in pursuit of eland and wildebeest again. Our bodies were worn-out. Our thoughts wrestled with the fact there were only a few hours left. Those hours were jammed with the numerous possibilities Africa offers. Such are the realities of final days.

I wrapped my arms around myself as the jeep rattled along the trail. The mornings were downright chilly some days. Though the blackness of night was graying, the sun had not yet made an appearance. I couldn't wait to get out and walk. The delay wasn't long. Even in the soft light we found where an eland crossed the road. Cold air tried to press in around us, but a long hike through the thorny bush warmed up the day in a hurry.

Three hours later we were sweating. We lost the eland's tracks in the rocks and were headed for the jeep, having seen little in the way of game. Optimism was suddenly difficult to come by. One morning the fields were full of wildlife as far as we could see – today it was almost lifeless. Our eyes began to drift from alertly scanning the land to staring at the monotonous ground before us.

It was then that the tracker stopped. He pointed and whispered, "Ngongoni."

"Wildebeest," Jack said, sticking his finger out next to the tracker's. "Do you see him Dick?"

Dick moved closer, following the indication of their aim. He stared for half a minute before spotting a dark shape at the base of a tree. He lifted his rifle to peer through the scope. The lone bull looked big, but then again, much of the game appeared big to us.

"Let's try to get closer."

The solitary bull seemed calm. The wind was perfect for a stalk. A herd would've made it more difficult – more eyes, ears, and noses. The bull's age was easily discernable by the heavily worn tips of his horns.

His bases were thick and had he not overused his headgear, the length would've been impressive. He was a good mature representative of the species.

The bull grazed, rarely lifting his head to examine his surroundings. When he did look up, he stared right toward us, but shortly went back to his grassy lunch. The blue wildebeest is a large antelope, often found in massive migrating herds. Bluish-gray in color, a mature male can weigh as much as 600 pounds. Sometimes referred to as the poor man's buffalo, these solid creatures have a much deserved reputation as being one of the toughest antelope in all of Africa.

We crouched for fifty yards, crawled fifty more. The bull's head popped up. He stopped chewing. Grass hung from his mouth. Dick quickly propped himself against a small tree. He clicked off the safety. Just as his finger touched the smooth trigger, the wildebeest let out a loud snort. A sudden breeze lifted the bull's mane from his neck. At that moment, this beast, this antelope, sometimes called ugly, was one of the most striking creatures I could imagine.

He turned his head for a brief moment, as if ready to run. That small hesitation offered Dick the perfect shoulder shot. He took it. The blast of the rifle was immediately followed by the *thwack* of a solid hit. The bull hunched forward and charged off in the same motion.

"Nice shot. Come on, let's go."

The shot looked good. Dick said it felt good. But the wildebeest ran far from sight. The trail was easy to find and easy to follow, sprayed with blood for 200 yards. Then it tapered off and disappeared. It was going to be a long day. One of the trackers took off after what appeared to be the wildebeest's tracks while the rest of us searched in wide circles for more blood.

We searched for over an hour, finding a tiny splotch of blood here and there. It was almost hopeless, but we couldn't give up. Sweat soaked our shirts. The worst looked to be a certainty. Then, the other tracker showed up. He waved us forward.

"Come, come," he said. "Ngongoni. Ngongoni."

"We've got him," Jack said. "We must hurry."

As we sprinted to keep up with the tracker, branches whipped at our heads and tangled grass threatened to trip us. We ran around a massive baobab tree and stopped.

The bull was fifty-yards away, lying alone in a patch of thick grass. We could only see his horns. When he turned his head in the golden pond of grass, it gave him the disturbing appearance of a Cape buffalo. He stared at us. Instantly, he pushed himself up and started to gallop off.

Dick snapped the firearm to his shoulder and squeezed off a shot. The wildebeest was quartering away. The bullet struck home.

"A little far back," Jack said. "Hit him again."

Dick jacked another shell into the chamber, but before he could fire, the bull's legs came out from under him.

"Sometimes these wildebeest can be tricky. Even when they're hit well they can go for hours. As hot as it is, I'd hate to be out here the rest of the afternoon chasing this one. Be ready, in case he decides he's not done yet."

He was done. The first shot penetrated both lungs. How he went as long as he did is beyond me.

The tracker who'd found the bull ran up to Dick. He reached out and took his hand. "Very good," he said. "Very good." He bared his teeth in a genuine smile. Everybody was smiling. It could've been a disaster.

Like always, the crew began to make short work of the bull.

"Would you look at that beautiful, long tail," I said.

"Yes, it is something isn't it? Some tribes use the tails as fly swatters. They swat them back and forth by their ears to keep the tsetse flies at bay," Jack said while one of the trackers demonstrated.

There were subtle times, like shortly after Dick had taken his wildebeest, when I almost felt as if I were in a National Geographic video. I didn't feel like the subject and it wasn't as if I were just watching one. It was more than that. I felt a genuine part of it. That if someone back home were watching at that moment, they would view me as a natural part of the scene. But, in truth, I was only a visitor. I'd be gone soon. These natives with their wildebeest fly swatters and their genuine love of life would remain among the mopane forest, among the animals and true hardships we can hardly imagine.

Little hunting is done during the heat of the day in much of Africa. Game can be found in all hours of the day, true, but like most big-game hunting, prime hours are at dawn and dusk. But this was the last day. We were tired and we were hot, but did we want to take a break? No way.

"I've got some paperwork to catch up on," Jack said after an hour lunch. "How is it if we meet at the truck in about an hour?"

"That'll be fine," we said.

What else could we say? If he had paperwork to do, he had paperwork to do. That's just the way it was. Like it or not, we accepted it. So we spent the next hour in our tent, peering out periodically to see if he was done with his paperwork. Eventually, the hour passed.

We were waiting by the jeep when Jack arrived.

"We're not going to take the jeep this afternoon. Mathew brought in another vehicle with supplies today. It's much better for hunting."

The vehicle was an old military model from Germany. It was beaten, but unbroken by Africa's unforgiving bush. Every door, the top half of the shell and the windshield of the army green 4x4 had been removed. Getting in and out was simple and, with the windshield gone, spotting game was never inhibited by bugs or dirt. Though the bugs and dirt we ate sometimes left us wishing for one.

Eland were proving to be an elusive bunch. We covered miles and miles of ground without finding a single track. We were over an hour from the vehicle, searching in vain. You'd think the largest antelope in the world wouldn't be all that hard to spot. Their cream coat blends in perfectly with the dry African bush and their nomadic behavior makes predicting their movements all but impossible. Unlike many mammals, eland are rarely territorial. They are much more content roaming vast areas of the bushveld.

As the African twilight began to bless us with another breathtaking sunset, we slowly realized an eland in Zimbabwe would be an unanswered wish.

"It's too late to continue on," Jack said. "But maybe on the way back to the vehicle we will see something."

It seemed unlikely. We'd seen very little since Dick shot the wildebeest. But there's a funny thing about hunting. Anticipation beckons the hunter to peer over the next rise, to walk just one more mile, to stay just one more minute. Dick and I were not overly convinced about the prospects of the final hour, but we shared a childlike wonderment of the possibilities beyond the next brush line – we shared hope.

Careful what you hope for.

The tracker stopped and crouched down pointing. "Mhene."

Steenbok.

We all hunkered when it darted from a patch of grass into some low bushes. It was a dainty little antelope with long slender legs and oversized ears. He was nimble, zipping from one patch of cover to the other. If I hadn't been looking in the right spot, I would've missed him completely.

"Can you see him, Mary?"

"Yes."

"Shoot him before he runs away."

I rushed the shot, but the tiny antelope dropped straight to the ground.

"Nice shot," Dick said.

I was a little surprised. I'd felt myself flinch. But I dropped it. Maybe I wasn't so bad shooting off the cuff. It wasn't a long shot, but it was quick. I had no rest and the target was tiny. Not too shabby.

"Let's go have a look, shall we?" Jack led the short distance to the small bush.

We were all caught off guard when the hardy little antelope took off. I was nearly devastated.

"Shoot him again. Hurry!"

By the time I reloaded, the steenbok was into another patch of shrubs. I just stared at the ground. "What happened?"

"You must've just grazed him. Almost any impact is enough to take down one of these little buggers. We had better get after him. Once darkness sets in we can forget about it," Jack said. "I just wish there was more blood to work with."

We knew it was going to happen, but when the steenbok flushed from the bushes I was caught off guard. I wished I had a shotgun – though I'm not sure it would've made a difference. The little antelope ran more than 100 yards before disappearing into the undergrowth. It didn't look good.

We had to keep after him. Blood was scarce and light was diminishing, but the tears in my eyes were all it took to convince the others to press on. Soon, we had our flashlights out, searching in vain for blood that wasn't there. We couldn't see, we weren't properly dressed for the icy fingers of the night air – we had no choice. We had to give up. I felt queasy.

"The cats will have him within the hour. Probably sooner," Jack said. "Nothing ever lasts long in Africa and nothing goes to waste. The scavengers make sure of that."

"I think I should give up hunting all together," I said to Dick on the way back to the vehicle, unable to hold back tears.

He didn't say anything. What could he say? He knew how I felt. Nothing he said or did was going to change it. He could've told me giving up hunting was a bad idea. That even the most accomplished hunters... but I was in no mood for logic. I was emotional and my husband knows when to leave well enough alone.

The road back to camp was silent. I knew much of that was my fault. Add to that the reality it would be the last night we drove back to camp and there wasn't much to say. I pulled the trigger. The sharp teeth of guilt pierced my stomach and gnawed at my conscience. I realized something on that long, silent ride. As hard as losing a wounded animal was, I think it might be an important part of what it means to be a hunter. Every hunter should feel the way I did – at least once. As humans, it is our nature to pursue game, but it is a serious undertaking. I knew that with certainty.

Customary conversation flowed at dinner, but the mood was toned down. We didn't speak of it, but it was at the forefront of all our thoughts. We'd be leaving in the morning. We'd most likely never see these people again. And though we didn't know it, we'd never be the same. Africa had given us so much, but it had taken a part of us that it would never return. That is the trade. We wouldn't have had it any other way.

It was around the fire, reminiscing about the successes and failures of the hunt that we realized just how much we'd miss the camp. It had been like our home. We wouldn't forget it. We waited for darkness to unfold around the dying fire before retiring.

Roars, rustles and shrieks filled our last night. It was a fitting. Those sounds had frightened me before. Now they were almost comforting – almost. If nothing else, they were familiar. I didn't want to forget them, but I knew the smells and sounds would fade first. The entire staff was there to bid us goodbye at 8:00 a.m. So many friendly faces – faces we'd never see again. I fought back tears.

The drive to Harare was three hours with three police road blocks to pass through. It was apparent the word police was used loosely. Only one of the stops actually looked official or seemed professional. At each stop however, they demanded to go through the vehicle and check our papers. It would've only been a small hassle had they not always pointed their assault rifles at us. They all appeared as if they were just itching for a reason to pull the trigger.

"That boy couldn't have been more than fourteen," I said.

"Yes, many are even younger. The leadership, if you can call it that, has found the young have very impressionable minds," Jack said as we drove away from the latest roadblock. "They are promised riches and glory and fed lies. Many of these children have been subjected to a murderous way of life since they were able to hold a gun. It's become all they know. You can't help but feel sorry for them. That is until you see them beat, or shoot to death an innocent, unarmed person because he or she refuses to give up their homes. Only seconds later, their barrels still hot, they light up a cigarette and laugh about it." Jack shook his head. "I've seen it happen too many times. I'm afraid the massive downfall this country is racing to will be irreversible."

The last roadblock was just outside Harare. Two "officers" donning loose-fitting, green, military fatigues pointed their weapons at us while forcing us to pull all our gear from the vehicle.

"Unzip the bags so we can see what's inside. And give us your papers so we may inspect them."

The older one did all the talking and spoke very good English. He kept his rifle pointed at us while his much younger subordinate took our papers and rummaged through our gear.

"Unlock and open the two cases there. What is in them?"

"Guns," Dick said.

"What do you have weapons for?"

"We've been hunting."

"Yes, very good. Now let me see them." He kept his gun pointed at one of us the entire time.

"Where is the ammunition?"

"In the bags."

"Are they loaded?"

"No, and the bolts are removed so they will not fire."

"Yes, but accidents happen."

"No, look," Dick pointed at the chamber of a rifle. "See, we've removed the bolts and put them in with the ammunition in the other bags. There's no way these rifles will work without bolts."

"Yes, I see what you are saying, but I have seen a weapon disassembled like this fire a bullet before."

That was impossible, but there was no use in arguing with him.

"We'll be careful," Dick said.

"Yes, you must be. It is my decision that everything is in order here. You may go on your way."

We said thank you, then spent the next half hour repacking the bags and the car, while vehicle after vehicle passed by with only the wave of a barrel by our two friendly "officers".

We finally made it to our hotel room around 8:30 that evening. We were tuckered out. It didn't matter. We tossed and turned all night long. One hour in the hard hotel bed made us realize we already missed the cramped tent, the laughing hyenas, and the savage beauty in the darkness. The noises had changed to honks, loud shouts and strange crashes – the midnight cacophony of any large city. Give us lions roaring and elephants snapping trees any day.

We were only one day removed and it already seemed so distant. We had an ace in the hole to keep our spirits up though – we were on our way to Botswana and a new adventure.

Botswana

A New Land: Dick

Botswana is a sparsely populated country in comparison to its African brethren. Landlocked, its borders touch Zimbabwe on the east, South Africa on the south and Namibia on the north and west. The southern part of the country, covered by the Kalahari Desert, is relatively dry for most of the year. Further north, the swamplands of the massive Okavango Delta reveal some of Africa's most unique game species, such as the swamp-dwelling sitatunga. This prime hunting land, teeming with wildlife, was once thought of by westerners as nothing but a wasteland. But one person's idea of a wasteland can be another's idea of paradise. We fell into the latter group. Wasteland? I don't think so.

It was warm with midday temperatures reaching as high as 85°. It seemed much warmer when we were out stalking game. At night it was usually a comfortable 40°; the cool morning air was always refreshing. For the most part, the weather was predictable. It was in direct contrast to the change-by-the-second weather patterns we were used to in Nebraska.

We spent one evening in Maun before heading for camp. We'd be hunting with a highly recommended outfit called Safari South. A staff truck with the company's insignia was waiting outside the hotel Friday morning. We were scheduled to make a brief stop at the city office to make sure everything was in order; of course, it wasn't.

"I'm sorry, but I do not have licenses for either of you. Are you sure you sent us your information?"

The young woman in the cramped office had sincere eyes, but it didn't change the fact that we'd traveled across the Atlantic to hunt in one of the world's great wildlife arenas and the licenses which were supposed to be waiting for us were absent.

"How could you not have our licenses? We sent in all the necessary paperwork months ago," Mary said.

The young woman rifled through every drawer and every pile of papers. "I can't understand what happened. Just let me make a quick phone call to see if I can't get this figured out for you."

Part of me wanted to yell, but what good would that do?

The young, dark-haired woman hung up the phone. "Great news Mr. and Mrs. Cabela. Everything is in order. The government just has not issued your licenses yet. They said they would have them ready and here within the hour."

"Isn't our charter flight scheduled to leave in thirty minutes?"

"The pilot will wait." She smiled before she sat down behind her desk.

Two hours later, a courier showed up with an envelope. He handed it to the young woman and walked out without a word. She glanced inside.

"Here you go. Everything is ready. The driver will take you to the airport now."

The plane wasn't there when we arrived. So, as we had done all day, we waited. In another hour an aircraft rolled up to the small hanger.

"Is that our plane?" Mary asked. "Do you think it's safe?"

"I don't know," I said. "There's only one way to find out."

"I don't know about this Dick."

The aircraft looked like an old Wright Brothers antique just recently dragged through a war zone. In Africa's unpredictable political climate, you could never be sure. Botswana was relatively stable compared to some of its neighbors, but it wasn't immune to periodic skirmishes along its borders.

The pilot opened his door and dropped a small wooden footstep down to the ground. Apparently, the steps had been lost.

"Good to meet you. Let me give you a hand with your baggage."

"How long is the flight?"

"Not long, maybe half an hour. First time in Botswana?"

"Yes it is. Should there be fluid leaking from there?" Mary pointed under the single engine.

"Oh, not again. Not to worry. It happens all the time." The pilot smiled. "She may not be much to look at, but she's a tough old gal." He slapped the door. "Come aboard. I'll try to keep her low enough for you to see some of the local wildlife. We'll be there before you know it."

We did see some wildlife, but the only species we could make out clearly were the long-necked giraffes.

"I just love watching them," Mary said over the puttering engine. "They move with such grace even though their gangly look makes them seem like they should tip over in the slightest breeze."

"There is our runway," the pilot yelled back to us.

All we saw was an open field. It looked more suitable for grazing cattle than landing airplanes. It even felt more suitable for cattle when the wheels touched down and bounced to a stop. At least we weren't susceptible to motion sickness.

The pilot turned and smiled at us. "Those warthogs have absolutely boiled the landing strip with all their digging and rooting. There's one of the little buggers right over there. I hope you shoot the lot of them."

"Would you look at those tusks," I said. "We never saw anything like that in Zimbabwe."

"Oh, that's just a little one," the pilot said.

"I can't wait to see a big one then," Mary said as the pilot opened the door and threw his little stepping stool out.

A big, green Toyota Land Cruiser drove up next to the plane. The driver was our professional hunter, Ronnie Kay.

"Hello Mr. and Mrs. Cabela. It's a pleasure to meet you. Here let me help you with that." We all grabbed some of the luggage and piled it into the back of the vehicle.

"Well, I'm off then," the pilot said. "Have a great hunt."

He waved to us before climbing back into his plane. The engine sounded as if it might cut out at first, but it held on. Before we knew it, he was airborne again. We were just glad we made it. The next thing we knew we were bouncing down another trail road carved into the landscape by the Land Cruiser traveling back and forth.

"How far to camp?"

"Oh, it's not far," Ronnie said. "Maybe 25 kilometers. We should be there in an hour."

The trail was in no condition for high-speed travel. Besides, it's difficult to spot game if you're moving too fast. The habitat was similar to what we'd seen in Zimbabwe with plains of high grass, mopane forests, scatterings of huge baobabs, lots of acacias and all sorts of other prickly brush.

"This is our on-site headquarters," Ronnie said as we pulled into camp just under an hour from the "landing strip".

Ronnie stepped away from the vehicle. "I need to go inside for a minute."

"Should we unload our gear?"

"Oh no, we will not hunt from here. It was my understanding you were interested in hunting both lion and leopard. The best cat hunting is at one of our spike camps."

"How far is that?"

"Not far, 45 minutes or so. We'll be there before you know it."

Ronnie was a thin man of average height. He was closing in on retirement age, but you'd never know it. He was in better physical condition than most people younger than him and he had a certain energetic disposition that made the years seem to fade away. He never wore any long pants, just khaki safari shorts – even in the thicker thorn brush. He had numerous scars and fresh scratches begging the question why.

"You get used to it," he said. "Everything in Africa either pokes or bites. There's really no use in fighting it." He paused for a moment as if in deep thought then said, "Of course, you might not want to take my word for it. Look at my legs."

We'd seen a few movies portraying professional hunters as ego maniacal and crass. In our naivety, I guess we'd probably expected that to be the case. But not with Ronnie. He was a soft-spoken man with an admirable humility that nearly caught us off guard.

We arrived at spike camp in time for lunch and a short rest. Our tent was roomy with two single beds, a clothes rack, a small table and a luggage bench. Private toilets and showers were just outside in small hut-like structures made of sorghum and grass. The showers had very little pressure, but it was always refreshing just to be able to take a shower so far from civilization. A shaded porch adorned the entrance to the tent where another small table with long legs held wash basins. There was even a mirror hanging on one of the porch poles. It may not have had all the amenities of home, but we were comfortable. It was more than enough for a hunting camp.

We'd seen a few animals on the ride to camp. There seemed to be plenty of game around. How different would this hunt be from Zimbabwe? At the time, we'd been highly impressed with what we'd seen there. It didn't take long, hunting with Ronnie, to see the differences between a mediocre operation and one that was top of the line.

Ronnie was a great hunter. He always hunted hard, genuinely striving to put us in position for very good representatives of the species we tackled. Our guide in Zimbabwe had been more interested in quantity than quality. He may've believed he would receive a better tip if we took as many animals as possible. We don't tip that way. Anyone who has ever guided us knows our tips are based more on effort and overall experience than on numbers in the bag. There are no guarantees in hunting. Wouldn't be much point in it if there were.

Ronnie had a bench mounted high on top of his Land Cruiser for spotting game. In one half day, we saw more animals than any whole day in Zimbabwe. Botswana doesn't by any means hold that much more game than Zimbabwe – sitting higher in the truck just allowed us to see above some of the smaller thorn bushes ubiquitously dotting the African savanna. Plus, Ronnie had a prime area, practiced sound wildlife management and worked vigorously with the authorities to quell any poaching problems.

"There's another herd of zebra," Mary said. "The game here is amazing. We've already seen zebra, warthog, giraffe, tsessebe, wildebeest, ostrich, Cape buffalo, impala reedbuck, steenbok, baboon, monkey, mongoose, kudu, jackal, hyena and leopard in just a few hours. Did I miss anything?"

"What about all the birds?" Ronnie said.

"That would be nearly impossible to count."

Ronnie smiled. "Too bad that leopard was a female. Had it been a male, we would've tried to put a sneak on it. Its okay to take a female, but a big tom is a much better trophy. We don't really like to shoot the females too often anyway."

"The trophy quality seems pretty good here," I said.

"Yes, it is. We haven't seen anything exceptional yet."

Most of the bulls we'd thus far seen were bigger than anything we'd taken in Zimbabwe.

"We're going to concentrate on lion and leopard this afternoon, but if we see something outstanding, we'll give it a second look," Ronnie said.

There are many ways to hunt the big cats. The most common is to

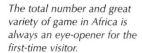

The total number and great variety of game in Africa is always an eye-opener for the first-time visitor.

wait over a bit of freshly killed bait from a blind or machan. Of course, we hadn't taken anything yet, so we would just do a little spot and stalk if we got lucky enough to come across something. We could get out to do some tracking, but Ronnie said he wanted to cover a lot of ground on the first day so we could get a feel for the area.

"The area we hunted in Zimbabwe had been hit by poachers pretty hard," I said. "Do you have that same problem here?"

"It is true most of Africa has a terrible poaching dilemma – especially where the political landscape is highly unstable or in countries where hunting is banned. The only thing in an area like this, so far removed from the cities, that curtails poaching, is hunting and other sound wildlife management. We are the only anti-poaching patrol around. The people here live simple, hard lives. We've found the best way to put a lid on poaching is to teach the value of conservation. At the same time, they see immediate benefits from the hunting revenues we generate."

"You seem to have it under control here," Mary said.

"For the most part we do. Sure, we get the occasional fellow who sets one small snare hoping to catch an animal to feed his family. We don't usually worry about those chaps. If it was me, I'd do the same for my family. It's the bands of poachers who cover the trails with snares, snagging every creature that crosses a field we hate."

They were bush meat poachers. It doesn't matter if it's an endangered species or an impala; everything is sold in the city merely as bush meat. The meat poaching industry has grown into a bigger problem than ivory poaching. Unlike the past, when poaching centered on one or two species, like the elephant or the rhino, today's meat poachers are indiscriminate. They'll take anything unlucky enough to step into a snare. The animals they take are not as glamorous as elephants, so they do not get the same press. That's why so few people outside the bush or hunting industry know about it.

Every hunting camp the world over has a gathering place. More often than not, that place is around the fire. After a hard day's hunt, there's nothing quite like the warmth of a gathering around the fire. Conversation sometimes ventures into more serious matters, but for the most part the campfire is a place to enjoy a few evening cocktails, relive past adventures and plan a course of action for the next day. It's usually light-hearted and the eyes are almost always heavy. But it's during the quiet moments around the crackling of the fire, when a lone hyena yips or a lion roars, that you know you belong. It's just something you feel. You can't explain it, but you know the others feel it too. There are few relaxing moments that can compare to those around a campfire after a long day of hunting.

Sleep came hard that first night. The sounds were familiar, but they seemed a little closer here; the tents seemed a little thinner when a leopard growled right outside. When the wake-up call came, we were tired, but we didn't delay. It was time to hunt. We left camp just as darkness was pushed away by pre-dawn light, as the sun gently warmed the morning.

Ten minutes from camp, Ronnie hit the brakes. Two elephants were crossing the road in front of us.

"We always yield right of way to them, as you can imagine." Ronnie smiled, but he kept a vigilant eye on the two bulls sauntering into the bush.

"They're beautiful," Mary said. "But I just wish they were a little further away."

A mere glimpse of these great kings of ivory in the wild instantly touches you. It's not the same on film or in a crowded zoo, where, too often, they've had their majesty all but stripped away. These massive mammals demanded respect, requiring all but the foolhardy to use caution when the feather of fear tickles their stomach. If you don't feel that tickle when you get too close, you've probably been watching too many cartoons.

A little further on, a roan crossed the road. These beautiful animals were scarce in this part of Africa and could not be hunted. But the animal's striking appearance was enough for us to stop.

"Their facial markings are similar to sable," Mary said.

"Yes," Ronnie said. "And they can be very aggressive like the sable, especially when wounded or cornered. A fight between two big bulls can be quite violent."

Lighter in color and with a more coarse hair than the black sable bulls or even the more reddish cow sable, roan do bear some resemblance to their longer-horned cousins. The black-and-white markings on the face and sweeping horns, although shorter, almost make them appear like a subspecies. Both male and female have horns. Like most horned animals, the male's are usually more massive. The roan's relative rarity in parts of Africa is normally accredited to the fact they are more vulnerable to changes in habitat than some of their African brethren.

The remaining morning hours passed by with numerous sightings of various species, some of which contained respectable representatives, but nothing truly outstanding. When it was time for lunch, we were ready. The temperature had risen from a pleasant warmth to a blistering heat. A two-to-three-hour break sounded just about right. The high temperatures drained us. We were used to hunting in the fall. Besides, most of the animals were less active during the midday heat. The extended break when everyone's bodies needed replenished with food, drink and rest was a rule, but if you were on a trail that rule could easily be broken.

We were still enjoying the latter part of our rest when one of the trackers spotted a big, bruiser warthog rubbing its side on a nearby tree. The boar had massive tusks.

"I know we are hunting cats this afternoon, but that is the kind of warthog that would give us nightmares if we passed him up. What do you say Mary? Do you want to put the sneak on him?"

Hunting in Africa is often an opportunistic game and opportunity only knocks so many times.

"Just lead the way," she said.

Warthogs have been described as ugly. To some extent it might be true, but they are also a unique and wonderful species. Most hogs around the world have tusks, but not like the warthog's. A warthog's display of teeth is impressive. They arc high and wide away from the mouth and, when necessary, can be used as capable and deadly weapons. From a distance the warthog seems almost bald. But closer inspection reveals a tuft of long hair running down their backs like an unkempt mohawk.

The warthog's entertainment value alone is worth the price of admission. When alarmed, their tails stick straight up in the air and their speedy little feet tear up the ground as they scamper away into cover.

Many of the warthogs in Ronnie's area were adorned with heavy tusks.

And who can't help but smile watching them wallow in the mud. Sometimes they can be downright cute.

Warthogs have also received an undeserved reputation for being a relatively easy wild hog to hunt. This is largely due to the fact that, unlike most wild pigs, warthogs are diurnal and are widespread with high population densities across much of Africa. In truth, exceptional warthogs are hard to come by. First of all, they must live long enough to grow heavy, long tusks and many predators consider the warthog delicious table fare. They also use their tusks to dig up roots and have a tendency to break them off. It is important for hunters to be careful to get a good look at both tusks before firing because very good warthogs with only one tusk are fairly common.

Poor eyesight is more than made up for by a keen sense of smell and good hearing. Mary and Ronnie's approach from downwind put them quickly within range. The boar's attention was focused on rubbing itself on the tree. It was totally unaware of their advance. Mary found herself a perfect rest in the crook of a small tree and fired. The warthog turned to run, but crashed to the ground lifeless within three yards.

"That is a fine, fine hog Mary. Congratulations."

"Thank you. I'm just glad I didn't wound him."

"Oh, I don't think you need to worry about that. In all my years of hunting, I haven't seen many shots as perfect as that."

"Well, I'm feeling lucky now," Ronnie said once we'd loaded the warthog into the truck. "What do you say we go find ourselves a cat – or two?"

Fifteen minutes later, Ronnie slammed on the brakes and all the trackers hopped from the back of the vehicle. Nobody had said a word, but Ronnie quickly joined them behind the truck, where they all pointed at the ground talking softly. Mary and I shrugged at each other then went back to see what was happening.

"Lion tracks," Ronnie said. "Two sets, both of them big. Problem is, they are two days old."

"At least it proves there are lions in the area."

"Yes, but there is no telling where they have gone off to. We'll just move along and find another track."

We didn't cut another track the rest of the afternoon. Nor did we put a stalk on any other animal. Still, Mary shot a nice warthog; we had to celebrate.

"We've taken several lion and leopard this year," Ronnie said the next morning. "The hunters who left camp before your arrival both took a leopard."

"I hope they didn't take the last two in the area," Mary said.

"Oh, there's no possibility of that. A regular count is done to determine how many of each species we can take from the area without doing any harm to the overall population. The quotas take into account predation loss and other natural deaths. We are not anywhere near our quota yet. The hunting pressure's been pretty heavy as of late though. I expect we will start to see more activity in the next few days. But you never can tell about cats."

"That's why they call it hunting," I said.

"Can't argue with that," Ronnie said. "It's the the challenge that makes it worth while."

He was right, of course, but it was more than that. It was the fresh air, the unending beauty of a unique sunset, the hope of what's around the next corner, the next hill, beyond the next sunrise.

The northern edge of Ronnie's hunting area was in the Okavango Delta. Largely made up of swampland, the Delta offers a chance at some of the more unusual antelope species like lechwe and sitatunga. We needed a break from the cat hunt, so we headed for the swamps to get a better look at a red lechwe bull feeding on the soft, wet ground at the marsh's edge.

"We need to be careful where we drive. Oh, bloody hell."

It only took a brief moment for the Land Cruiser's tires to sink into the swamp's tight grip.

"Keep watch on the lechwe while I try to get us out of here," Ronnie said.

He revved the engine, spun the tires and flung mud everywhere. The lone red lechwe bull didn't lift its head. It was upwind and so far away, I had to use my binoculars to keep an eye on him. How Kidane, one of the trackers, spotted it without the aid of any optics was beyond me.

"Where's our bull, Dick?"

"He hasn't moved. Didn't even look over here when the engine was cranked."

"Good. He's not going anywhere. I'm sorry about this. I know you are supposed to be on holiday, but if I could ask everyone to get out and push from the front we might just get out of this mess. I just need to find something to tie the wench up to first."

With a lot of grunting, pushing and cranking, we finally freed the vehicle from its mucky prison.

A few miles to the south, the plains were dry, the ground scorched hard. Here, two-and-three-foot high grass was still green even though it was a dry year. Much of the ground was also covered in shallow water. It was impossible to walk quietly; the standing marshland grabbed our boots, making a swishing pop, like a child smacking his food, but with more volume. Ronnie drove as far as he could. We found ourselves stuck more than once. The wench paid for itself in one day.

As Ronnie revved the engine and the tires spun, a small group of female lechwes we hadn't seen went running with their noses close to the ground, their ears flat against their backs. It almost appeared as if they were ducking when they charged off for thicker cover and deeper water. The local lion population preyed on lechwe often. Being the good swimmers they are, the handsome antelope looked to water for their escape.

To encounter a lone red lechwe like we had was somewhat uncommon. They are normally a highly gregarious animal. This anomaly may very well have presented us with a better opportunity to close the distance – one set of eyes is easier to fool than one hundred sets. The lechwe's preferred habitat made it most difficult to follow when it turned its back and bounded through the grassy lagoon. Its splayed hooves are designed for this kind of travel – not splayed as wide as the sitatunga, but still enough that they can move around in the marshy ground with not only ease, but grace. I cannot count how many times we stumbled and fell. The marshy ground was like suction cups on our boots.

Lechwe are wary, reclusive antelope, living in wide open marshlands that don't offer much in the way of cover. We hadn't sloshed far before Ronnie said, "This is about as close as we are going to get."

"Let's do it then."

Although I'd been hunting in one form or another all my life, it was still necessary to spend countless hours at the shooting range before our first African safari. I knew my shooting abilities would be challenged by a number of different situations. The shot was long, but I was confident.

Ronnie handed over the shooting sticks. I steadied the rifle in them. The mud schloped when I moved my right foot for better support and a red-eyed dove *hoop-ooed* off in the distance. I blocked it out. Then I didn't hear anything. That brief moment before I squeezed off, time stood still. It was just me and the lechwe. I knew the time was right, everything was perfect, I couldn't miss. When the 7mm jerked against my shoulder, it couldn't have felt more right.

The bull's reaction to the bullet impact was immediate and telling. He dropped hard, his legs flinging out from under him as he disappeared in the wet grass. We watched him for a moment to be sure. As we learned from Mary's steenbok, those quick-dropping animals can be deceptive.

"He isn't going anywhere," Ronnie finally said. "Great shot, Dick. Now let's get back to the truck. Dragging a 200-pound lechwe through this muck will not be as pleasurable as it sounds."

We managed to get the Land Cruiser stuck twice on the way, but we closed the gap. The soft ground made the going slow. Each time the swamp grabbed the tires in its muck, the distance seemed to double. On the fringes of the swamp, it was too shallow to skip across in a boat, but also inundated with too many deep holes for easy navigation in a vehicle. Two hundred yards was as close as we were going to get. The bull was dragged the rest of the way by sheer manpower. Though I tried to help, Kidane and Kadoni did most of the work.

We'd earned a long break for lunch, but were so fired up we barely took enough time to eat before heading back out. It had taken too long to retrieve the lechwe. We didn't eat until three – right on the truck, stranded in the middle of the swamp. The food was fulfilling, but it was no picnic pushing and pulling the truck after lunch.

When we'd finally freed the truck, Ronnie drove all of ten yards before hitting the brakes.

"There's another good bull." He pointed across the marsh. "Two lone bulls in one day. What luck."

He said this as sweat dripped off my chin in a steady stream.

"We can get a bit closer if we use that tall grass there, but we can't cut the distance by much. Do you think you can shoot that far Mary?"

"Oh, I don't think I even want to try. I wouldn't want to wound him. That would be terrible in the swamps."

"I'm sure you can do it," Ronnie said. "Just concentrate on one spot, high on his shoulder and gently squeeze the trigger. It's a piece of cake."

"Okay, I'll give it a try."

We left the vehicle and made our way through the high grass. We

Getting the vehicle stuck in the marsh couldn't prevent Mary from setting her sights on a red lechwe.

had to stay inside the wall of greenery or we'd be busted, so Mary pushed her barrel into the open to take the shot. The big bull jumped and spun, running in a mad dash straight to us. He was closing distance quickly until he staggered and fell. His horns were larger than the one I'd taken that morning. Best of all, we were able to drive the Land Cruiser right to it. Kadoni and Kidane were quite pleased.

Within 100 feet of leaving the delta, the air turned black with ash and smoke. The land went from marshy to dry and barren with very little transition. As far as we could see, the ground was black and smoldering.

"The fires help promote new grass, which the animals feed on," Ronnie said. "It also opens up some of the walls of long grass, giving us a better line of sight. The truth is that, although a bit unsightly and uncomfortable, it greatly benefits wildlife and does little if any damage to habitat. New growth is great nutrition for the plains animals which, in turn, are great nutrition for the larger predators and thus the burns help continue the circle. I am sorry we have to travel through these burned areas. They are a bit hard on the lungs and cover your body with soot, but it is positive for the animals and good for hunting."

We arrived back at Camp Motsaoudi a filthy bunch of characters – mud on our legs and boots, dirt, soot and black ash all over our faces, hands and clothes. It looked more like we'd been out battling brush fires all day instead of hunting. Long showers and deep drinks by the fire never sounded more pleasurable.

"I hope it's not rude of me to ask, but what happened to Kadoni's arm?" Mary said as we sat around the fire.

"Buffalo," Ronnie said. "Wounded bugger came right out of nowhere to gore him. It was wounded by another bull most likely. They can get pretty touchy when they're uncomfortable. Kadoni just happened to walk by at the wrong time. He lost his arm up to the elbow."

Ronnie was quiet for a moment, then glanced over to the skinning shed. "Still one of the best trackers I've ever seen. You'd think after something like that a guy would be afraid to go back into the deep bush. Not old Kadoni. As soon as he healed up, he was right back out tracking. I was a bit worried when we were on our first wounded buffalo, but he tracked him into the thick stuff. We've been in some hairy situations, him and I. I trust him. He trusts me. That's the way it has to be. Otherwise you could find yourself dead pretty quick in this business."

Every night around the fire Ronnie had great stories to tell. Many involved renowned professional hunter Harry Selby, whom he partnered with in Safari South. Ronnie was one of the last old professional hunters of Ruark's time, when hunting in Africa was near its height.

"Harry and I used to go to the Duck Inn, Peter Capstick's bar in Maun. We'd get to putting a few drinks back and start talking about our last adventures. Well, some of the stories in Peter's books seemed awfully familiar. Ol' Peter could sure tell a story though. Nobody can argue that."

We enjoyed his stories, tried to absorb the plethora of knowledge about the local plants, animals and people he willingly shared. And he was one heck of a story teller in his own right. But long, hard days always end in short nights. We were mesmerized by Ronnie's stories, but we didn't fight rest.

There isn't much of a schedule to live by in the bush. You easily forget what time it is and rarely glance down at your watch (if you're wearing one). I found myself forgetting what day it was. With no reason to care, I hardly ever asked. We lived by Africa's time – a schedule dictated almost entirely by the location of the sun. When the sun closed her eye for a long wink, we knew it was almost time to retire. About the same time many of the inhabitants of the veld awakened to begin hunts of their own. The bush never sleeps. When a lion starts to roar and a hyena laughs and a leopard saws through a pack of screaming baboons and an elephant rips down trees, I sometimes wish I didn't have to.

The Zebras Cry: Mary

I'd been sleeping as well as I had since we left Nebraska, when around 1:45 a.m. some kind of owl must've perched right above our tent and started hooting. That thing hooted all night long. I didn't get a wink of sleep. Of course, Dick slept like a log. Between his ground-shaking snores and the owl's incessant hooting, I didn't stand a chance.

I heard the camp staff before 6:00 a.m. Our wake up call was to come at 6:30. Since I was already awake, I woke Dick as soon as we were called for. We skipped breakfast, opting only for a small cup of tea. Lions retire early in the morning. It was in our best interest not to dilly-dally. I wanted Dick to take a big-maned male, but lion hunting was frustrating. Lions regularly feed at night so the first few moments after dawn and the last few moments before dark comprised our best chances. Did it keep us from trying all day? Heck no. Most days we were lucky if we saw any spoor, let alone an actual lion. Part of me wanted to hunt one too, but the apprehensive part was always a little relieved when the day ended without a close call with the king of the jungle.

Most of the morning was a luckless affair. No good luck, no bad luck – just no luck. It dragged along until the tall grass waved to us, pushed by a wind that rustled the trees. It brought with it a burst of cold air that decided to stay for a few days. Along with the wind, the landscape changed. It went from a fire-blackened savanna to more of jungle-like greenery which closed in around us. The trees stretched higher and the undergrowth was almost impenetrably thick.

Some days were filled with so much action we almost found ourselves hoping for a break – almost. Other days, we wouldn't see anything for hours. We'd been hunting lion all morning without seeing so much as a track. The change of scenery was a welcome distraction. We stopped for an almost tranquil lunch – almost. The menacing tsetse flies stung right through our clothes, refusing to be satisfied until every inch of our bodies were decorated with lovely, itchy, red welts. We rested under a canopy of verdant trees surrounded by the varied orchestrations of song birds. I was so relaxed from it all that I took a short nap after eating. Despite the tsetse flies, it was the best sleep I'd enjoyed in some time.

I awoke to a gentle nudge from Dick. "It's time to hunt," he said.

My, what a difference an hour can make. We were rejuvenated, but more importantly, it seemed as if the game received its own wake up call. There were animals everywhere. Big bulls of many antelope species were scattered in relatively close proximity. It wasn't a question of whether or not we could find a good one, but of which good one was better.

Right away we encountered a massive reedbuck by the swamp's edge, which Dick put down almost effortlessly. Before we could get it loaded into the back of the vehicle, a big old tsessebe poked its head from the brush. Kadoni tapped Ronnie on the shoulder and pointed. Ronnie took a look at him through his binoculars.

"He's a shooter. Would you like to go after him Dick?"

"Let's do it," Dick said.

"I think we can get a little closer if we use those trees over there for cover." Ronnie started for a cluster of small acacias with Dick and I right on his heels. He turned back to Kadoni. "Load up the reedbuck and wait here by the truck," he said before we hurried to the trees.

The tsessebe watched us the whole way. I think it even watched us sneak through the trees, but it didn't run. In point of fact, it took a few steps toward us until we entered into his danger zone and he ran a little ways in the other direction. When he stopped, he turned broadside giving Dick an opportunity. But Dick yanked and flinched. He hardly ever yanks and flinches. The bull ran into the brush.

"You hit him," Ronnie said.

"I'm surprised. I flinched pretty badly. I should've taken more time."

"It was a bit high, but I thought it was a solid hit. Just the same, put another bullet in and keep it on safe. I've seen too many animals go for hours when not hit properly and sometimes even when they are. Just be ready."

I could see Dick was upset with himself. It was time to prepare myself for a long day of tracking.

"There he is right over there," Ronnie said, pointing. "Looks like you may have hit him better than I thought. Let's keep it ready though, just in case."

We couldn't believe it when we saw him lying with his head on the ground. We were sure he'd pop up and try to run. He didn't move.

"Look here," Ronnie said, pointing to the wound. "You hit him pretty high. I'm a little surprised he didn't go further. He is an old bull though. He might have been a bit weak."

The bullet hit the shoulder, but was way too high. It shouldn't have put him down as easily as it did – he was scarcely 30 yards from where Dick shot him. I can't explain my relief. Wounded animals are the worst.

We had both antelope field dressed just before sunset. Vultures were on them immediately. They had every single morsel devoured within seconds. I don't know how they home in on a kill like they do. It sure is something to see.

We took the roundabout route to camp. Halfway back Kadoni said something to Ronnie.

"Yes, I see it," Ronnie said softly.

We could see what they pointed at. It looked like a huge boulder – until we closed the distance. It was much more sinister. It was a dead elephant.

"Bloody poachers. They didn't even take any meat. Just ripped away the ivory and left the rest to rot."

"It looks fairly fresh," Dick said.

"Yes, I'd say less than a day. Probably last night. Just when you think you've got it under control, the bastards sneak in, steal their gold and disappear. I must warn you, we will go after these poachers if we see them."

"Will they be armed?"

"Probably not, they usually kill with snares. But just the same, I'd prefer if you stayed in the truck with Kadoni if we catch up to them."

We never crossed paths with the poachers. I'm glad we didn't. I really didn't want to be part of a shootout if they did have firearms. I can't say I wasn't angry. I wanted to cry.

"I'm sorry you had to see that. I know it's not much of a consolation, but it will not go to waste – nothing in Africa does. The hyenas, vultures and lions will make short work of the carcass. We really are getting the problem under control. It used to be much worse. All that's left of the elephant poachers around here are a few small bands – we'll get them. I'll report this. The authorities will come in and put pressure on the local population. They will eventually give up the responsible parties."

The dead elephant weighed heavily on our minds that evening. It was such a waste. However, it didn't keep us from the over-indulgence we cursed ourselves with on a nightly basis. It was lechwe soup, lechwe burgers, mashed potatoes, onion gravy, squash, and peas. We ate too much. We initially believed we might lose a few pounds on safari, but at this rate we'd be really fat by the time we went home.

The next morning our wakeup call came at the scheduled time, but we found Ronnie hard at work on the Land Cruiser. We ate a leisurely breakfast, sighted in our guns – one of them was way off – and loafed around until he was ready. It was nice not to be so rushed for once. We were slowly acclimating ourselves to Africa's pace. It was a relaxed tempo. You just took things as they came. If the Land Cruiser needed work, you worked on it. The lack of stress was pleasant.

"Thanks for waiting. The vehicle is ready now. Since I've wasted much of the morning, I think we should take it easy today. We'll just go out to have a look around. Maybe fill some of those plains game licenses. You never know."

We didn't see much. The animals must've been resting as the sun scorched the plain. We did eventually encounter a nice warthog, but I missed him. So much for sighting in the rifles. The morning was gone before we knew it.

"What do you say we eat lunch by the water today? It's not exactly the beach, but early afternoon is a good time to catch game coming in for a drink. This area is really dry. The water holes are few and far between this far south of the Delta and they become like cafeterias for game to congregate." Ronnie waited a moment then shrugged. "Of course that doesn't mean there will be anything there today."

The beach was nothing more than a small mud-hole surrounded by vegetation. Sure there was water, but it didn't look like enough to quench the thirst of an impala. Ronnie and Kadoni went right to work gathering small bushes and grass to build a temporary blind about 50 yards from the edge of the drying puddle. Despite the one arm handicap, Kadoni was impressive in his ability to use a machete. He did the work of two men. His swift, powerful swings soon had enough thorny thicket and grass to break up our outline. We were well hidden and more comfortable than we could've expected.

"Now if we just wait a while, we should have a few animals come in for a drink after their noon rest," Ronnie said while he unpacked lunch.

We'd barely taken a bite when Ronnie interrupted us. "Now that's a warthog," he said softly. "Why don't you slowly get into position to take him Mary?"

Me? Hadn't I missed one earlier? Shouldn't I let Dick take this one? My confidence may've been shot, but the hunter in me took over. I couldn't have fought it if I wanted to. The big tusker took small tentative steps toward the water, then he'd scamper away only to sneak back up. Waterholes had always been dangerous ground. He eventually put his mouth to the water. He was facing straight at us. It would have to be a head shot or nothing. I chose nothing. I just wasn't comfortable with it. Besides, I was a patient shooter, he had to move sometime. It was a chance I thought worth taking.

"Whenever you're ready," Ronnie said.

The big boar rolled around in the mud like he was grooming himself for a hot date. He meticulously made sure he had his backside covered and his belly nicely caked. When he finally finished, he stood and turned broadside.

The angle was good, but I was shaking. I didn't want to miss again. Goodness sakes, I couldn't steady my trembling hands. Then, against all my better judgment, I took the shot anyway. I shouldn't have, but I did. The bullet smacked the biggest warthog we'd seen right in the back leg. He took off on a tear. Ronnie and Dick kept their binoculars on him, watching him run nearly 500 yards before he fell.

We waited. When he didn't move for a few minutes we decided to go have a look. Was it possible I'd hit a vital or severed an artery somehow? That would be fortuitous. When we closed within 50 yards, the boar saw us and struggled to his feet.

"Shoot him again Mary," Ronnie said.

I brought the rifle to shoulder, flipped off the safety and squeezed in one full motion.

I hit him right in the heart. It was over.

No trembling whatsoever. I didn't have time. I guess I shouldn't take so long trying to steady myself. The mud-caked boar was fat with eleven-and-a-half inch tusks – a real brute.

We were back in the blind trying to finish our lunch in short order. On my second-to-last bite of a lechwe sandwich, ten zebras wandered into the waterhole for a drink.

"Grab your rifle Mary," Ronnie whispered. He never took his eyes off the big stallion in the group. "He's the third one from the right. Load your gun and find him in your scope. Take a deep breath. Just wait for it. When it feels good, squeeze the shot."

Zebras are some of the most striking animals on the planet. Their horse-like bodies are decorated with a beautiful array of black and white stripes, individually unique like a fingerprint. They are also one of the most identifiable animals in the world – everybody knows what a zebra is. Although similar in appearance, zebras are not horses. Most attempts to domesticate zebras have failed miserably. Make no mistake about it; a zebra is a wild animal. They are tough with powerful speed and endurance and will not come to eat a carrot out of your hand. They are not easy to put down with one shot, but like any big-game animal, a well placed first bullet shouldn't allow them to go far.

I knew when I squeezed the trigger; it was a perfect shot. The stallion ran less than 25 yards before collapsing. Still, I surprised myself. My confidence level was about as low as it could get with the lousy shooting I'd been doing. This was a huge step in the right direction. I could almost feel myself rising; suddenly I could conquer the world.

What happened next, I never witnessed again in nearly 20 years of hunting in Africa.

When that stallion went down, all the females in the herd began running around in confusion, crying. Zebras often produce high-pitched barks, neighs and squeals, but this appeared to be something entirely different; their whines had an almost somber sound to them. It was heart rending. I couldn't hold back my own tears. It wasn't until we exposed ourselves they finally ran off in alarm. I've taken many zebras since then, have been along when Dick or one of our children has taken one and have not observed anything even remotely similar to this. For that, I am grateful. It was almost enough to make me quit hunting. I would've missed out on way too much.

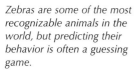

Zebras are some of the most recognizable animals in the world, but predicting their behavior is often a guessing game.

<u>First Nyati:</u> Dick

Oppressive afternoon heat and a slight breeze evaporated our sweat before a bead could gather to slide down the side of our faces. Dry air insisted we keep our mouths wet with occasional sips from our water bottles. Dust and dark soot from burned fields gathered in our nostrils, around our eyes and in our throats, adding to a thirst we could not quench.

Wildebeest seemed to be in short supply. With dusk approaching, we decided to hunt back to camp. The sunset's orange glow was awe-inspiring almost every evening. If it wasn't for two old, bachelor Cape buffalo, my eyes would've been glued to God's magnificent display of fading daylight until it was covered by a blanket of darkness. But God also created a magnificent creature called buffalo. And so, for the moment, the solidly built horned beast with his fiery stare trumped all else.

"He's a shooter Dick. I think we should give him a go." Ronnie's binoculars were stuck to his eyes.

How could I refuse? It was a Cape buffalo – Black Death – or, in Kadoni's native tongue, nyati. The dangers of buffalo hunting are legendary. Though I had no desire to add to the legend with my own skin, I was pulled from the Land Cruiser by an unseen force to give chase. Was it bravery? I wouldn't go that far. A fascinating desire had a hold on me for some time. I could never read enough spine-tingling, near death stories of charging buffalo. Now it was my turn.

As we closed the distance, a minor tremble found its way to my hands. I forced my legs to take the next step.

Was I really prepared for a showdown with a Cape buffalo? It didn't matter; I was committed. I had confidence in my .375 and if things got too hairy, I trusted in Ronnie's vast experience.

We inched closer. The old pair glared at us, their noses in the air. There was no mistaking which bull we were after. Both sets of headgear were ominous, but our bull's horns were longer, deeper and heavier.

I wasn't sure what to expect. Would he charge? Would he run? I suspected the latter, but I was under no illusions about the temperament of nyati – unpredictable.

The big bull turned.

"He's about to run, Dick. Take him."

Both buffalo bolted at the blast, but stopped and turned after only 50 yards. I felt good about my aim, so we waited. Then the big-bossed buff confirmed it when he swayed, stumbled and finally fell. A calm relief wiggled its way into my thumping heart. Thank heaven there was no belligerent charge.

"It's the dead ones that kill you," Ronnie reminded me. I think he could sense me start to let my guard down. "Let's go have a closer look to make sure. We haven't much light left."

That calm relief was barreled over by trepidation. We approached slowly. Then at 20 yards, the bull shifted and tried to stand.

"Put another one in him Dick."

I gave him another 200-grain dose of lead poisoning, with little effect.

"Again!"

He never moved after that.

We moved in to retrieve the buff, but our advance was stalled by a 1500-pound bull with an attitude. The other buffalo decided to stand his ground between us and his fallen comrade. Kadoni leaned over to grab a small stone. He tossed it toward the buffalo. The rock bounced to a stop on the ground by his front hooves. He didn't give it a glance. He took a step toward us.

Ronnie and I kept a bead on him while Kadoni and Kebone threw stones. He snorted and shook his head. The two natives backed away as the buff advanced. They threw everything they could get their hands on, but he wouldn't be deterred. Finally, when the lane was clear, Ronnie fired a round at the bull's feet. The fire in his conviction extinguished immediately and he hurried off into the tall grass.

It was one of the most unexplainable feelings I'd ever had. I could

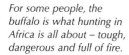

For some people, the buffalo is what hunting in Africa is all about – tough, dangerous and full of fire.

literally feel blood pumping through my body. The rush didn't begin to taper until we finished with the pictures. It stayed with me long after.

I think it was then I decided we'd be coming back to Africa. Oh yes, we'd be coming back to Africa soon, no matter what.

Risk. It's one of the   alluring aspects of hunting dangerous game. Your life might depend on your abilities. The outcome is never 100% knowable. Sure, I'd questioned the strange desire to put myself in such a situation. I can't explain why. I don't know if anybody could. What I do know is there are few times in my life I've felt more alive than when hunting one of the Big Five.

Stars began to sprinkle the sky as Ronnie, Kadoni, Kebone and the others went to work. I helped load some of the meat, but spent the greater part of the next hour and a half as a spectator. The others caped, field dressed and cut up the buffalo for camp meat with precision knife work. As always, all extra cuts were divided amongst the local people.

We had a late start and had planned a relaxed day of hunting. Now it was late. We pulled into camp at 9 p.m. The fresh, cool air blowing in our faces during the long, quiet ride back gave us ample time to reflect on the day. We'd taken three fine animals – one happened to be my first of the Big Five. That night I slept like a log; vivid pictures of Cape buffalo kept me company in my dreams.

Early the next morning, we started off for lion. Luck was in the air, our confidence soaring from our earlier successes. Our thoughts of good fortune reached epic proportions when we found fresh lion tracks almost immediately – four females and one big male.

The African bush's quickest and most effective lines of communication travel through the voices of swift native whispers that seem to ride on the wind. The speed with which information travels great distances on nothing more than fleet feet and quick voices would make the Pony Express jealous. It was upon these communication lines that Ronnie learned lion roars had been heard outside the next camp. We picked up the trail less than 500 yards from the living quarters. Lions had been here not long ago. With any luck, we could catch up to them shortly.

"I think it might be best if you stay at the truck with Kebone and Danger," Ronnie said to Mary. "Dick, Kadoni and I will stay on the tracks. Lions have acute senses of sight, smell and hearing. Too many bodies could give our stalk away before it starts."

So off we went in search of danger, the thrill of the chase, that ageless journey following the same path the earliest human did when he took his spears to follow an instinct connecting him to the earth in the most honest way. On the trail, my mind was consumed by thoughts of the lion's brute strength, rapier claws and flesh-tearing teeth. A storm was beginning to brew in the pit of my stomach. It felt good.

Kadoni's eyes rarely left the ground. He read the lion sign like a book – a book without an ending. There were long stretches where I didn't see a track, but Kadoni never slowed his pace. It was almost as if he could smell them on the breeze. Sometimes we followed the spoor through open fields where we could see for vast distances. Other times, times when my heart beat like Zulu battle drums and my stomach slithered into my throat, we could see no farther than four feet in every direction. Those times, when the lions led us into the thicket or the long grass, the hot sun, dry air, and slight breeze couldn't evaporate the sweat from my brow.

Every once in a while, I thought I could feel them watching us. It felt like a spider creeping up the back of my neck.

We followed their tracks for miles, but when they entered a labyrinth of thick thorns our better judgment grabbed hold on the back of our collars and pulled us from the stalk.

"Bloody wind. It keeps changing direction on us, alerting them to our presence every time we start to close the distance."

I could see the disappointment in Ronnie's eyes.

I wonder if he could see anything in mine – like that small part of me that felt relief when he decided we wouldn't crawl through the thick stuff. The lion had won another round; we were knocked down, but we weren't out.

We never saw the lions, but to know they are there, ahead of you, maybe in the next bush, your senses are in a higher state of awareness. I knew I'd miss that feeling. I didn't realize it until we were headed back for the vehicle, but we'd hiked several miles chasing those lions. The walk back took the rest of the morning. We never saw another person, but we did spook the occasional antelope and had to detour around a small herd of elephants.

My kind of walk.

My Feet Get Wet At Camp Shindi: Mary

I was well rested when Dick and the others dragged themselves back to the Land Cruiser. I had time to finish my prayers, write a letter and enjoy the entertainment of three impalas – two rams and a ewe – all before taking a short nap. The two rams would touch horns every once in a while in an attempt to show off for the ewe. She was snobbishly disinterested. The fight never became too aggressive though. It seemed more playful than anything. One thing is for sure, that female never gave them a second look.

The guys were gone so long, I was sure they'd return with a grand tale of a thick-maned lion. Their tired faces told a different story. The stalk had not been as fruitful as was hoped. We'd only stay at this particular camp one more day, so if this is where Dick would take his first lion, it would have to be quick.

Lions are usually reclusive, but can, in certain situations, be quite dangerous. Wounded lions, lions that are surprised or feel threatened and a lioness with young cubs are all lions best approached with the utmost caution.

"Two villagers were killed by a lion in this area just two years ago," Ronnie said. "It was an odd incident. He never attacked again and we never found him. Often a big cat will acquire a taste for human flesh once he figures out how easy we are to kill. I doubt we taste any better than buffalo, but we're slow, we're weak, our sense of smell isn't worth a darn, we don't hear well at all and we don't have sharp horns. We can think and make tools. Those are our only defenses. Without that, the human race would've been extinct long ago. Not to worry though. For the most part, lions keep to themselves. It's the very old or crippled that usually turn to man-eating. They can't catch antelope anymore."

Just the same, I didn't tend to let my guard down in lion country. I wanted Dick to get his lion, but I have to admit, when he was on a trail, I was worried. I would be relieved when it was all done with. I did wish for Dick to have a chance, but our days were dwindling. Maybe we weren't meant to tangle with the "king of beasts". Fortunately, we could hunt them at the next camp as well – Camp Splash. Ronnie didn't seem too worried yet.

The next day began with a chill in the air. It was cooler than most mornings – so cold we could see our breath. We quick-stepped it to the campfire to warm our hands while we waited for Ronnie and the others.

We hadn't visited the far eastern edge of the concession yet, but Ronnie was confident we could find lions there. The habitat was strikingly dissimilar to any of the other areas. It was lush and green; water was everywhere and small palm islands were abundant.

"Lions sometimes like to rest on the small islands there. We often see pockets like this before the Okavango Delta. It's not quite a marsh, nor is it as dry as the grasslands," Ronnie said.

"It sure is pretty here," I said.

I was surprised we hadn't visited this place before. It was our last day. The urge to explore this verdant beauty at the edge of such a vast, dry veldt would be held in check.

We spent all morning traipsing through the area, with little in the way of luck. We didn't see much game. I thought that was strange with all the fresh greenery surrounding us. The area was obviously frequented by animals. The substantial prevalence of droppings and spoor provided ample proof. We saw few of these creatures that left those tell-tale signs. Thick vegetation gave them cover and escape routes to duck into when they were alerted to our presence. We may not have seen many of them, but they knew we were there. They saw us, they heard us, and they smelled us – they always do.

Ronnie smiled when it was time for lunch. "We still have the afternoon left. Plus, there are lions at the other camp, just not as many and the quality is not as good on average. I think we should eat lunch over there under that strangling fig tree."

"What kind of tree?"

"A strangling fig. It finds another tree and begins to grow around that tree until its roots have strangled and choked it, leaving mostly just the fig with anything resembling life. It's quite fascinating really."

Ronnie was more than a dedicated professional hunter; he had the knowledge of a biologist and though he may not have known it, he was also a poet, for only a poet could see with such clarity, fascination in nature's cruel ways – like the slow strangling death of a tree. Ronnie was more than just a professional hunter – he was a man with an unyielding affection for the plants and animals he lived among.

One of these regaled us with his presence over lunch. The gray lourie – the go-away bird. This particular feathered guest, invited or otherwise, perched high in the branches of a nearby umbrella tree, telling us in no uncertain terms what he thought of us. *"Goaway,*

goaway," he said. We heard, but we did not listen.

Our keen-eyed tracker glared into the umbrella tree.

"Kadoni doesn't like the go-away bird much," Ronnie said.

"Why's that?"

"He says they sit there on top of trees, warning all the animals you are there. He says that's why we haven't seen any game come to the water. He says you can kill the go away bird, but another will take its place and cry with double the tenacity." Ronnie laughed. "Kadoni says he still wants to shoot him."

The lion continued to evade our search. The day and our stay at Camp Motsaoudi ended without a lion. A new adventure at a new camp would have to be an acceptable consolation. Ronnie, Kadoni and two skinners would accompany us to Camp Shindi and Camp Splash – the rest, we'd never see again.

We took a Polaroid of everyone in camp the following morning, giving each person a picture of themselves as well as a tip and a small gift of appreciation. Then we said our goodbyes. The entire camp staff gathered to see us off. The truck pulled away as we waved to them with the certain knowledge we would never see them again. It was a strange moment. I was excited to embark upon our new journey, yet it was these contented faces fading with the distance I would miss. I couldn't help but wonder, would they remember us?"

Camp Shindi was a photography-only camp. It was a modern tent camp with running water and flush stools – all the amenities of home. Well, close enough.

"What do you say we do a spot of fishing this morning?" Ronnie asked.

Dick and I loaded ourselves into the boat while the fishing gear was tossed in.

"I think we might want to leave one of our spring catalogs here," Dick said.

He pointed to the old, worn out, rusty tackle. It was weathered and tired, leaving much to be desired, but it was its weathered, tired, rusty, tooth-marked nature that proved its reliability.

On his second cast, Dick hooked a tiger fish. The violent fight ended quickly when the aptly named fish snapped the line. Tiger fish are endowed with massive razor-like teeth capable of snapping off a finger; 20-lb. monofilament would be more like a toothpick attempting to stop Paul Bunyan's ax. The steel leaders tied to the end of our line were not nearly long enough. Despite the tackle's self-proclaimed reputation, we didn't hook another fish during the remainder of the afternoon. So, when the bugs came out like a full-force hurricane, we tucked our tails and headed for camp.

A single cognac at the fireside that evening hit the spot. Sleep was a foregone conclusion, though it didn't last. It was one o'clock when I heard my first lion roar.

"Dick did you hear that?"

I dared not talk above a whisper lest I accidentally gain the lion's attention.

"Dick, wake up."

He kept snoring. How could he sleep through that blood-curdling echo? That deep guttural challenge to the world was as primitive as life itself. The lion's roar is the spice of nightmares. Dick slept through it all. His snores deep and loud like the lion's roar. How I hoped the predator wouldn't see them as reason to come investigate.

"Dick, wake up now!"

"Wha – what is it?"

"Did you hear that?"

"Hear what?"

"A lion just roared right outside our tent. Come over here and squeeze into my bed."

The discomfort of two bodies in a single-occupancy bed were outweighed by feeling safe.

I eventually came to enjoy the sound of a lion roaring in the night – as long as it wasn't too close – and even sometimes missed it when safe at home in Nebraska in our king-sized bed. But that night, our first night at Camp Shindi, I did not enjoy the lion's roar. I did not enjoy it at all.

"Did you hear the lion roar last night?" Ronnie asked. He seemed quite delighted with it.

"It scared the hairs on the back of my neck stiff. But Dick didn't wake up."

"Not to worry Mary. They had most likely just made a kill and were merely expressing their satisfaction with themselves."

"They sounded hungry to me," I said.

Ronnie chuckled. "I have to do some work today in camp. Dick has expressed to me you would like to see the sitatunga – a treat I assure you. I will send you with our local pole guide, Mathew. If anyone can locate a sitatunga on command, it is him."

So Dick and I joined Mathew in a small dugout and headed into the marshes. Mathew was a thin, quiet man who showed us great respect and kindness. He had a constant smile that went well with his constant push of the dugout and alert eyes. He was working hard, but we came away with the distinct feeling he was enjoying himself, like he wanted to find a sitatunga too.

The elusive sitatunga is a diurnal, almost aquatic antelope. It spends most of its day standing in water. Their unique hooves are quite long and splay out. This makes their movements much easier in their preferred wet habitat. A sitatunga can, at times, submerse itself leaving only its nose visible in order to avoid detection. It would be amazing if they'd have to use this little trick. Tall green reeds grow thick throughout the marsh. An antelope, even a diurnal sort such as the sitatunga, most likely could avoid detection without snorkeling. Either way, we couldn't find one.

Mathew poled us leisurely through the open waterways between reeds. If not for the endless expanse of tall grass and a setting so much more beautiful and moving, we might've been in Venice. The morning sun glistened orange diamonds off the gently rippling blue water. Green and golden reeds bent slightly in the breeze above us. If we peered over the edge of the boat, we could see them drifting under the water. The splendid view intensified when an elephant herd waded across the water. The smaller ones had to lift their trunks high and swim across. The matriarch and other adults pushed through with ease and grace. It couldn't have been a more peaceful scene, something an artist should've witnessed.

We took a few photographs before deciding it was time to head back to camp. Around the next bend was a massive bull elephant. He blocked our pathway and took immediate offense to our presence. He stuck his head high in the air, giving us an icy glare. Then he came.

Mathew flung himself from the dugout to push us as fast as he could into the reeds.

"Oh my God, Dick! He's right there! He's charging! Oh my God! Oh my God!"

He was right on top of us. Then, this modern-day mammoth raised his trunk, flapped his ears and let loose a thundering trumpet. It only took him mere seconds to close to within a few yards. I did a frantic monkey-bar climb over Dick; he was calmly filming the entire episode. I didn't know what I was doing or where I was going, I just knew I had to get away from the hot, stinking breath of the beast bearing down on us. I scaled my husband and jumped from the boat, splashing one leg in the water and leaving the other stuck in the dugout.

"Oh my God! Oh my God!"

Mathew grabbed me, trying to hold me in the boat. "Wait, wait," he said.

Wait? This elephant was only a few feet away, snorting and still coming like a banshee. He wanted me to wait? I was fighting to get away, the guide was fighting to push the boat, while at the same time trying to keep me in it and Dick was trying to pick up the video camera I'd knocked from his hands clawing my way over him. I couldn't breathe, I couldn't move, I was shaking uncontrollably; and to top it all off, I

A close encounter with an enraged elephant can cause rash decisions.

thought I was about to die – for all I knew, I already was dead.

When the bull was close enough for us to reach out and touch him, he snorted one last time. It was like a quick burst of hot wind that almost tipped the dugout. Then, just like that, he was gone – swallowed by reeds.

I couldn't move, one foot stuck in the mud, the other stuck on the edge of the boat, all my fingers imbedded with a death grip in the hard wood. Dick and Mathew literally lifted me back into the dugout and put me in my seat.

That's when I realized I'd lost my shoe. It was stuck in the mud where I'd tried to display my water ballet skills. Our diligent, highly understanding guide eventually found my shoe in the bottom of the lagoon. Then we headed straight back to camp. Nobody said a word.

It was a mock charge all along. How was I to know? I knew very little of Africa, had never seen real elephants, other than in a zoo. I'd certainly never been charged by one – mock or otherwise. I thought I'd be happy if I never laid eyes on another elephant, but I was only kidding myself. For a long time though, I was terrified every time I saw an elephant. I don't care if a charge is mock or not, it's impossible for me not to shake when a 12,000-pound freight train of muscle is rushing toward me.

I needed two stiff drinks back at camp just to help the trembling subside.

"How can you remain so calm, Dick?" I asked.

"Calm? I thought my heart stopped. But what are you supposed to do? I couldn't have outrun him on land, let alone wading in a swamp. Besides, how many people can actually say they've been charged by an elephant? It was pretty awesome wasn't it?"

"I don't know if that's the word I'd use to describe it."

"You have to admit it was exciting though."

He was right. It was exciting enough to make my hair turn gray and make me overly jittery the rest of my life. Yeah, it was exciting – if you like that sort of thing.

Nyati Number 2: Dick

A small charter plane picked us up on a dirt runway. The pilot's landing – like that of a skipped rock – was almost as frightening as finding yourself confined to a small dugout while a charging elephant runs you down. He did a near-vertical nose dive straight for the runway before pulling up at the last second. He'd promised us a smooth ride to Camp Splash; he delivered a roller coaster flight of terror.

Three people greeted us on the runway – a married couple and their young son, who were just finishing a safari. We tried to warn them of the pilot's skills – or lack thereof. I'm not sure they were listening.

"Wow, Dad," the young man said. "They own Cabela's. That's our favorite catalog."

It's always nice to meet customers who've been satisfied with the level of service and quality of merchandise they've received. It's equally enjoyable to meet other fine people who share the same interests and passions as we do.

"Dad got a lion and a leopard. Have you ever shot a lion or a leopard?"

"Not yet," I said. "But I hope to get one here."

"Oh you will for sure Mr. Cabela. They're everywhere. The one's my dad shot were huge."

"How long were you here?" I asked the father.

"Ten days. I've never seen so much cat sign. I think you're in the right place. I hope you have great luck."

"Thank you. Have a safe trip home."

The next thing we knew, we were nestled in bed at our new camp, listening to the night life. It was a bit more vivacious here, or maybe activities took place closer to our tent. I'm not sure, but as soon as the sun went down barks, shrieks, snorts, growls, stomps, rustles, and roars made sleep hard to come by. There was a huge party outside our tent, the whole of the animal kingdom invited. It didn't bother me too much and I eventually fell asleep. Mary, on the other hand...

"I don't know how you can sleep through all those frightening sounds," she said the next morning. "Something actually bumped into our tent a few times. You didn't hear that? A lion roared, the hyenas were laughing, I don't know how many baboons were barking and shrieking and I heard what sounded like a big hog grunting right next to the tent."

"That was no hog, Mary," Ronnie said over the top of his coffee mug. "There was a leopard in camp last night. I imagine that is why the baboons were making such a ruckus."

"A leopard? Right next to our tent? Oh, I won't be able to sleep at all now."

"He's just prowling around. Not to worry, he won't bother us."

"Yeah, well I wish I had your confidence."

"Really, Mary. The leopard will not bother you. Just make sure to zip your tent all the way." Ronnie chuckled, finished off his coffee and headed for the truck.

We encountered an elephant shortly after leaving. Mary's face went pale immediately and her hands began to tremble. She was obviously more shook up from our previous encounter than I thought. The solitary bull we came upon was never closer than 100 yards, but Mary was clearly uncomfortable.

The greater portion of the day was spent in the vehicle. A long, bumpy ride in a hot, cramped truck. We encountered plenty of game, but nothing worth pursuing. Our hopes for lion were hanging by the thinnest of threads. The Land Cruiser came to a jolting stop just before I dozed off.

What the?

"Lions." Ronnie pointed.

At the edge of an open field, near a meadow waving with long, golden grass, two lionesses were soaking up the sun's rays. Finally, lions. One female was lying on her side, completely bored with the world around her. The other sat upright. She had the look of pure concentration; her stare was intense, unwavering. Her sleek golden coat was highlighted by well-formed, rippling muscles honed from a life which revolved around a necessity to hunt. She was a sentry – keeping watch, forever on the lookout for easy prey. They tolerated a few photos before disappearing into the thick wall of grass.

A renewed sense of hope smacked lethargy with a backhand. It filled the air like smoke from a grassfire. Lions. There's nothing like a wild lion, free and unencumbered by hoards of vehicles crowding in around them. No, these lions had something you cannot find on a video series or in a zoo. They have an arrogance unmatched by any creature I've ever seen. And they are wild. There is no cage, no Plexiglas partition, no television screen dividing you from one of the fiercest predators on earth. A stroll in this untamed land could put you face-to-face with beasts whose entire physical being is made for one purpose – to kill. Split decisions can make all the difference.

I was suddenly alert – my confidence rising like a mist from a river. Still, we didn't see another lion that day. It didn't matter, we'd had a sighting, there were lions nearby. Later that night, like a personal challenge, a lion roared as we slipped into bed. At that moment, it was as if we both knew we were destined to meet. I couldn't wait.

Crisp early mornings in the bush are always filled with the promise of a new day. Some folks may feel the same way about the city, but not me. The confines of monotonous city days are too predictable. Day in and day out, cursing traffic to and from a day, more or less, the same as the day before, trapped by a need to provide, a responsibility to pay the bills, a desire to get ahead. Out in the bush it all goes away – all the worries, all the stress, if only for a little while. An engrossing focus, an enlightening awareness and an unwavering drive to go one more step gives new meaning to the word alive.

An hour into the new day, anticipation switched gears to excitement. Lion tracks.

Four lionesses and one male left their mark on the dusty ground. A trained eye knew something of the predator's past without ever having seen it. Kadoni couldn't read a book, but he could read the words nature wrote down better than most. He deciphered its clues, translating their meanings with an expertise unteachable in a classroom.

Tracking is a meticulous, often sluggish endeavor, but tracking dangerous game demands much more than just reading clues. The buffalo or lion, especially if wounded, could be lurking nearby in the brush – waiting. An animal with a wound will often hide and lie in wait, unmoving until the last second when they can burst from mere feet. Awareness is key when on the trail of dangerous game.

Kadoni's head was bowed reading the lion spoor, but he intermittently glanced up to scan the area. Ronnie concentrated less on the ground than ahead of us, but like his native counterpart, he was all business.

We found the tracks at 9:30 a.m. It wasn't until 12:30 p.m. when we finally caught up to the lions. They'd traveled in a big circle and, wouldn't you know it, weren't too far from where we'd parked the truck. We pushed our way through the bushes and almost stepped right into them.

We froze. The lions stared at us. I raised my rifle, but Ronnie stopped

A lion in the wild is an awesome sight. It's best to keep your guard up.

me with a whisper.

"He's too young. We can do better. Let's just back off real slowly."

As we backed away, the male and two lionesses trickled away, but one lioness's intense piercing stare never wavered. Her look was threatening, bordering on evil. Without warning, she jumped to all fours, took a step forward, and let out a deafening guttural roar. I had to gulp hard to get my heart back down from my throat.

Then, like a ghost, the lioness glided away, disappearing as if she was never there.

Mary was a bit shaken by the ordeal. On top of that, she couldn't get enough liquids into her system. The heat, the excitement and the overall exhaustion made it hard for her to hydrate herself sufficiently. Our hike had been long during the heat of late morning. Two small bottles of water were not nearly enough. There was plenty in the vehicle, but by the time we reached into the cooler, the sun had already taken its toll.

"I think we should eat a bite and take a rest," Ronnie said. I saw him quickly glance at Mary with a look of concern. "I'm beat," he said. "I don't know if I could walk another minute in this heat."

It wasn't long before Ronnie was napping. Kadoni, Danger and Kebonne disappeared somewhere, Mary wrote in her journal and I couldn't sleep. I had found an ivory nut earlier and decided to pass the time whittling away on it. I tried to sleep, but it was just too hot. It was an oppressive heat despite its dryness. It was the kind of heat that beat you down and drained your energy. There was no escape. The shade offered some respite, but very little. It wasn't until Ronnie awoke and started the Land Cruiser that I remembered and appreciated the refreshing feel of a breeze. Sure, it was a dry, warm breeze, but it was still a breeze. We bumped and bounced along the trail for most of the afternoon. It didn't take long for my eyes to get heavy; I'd missed my afternoon nap after all.

My eyes popped open when Ronnie stopped the vehicle. I looked around, but didn't see anything.

"Let's you and I go after that zebra, Mary," Ronnie said. "What do you say?"

She answered with a reluctant nod. Even after the last time. She was willing to get back on her feet and try again.

"Good luck," I said.

I stayed in the truck while they went on the stalk. I still hadn't seen the zebra, but as I watched their progress, I saw Ronnie point. They all crouched and their pace slowed. Then I finally saw the zebra. It was all alone over 200 yards across an open field. When Mary set up to shoot, I thought it was awfully far, but considering the lack of cover, getting closer may not have been practical. I watched the zebra through my binoculars, waiting for the shot. It seemed like a long time – too long. In my impatience, I lowered the binoculars to see what was going on. At that same moment, she fired. Mary never shot hastily. I knew this. I found the zebra right away. He'd run toward the acacias, but stopped short of entering. He appeared unharmed. Then Mary shot again. The zebra ran into the trees; this time I knew she'd missed.

I don't believe it was merely the distance that caused her to miss her target. It hadn't been long since her encounter with the zebra herd by the water hole. Maybe she didn't want to shoot the stallion or maybe she just didn't care. Either way, I'd seen her shoot at such distances and knew she could hit a smaller target than a zebra. To her credit, she made no excuses. Upon her return to the vehicle, she just shrugged.

"Maybe next time," she said.

I think her mind was elsewhere anyway.

"I wonder how mother is doing today," Mary said before bed. It was August 31st, her mother's birthday. "I said an extra rosary for her; hope she has a happy day."

Mary had become acclimated to the nighttime sounds, but had a hard time getting to sleep that night. It was too quiet.

"I kept thinking it shouldn't be this quiet. Nothing was making a sound," she said. "I stayed awake because I wanted to hear something. Then, about 4 a.m. a leopard snorted, stirring everything up. The birds made all kinds of strange noises, the hyenas barked and *wooo-ooted* and the baboons wreaked havoc. I couldn't sleep then because it was too loud. So I didn't get any rest last night. I think I'm starting to get used to the leopard though. At least that's something."

If she was tired the next morning, I couldn't tell. She didn't seem fatigued at all. I don't know how she does it. I would've been sleeping the second the Land Cruiser pulled away from camp. But it's hard to sleep, even if you're dead tired, when the quarry for the day is Cape buffalo. It was a welcome change of pace. Buffalo are always exciting.

Early in the morning, we came around a corner and ran right into a big herd of buffalo. We almost drove into them. They'd definitely caught us off guard, but we'd caught them off guard too. In the confusion, they scattered in different directions. One huge bull gave the truck a charge, but backed off after a few yards. When the dust settled, they regrouped and stampeded into the bush.

"There were a couple really nice bulls in that herd Dick." Ronnie's eyes were wide. "I think we should give them a few minutes to calm down, then go after them. We'll park under that tree over there."

"Whatever you think," I said. "You're the buffalo expert."

We sat in the truck, without a word, for ten minutes. I kept turning to look into the thorn bushes where the buffalo had gone, but Ronnie was nowhere near as anxious as I.

Finally, Ronnie said, "If you do not mind Mary, I think it would be best if just Dick went on this one."

"I'll be fine," she said.

"Are you sure?" Ronnie and I both asked.

"Yes, I'm sure. You go on ahead. Get a good one honey."

We walked away from the Land Cruiser, leaving Mary with one of the camp skinners.

"Kadoni believes the buffalo are heading to the river. If we hurry, we should be able to cut them off," Ronnie said.

The pace was quick. At times, I had difficulty keeping up. I tried to suck in air, panting heavily during each short break, but our goal was clear. An urgency to reach the massive herd before they made it to the river kept our tiny rests to a minimum. We pushed on. Would we ever make it to the river? I didn't know if I would. My legs were tiring and my weak knee tried to give out on me more than once. Why subject myself to such pain? Just one more mile. My conviction thought about waning.

"We should have been able to get ahead of them by now," Ronnie said softly. "We need to catch them long before they reach the river; that is our boundary. The last thing we want to do is shoot one and have it cross over. We would have to give too many bribes just to step foot over there. It is unfortunate, but the steward there is a bit of a crook. It's best

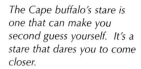

The Cape buffalo's stare is one that can make you second guess yourself. It's a stare that dares you to come closer.

if we can stay on our side."

I was breathing heavily, sweating a river. I couldn't say okay; I couldn't say yes; I could barely, just barely, nod. So, we pressed on. I couldn't see it, but knew the river wasn't too far to our north. My fatigue grabbed hold of my optimism with the grip of a wrench and with each new, painful step twisted it into a gnarled mass of pessimism. The herd must've beaten us to the river.

"Bwana," Kadoni pointed. "Nyati," he said. Buffalo. A cloud of dust was rising on the horizon.

One foreign word. That's all it takes. Weariness is swept away, instantly. Kadoni knew that word. When he spoke it everything changed. Nyati – all other thoughts just went away. It was time for hunting – time for buffalo. How could a dust cloud evoke such emotion? I don't know, but this one held the promise of adventure and it was coming our way.

"Come, Dick. We'll hide under that bush over there." Ronnie pointed to a medium-sized thorn bush. "Hurry, before they see us."

We rushed to duck under the bush. With rapier fury, the bush protested, but we ignored the burning scratches. I was too engrossed by the approaching buffalo to feel much at all. The rising dust expanded in size. A few black spots began to trickle to the forefront, leading a great herd to greener pastures. Like they had done before, the buffalo pressed on in the relentless heat of the day, pushed by an unseen force toward an unknown objective.

Their current line of approach would bring them right on top of us. The enormous herd moved as one, almost like a giant serpent slithering along the savanna – a few lead buffalo as the head and a few dawdling stragglers as the tail. The closer they came, the more certain it seemed we'd be swallowed into the belly of the slow moving mass of dangerous beasts.

Before I knew it, we were being passed by more than 500 Cape buffalo. We watched silently from less than 25 feet away as cows, calves and old and young bulls, sauntered along, aimlessly following the buffalo ahead, oblivious to our presence. It was an awesome sight.

And we saw bulls. Most of them were still young or carried headgear that was average at best, but in a herd that large an exceptional old bull was bound to come by, so we waited.

After we waited, hunkered down in the bushes watching hundreds of buffalo go by, we waited some more. They never knew we were there, hidden in the thorns. They were close, but their concentration so focused on reaching their destination, they failed to detect us. Plus, they seemed to understand the concept of safety in numbers. So they ambled along in apparent apathy.

The ground rumbled beneath us, dust rose all around, but we remained steadfast. Steadfast, but not without fear. Fear is essential. It keeps you honest. You must control your apprehension, your excitement or whatever emotion tends to grab hold of you in such situations and focus on the task ahead. Our task was buffalo. My leg burned with pain from the constant crouch, yet I couldn't move. We had to remain silent. We had to wait.

Finally, near the tail end of the herd we spotted a nice bull.

"Get ready Dick," Ronnie said as loud as he dared.

I leaned over so he could hear me. "Which one? I see two big bulls."

"He's the one off to the right a little bit. With his head hanging low, like his horns are too heavy. Do you see him now?"

"Yes, I see him."

Boy did I see him. It was neither of the two I saw; his horns were much more massive. The difference between his headgear and that of the others in the unending herd was unmistakable; especially the boss. Many young bulls had soft bosses or no boss at all. His was thick and full – solid.

"As soon as you get a clear shot, take him."

It only took a moment for him to step into the clear. The entire herd charged off at the blast. Thank goodness they didn't stampede over us.

Wounded, the old bull didn't go far. He stayed to confront his attackers, still stooped in the thorny brush. I worked the bolt and put another one right in his shoulder. He staggered before turning to face us

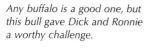

Any buffalo is a good one, but this bull gave Dick and Ronnie a worthy challenge.

head on, now sure which direction the last bullet had come from. The .375 held three bullets. When I put the third one in the center of his chest, I was certain he'd go down. He only stumbled a few yards closer, almost like he was drunk – discombobulated, but not finished by any means. I fumbled into my pocket for more bullets, jammed three more into the magazine and popped the first one into the chamber. I raised the barrel, but at that moment, the old, stubborn, warrior finally fell. Relief was the first to touch my heart, slowing each beat with its calming ability.

We pulled away the few thorns that had imbedded themselves to our clothes and stood up. My half-smile was greeted with wide, sincere con-gratulatory smiles from Ronnie and Kadoni. Just as Kadoni reached out with his good arm to shake my hand, we heard a thump. All three of us wheeled around.

The bull struggled back to his feet. Three big pieces of lead weren't enough to keep this brute down. When he glared at us, there was a fire in his eyes, a commitment to take us with him. He was locked on. If he could get his feet under him, he'd come – full bore.

"Give him another Dick. Quickly."

In one constant motion, I raised the barrel, clicked off the safety and fired. He fell in a hump. Then, a few seconds later, he let out his death bellow, a somber last gasp of air from a worthy, old bull. It was the last bullet I had to fire at my second Cape buffalo. The obstinate old fellow gave me an adventure only surpassed on extreme rare occasions.

The Push of Hope: Mary

Dick and Ronnie had left me with the camp skinner. I tried to talk to him for a few minutes, but he didn't answer. Then he just disappeared behind a tree or termite mound or somewhere. Oh well. Maybe he didn't like me.

After some time, I heard a shot, quickly followed by two more and then, a bit later, a fourth. The way I saw it in my head was the first shot ignited a charge, the next two were fired out of fear of being trampled and the final delayed blast was insurance.

They returned a short while afterwards.

"No, he didn't charge Mary. Dick shot him well with the first bullet, but he was a stubborn old bugger." Ronnie began loading the vehicle, but stopped short and looked around. "Where's Kebone?" he asked.

"He disappeared shortly after you left. I guess he found our conversation boring."

"Your conversation?"

"Yes, I tried to ask him if he wanted something to drink. He just got up and walked away."

Ronnie laughed.

"He didn't think you were boring, Mary. He couldn't hear you. Kebone is deaf and mute. He probably just went to take a nap. I'll have Kadoni and Danger go find him. Sorry about that, I guess I should've warned you. Once they find him, we'll drive over and take some photos before we load Dick's bull."

The boys took pictures, cleaned, skinned and cut up the meat for the better part of two hours. It gave me a chance to catch up in my journal, but the unbearable midday heat allowed for a less pleasant two hours. The three natives made the work look light. Their skill with rustic homemade knives was unmatched. The way they worked as one was impressive. They could accomplish so much with so little. We have all the creature comforts in the world back home and it's never enough. The villagers in Botswana reminded us people can and do live rather contentedly with relatively little compared to almost anyone in our own country. They knew how to enjoy life.

With the skin and meat loaded, we made our way back to camp for lunch and a rest. The food was good as always, but resting was difficult. There was no escape from the excessive afternoon heat. The African sun burned right through the shade with its suffocating, breezeless, outdoor tanning lamp. The hot, dry air wicked away our sweat before it could bead up, doing its best to drain our energy.

It wasn't easy finding motivation for the afternoon hunt. The heat had our spirits barely hanging on. But as we rolled along the trail-road, the wind caressed our faces and renewed our vigor – well, at least it kept us awake.

"We are going to drive a bit further today," Ronnie said. "It's an area just full of leopards. Kadoni tells me his brother has seen a big tom just before dusk two evenings in a row."

The big cats had, thus far, managed to elude us completely. The tip from Kadoni's brother was the best lead we'd had; we were going to follow it.

The area was lush with green life, water everywhere. Numerous palm islands added to an indescribable beauty. We hunted buffalo in a dry, desolate and dead looking place – not that it wasn't full of beauty, it was – you just had to look for it. The colorful, untouched leopard area took its verdant brush and whacked you over the head with it. How could two places only a few miles apart be so dissimilar? At least it kept any monotony at bay. As if monotonous days were a problem.

The afternoon's high drama occurred while we rode along on one of the few trail roads Ronnie created with repetitive travels across the ground. We passed a clump of bushes about the size of two Land Cruisers when Kadoni pointed out a Cape buffalo lying under its shade. Dick grabbed the camera for a photo, but Ronnie hadn't seen the bull; he never took his foot off the gas.

Kadoni laughed, tapped Ronnie on the shoulder and had him back up. We rounded the corner in reverse. When the callous old buffalo saw us coming back, he jerked his head up.

"Go! Go! Go!" Kadoni was frantically waving at Ronnie.

The buffalo didn't hesitate. He charged a metal beast twice his size without fear, without a second thought. He had a determined, hateful look in his eye. We were headed for collision. I braced myself for impact. Ronnie changed gears just in time to avoid major damage, but the buffalo raised his horns at the last second and clipped the tailgate. He lifted the back of the vehicle with a simple twist of his neck. We started to pull away, but the buffalo grunted and gave chase. I tried to cling on for dear life, but my hands, my whole body, in fact, shook uncontrollably. Danger, who started out in the very back, had nearly wedged himself under my seat. And, Dick, of course, calmly sat, snapping photos at point-blank range. I even think he might've been laughing. Typical.

The bull finally decided he wasn't going to catch us and gave up. He shook his head, snorted one last time, then stood defiantly in triumph in the middle of the road as we sped off. It wasn't until long after he faded away in the distance that the trembling in my hands began to taper.

"I guess he didn't want his picture taken," Ronnie said.

By the time the dust settled over my nerves, the day was fading to dusk. A shower and a stiff drink followed. I needed them both just so I could sleep.

The next morning proved sluggish for all. Most of the adrenalin and excitement was used up on buffalo. It was also miserably hot with a gale force wind. The weather affected the wildlife strangely. A wind like that might cause the animals to hunker down until it passed, but not on this day. Maybe the odd weather had them confused. There were animals moving everywhere. We saw just about every species out wandering around. We even saw a few cheetahs, which we hadn't seen before. We saw almost everything – except lion. Poor Ronnie; he'd been breaking his back trying to find a lion. His efforts were admirable, but you just never know with the big cats. I think we were all a little down, but what can you do?

Hunting isn't a guaranteed endeavor and I hope it never is. The high chance you will not find your prey is an important element to the hunter's lifestyle. It's a possibility of success that keeps us coming back for more. We return to the field each day because if we push ourselves hard enough, we might just encounter something we've never seen before. If we're really lucky, that monster we've been striving for might make a mistake, but he probably won't, so we'll be back again tomorrow. I could go without shooting, but I'd never understand the true natural experience connecting us to the land and its creatures and why conserving them is so important. We knew who we were and understood life's circle with clarity.

With only two hunting days remaining, the possibility of the king of the jungle keeping his crown became increasingly probable. But we couldn't give in just yet. We hadn't packed up our bags for home had we? No, it wasn't over. But two days? Hope was little more than tiny drops in the bottom of a bucket. The bucket had been overfilled on day one and now was almost dry. Each day a little more was taken – some more than others, like the days we followed a track for miles only to come upon an immature cat. The last two days are the worst. You reach into an empty pail, searching for that last drop of hope. If you find it, you are reluctant to use it up – you may need it later.

Ronnie was particularly quiet today. He drove with more of a purpose – he didn't stop to look at tracks, didn't watch the bush so intensely, didn't drive slowly. Who could blame him, the area was desolate. An elephant herd had knocked down almost every tree. What little vegetation there was on the barren ground was in a struggle to survive. Water was non-existent. Dry, dusty air made the simple task of breathing a chore. We weren't too far from the Kalahari, which covers nearly 85% of Botswana. The sharp contrasts in the landscape between the Okavango Delta and the Kalahari never ceases to amaze. The trees, grasses and all vegetation, as well as many of the animals and birds could often be found in one place and not the other.

At one point, Ronnie looked back over his shoulder. "I would like to stop at a nearby camp and talk to another hunter. He may have seen a lion or two about. It shouldn't take long."

He was speeding faster than he had the entire safari. There was very little game to be found in such a dry wasteland; with no water or food to sustain them, the animals wouldn't last long. He never said as much, but he most likely didn't care for the depressing area, wishing to pass through it as quickly as possible.

When we pulled into the camp, a tall, slender man with coal black hair and a hard, weathered face emerged from a canvas tent to greet us. He shifted the big, green, safari hat he wore. Ronnie jumped from the truck to shake his hand.

"How is it Jack?"

"Good Ronnie. We've got a couple chaps from Texas in camp right now and we've done quite well. Taken some fine trophies."

"This is Dick and Mary Cabela."

"Pleased to meet you folks." Jack reached out to shake our hands. "Your catalog is impressive. The two old boys in camp this week are fitted up with all kinds of your gear. So Ronnie, what brings you out here?"

"Lion."

"Looking for a big old cat are you? We took one early in the hunt. They only had one on license."

"Have you seen any in the area," Ronnie asked.

Jack took off his hat and rubbed the rim. "Well, there is one old boy we're going to have to take care of sooner or later. He's getting too old to hunt. Been carrying livestock off from the local villages at night. It's just a matter of time before he snatches a person. One of the boys said he saw him yesterday; said he was limping, favoring his right, back leg. If he is wounded, it would help explain his aggressive behavior. You best be cautious. You know old, wounded lions near the end – they sometimes refuse to go quietly. They can make a pleasant situation hairy in a moment." He placed the hat back on his head and shifted it into place. "Why don't you have Kadoni run over to the skinning shed to ask Mathew where he saw the lion?"

Kadoni and Danger both went to make sure they clearly understood Mathew's directions. Dick and I shared a Diet Coke while waiting by the truck. We climbed back into the Land Cruiser when we saw them running back. We thanked Jack, said goodbye and held on tight as Ronnie sped off.

We clung on to that last drop of hope and gulped it down; certain this was our last chance. We flew through another dead looking area,

You never know what lurks in Africa's grass. Watch your step.

then by a village and right on past a small green water hole before slowing down. I had to pry my fingers from their vise-like grip on the roll bar. He was going a bit too fast. He was in a hurry to find a lion we all wanted, so I didn't say anything. And just like that, we went from Africa's trail-road version of the Daytona 500 to the pace of a snail.

At one point, we stopped and Ronnie, Danger and Kadoni hopped out to look at the road. They pointed at the ground, walked around with their heads down, arguing for nearly 10 minutes. We couldn't hear them very well; they were speaking in their native tongue anyway. Finally, they returned to the truck and we were off again.

"There were some lion tracks there, but they weren't very big," Ronnie said. "One of them could have been a young male, but Jack said this boy is a loner and we know he's big. I'm afraid if we followed those tracks we would have been wasting our time on a cat we would not want to shoot. Besides, the place where he was seen is still up here a bit."

After 15 minutes of slow driving, Kadoni tapped Ronnie on the shoulder. "Stop Bwana," he said, pointing to the ground just behind the truck.

"More tracks?" Dick peered over the edge of the truck.

"We'll just have a look. This could be our boy."

Once again, an animated discussion ensued as Ronnie, Kadoni and Danger peered to the ground and followed the tracks for a few yards. A few minutes later, Ronnie walked back.

"Grab your rifle Dick. Load it and put it on safe." His voice had softened to almost a whisper. "I think this is him. The tracks are fresh. They lead just into the brush over there. If he is injured like they think, he probably hasn't gone far. Be ready just in case."

The tracks led away from the river. The road followed the river and just across the water was a National Park. Every now and again, we'd see a truck full of people on photographic safari on the other side. Out of courtesy, we made sure our rifles were not in plain sight whenever we were near the river. We didn't want to offend anybody. A strict rule not to shoot toward the river was always followed and most often, if we did come upon a vehicle across the river, we ceased hunting all together until we were far enough away that the blast from a shot wouldn't bother any animals they hoped to catch in a picture. After all, we wouldn't want someone coming by making a lot of racket if we were on a stalk. But these tracks led away from the river and we couldn't even see the other side at the moment. We didn't think anyone would hear the shot, but for a lion, it was a chance worth taking.

Dick pulled his rifle from the vehicle, loaded and waited as our diligent PH leaned into the truck to get his own. Kadoni and Danger never left the lion spoor. They slowly worked the trail back and forth, following it nearly 150 yards toward the brush.

Suddenly, we heard a scream – loud and drawn out. We looked up to see Kadoni and Danger racing toward us in a frantic dash, their feet kicking up dust. Their speed would've given an Olympic sprinter a run for his money. They didn't run for glory or medals. They ran for their lives.

Less than 75 yards behind them, a huge male lion crashed from the thorns. His speed wasn't overly impressive. A limp from one of his back legs held him back. It was him.

It all happened in slow motion. At least that's how I remember it. Kadoni and Danger ran, waving and yelling. The lion exploded from the brush behind them, his long thick mane flowing in unison with his bounds; fire blazed in his eyes. He appeared a little bony as if he hadn't had much to eat for some time. Favoring his back, right leg, he didn't move as fast as would be expected, but he was closing the distance on his two-legged meals. He was the very essence of power. I was terrified.

Ronnie shouted. "Shoot him Dick. Shoot him!"

I didn't see Dick shoot. I was focused on the lion and two wide-eyed desperate men, who in all their amazing speed could never outrun even a lame lion. When the blast came and the impact of the bullet slammed into the charging lion, the scene continued in slow motion. The old beast rolled over once before landing in a heap.

When lion hunting, split decisions can make all the difference.

"Great shot Dick. Let's go make sure the old boy's dead," Ronnie said.

He led Dick toward his lion, but Kadoni and Danger didn't slow down or look back until they put the men with the guns between them and the hungry lion. Ronnie carried the big gun, Dick walking tall beside him with his Dakota Arms .375, but the lion didn't move. The bullet struck him square in the chest. In the aging cat's weakened and injured condition, he didn't have the strength to fight off death any longer. Thank God.

It had been a long, hard hunt. When we'd finally found the lion, we faced him in the most thrilling way. I'd rather not have to deal with that kind of excitement again.

"I hoped for your hunt to be thrilling, but I didn't mean to over do it." Ronnie's face was glowing.

He'd worked so hard to find Dick a lion. I don't know who was more pleased – Ronnie or Dick, but they were both on cloud nine. Kadoni and Danger each grabbed Dick's hand and shook it – smiles, congratulations and thank yous. It was a long time before Danger let Dick's hand go. The drastic mood change was written in the faces of our whole group, but underneath the wide grins and bright eyes, below the laughing and admiration for the lion was the sense our hunt was nearly over. Our time with those wonderful people was almost at an end. We were all in celebration mode. Although we knew our last day approached with alarming speed, we were too high to be brought down.

At camp, the setting sun colored the horizon with melding hues of pale orange, yellow and red. From a perfect, hot, glowing sphere, God gave us a breathtaking end to an indescribable day. It was just one of the simple pleasures he gave us everyday, like sunrises and sunsets, or the refreshing tickle of a subtle breeze. We were surrounded by the splendors of life and little was asked of us in return. Yes, we have been blessed.

Saying Goodbye: Dick

Thursday, September 3rd wasn't our last day, but it was close. We'd hunt half a day Friday and that would be it. Our safari would be over. We'd leave with the hope our new memories would stay with us, not fade into blurry pictures collecting dust in the back of our minds. It happens too often with things we wish to remember most.

We were up at just after six, ready to go well before seven, but circumstances had other ideas. At some point the day before, we'd managed to puncture a tire with one of those ubiquitous thorns.

"Everything in Africa either bites, stings or pokes. I would say we got poked yesterday." Despite the setback and hard work required to replace the tire, Ronnie was in good spirits. "We go by a different pace here in the bush. You have to be able to take what she throws at you with a relaxed attitude, otherwise you will go insane."

We weren't required to do anything. We offered what help we could, but Ronnie was one of the really good operators. The good outfitters and guides have learned their industry is competitive. Those who offer not only a great hunt, but also superb service, will be able to charge a premium and can be assured of return customers.

The skills an experienced professional hunter must possess are numerous. First and foremost, he must be a good hunter with extensive knowledge of the land and its animals. For guys who live for this sort of thing (and they are the only kind you will ever find in the profession), that is the easy part. The pay isn't great and the work is hard. The impressive part comes in everything else they must know and be good at. A good PH needs to be a mechanic, he needs to have basic first aid skills, to be a good host, to know how to take care of delicate skins, to know how to cook, to have diplomatic skills and be able to communicate with the local tribes, to know basic carpentry and to understand accounting, just to name a few. All this while looking after, not only the safety of his clients, but their comfort as well.

It was almost nine by the time Ronnie had the new tire on and the punctured one sealed. We left in a hurry, trying to make up for lost time – an impossible feat, yet something we all hope to do at some point in our lives on both small and large scales alike. Our destination was over an hour's drive. By the time we started hunting, the morning would be mostly over. We decided to eat a late lunch to give ourselves a little extra time.

I shot a zebra and after the trackers and skinners made short work of it, the vultures came in like dive bombers, devouring what was left within seconds.

The cool morning air was bullied aside by another oppressive midday heat that pressed down on our shoulders. It was soon time for lunch. We took it slow, hunting our way back. We weren't hunting for anything in particular, but hoped for a classic spot and stalk on any number of plains game if we happened to catch sight of something impressive. Wildebeest or impala were overly abundant in the area. We saw many animals, but nothing of exceptional quality, so we passed.

I was particularly interested in a big, old wildebeest or a long-horned impala ram. But it was the diminutive steenbok with horns surpassing four inches that demanded our attention. Kadoni spotted him first. They are small, speedy and tend to blend in well with their surroundings. I didn't see him until he took off. His path led him 50 yards into the brush.

"He's a good steenbok Dick. I know it's hot and we're all hungry, but I think we should give him a go. What do you say?"

"We can sure try. If he gets too far ahead, we can always turn back."

Within a few yards it exploded from a bush, like a flushing pheasant. I tried to follow his quick darts in my scope, managing to get a shot off when he stopped. I didn't have time to aim. I thought I jerked some, but the ram dropped hard. I actually hit him. But Mary's had fallen quickly too, only to run off forever. I kept my rifle shouldered as we approached, but he wasn't going anywhere.

"Better safe than sorry." I lowered the barrel.

We never expected to find a steenbok of this caliber.

"They're plentiful here, but this area doesn't produce many big males," Ronnie had said.

We were lucky. You can put in your time, hunt hard, do everything right to increase your chances, but there's really no substitute for good old-fashioned luck.

We had buffalo tongue for lunch, then took a short nap before the afternoon hunt. We ended up in an area where everything was alive with color, but game was scarce. We did happen upon a small herd of sable bulls; one had massive sweeping horns. We didn't have one on license, but still enjoyed the moment. The big boy seemed to know we couldn't hunt him. He strutted around in the open like a big tom turkey trying to impress a hot hen. Finally, they slipped into the brush. With their sleek, shiny, jet black coats; distinctive white facial markings; thick horns, sweeping back like scimitars and the grace of a ballet dancer, sable are one of the most beautiful antelope in the world. They left us breathless.

"I just don't understand it," Ronnie said. "Whenever we're hot on the trail of some other animal, the wildebeest are everywhere. Now that we are after one, they're nowhere to be found. Just our luck."

The sun was well on its daily journey to the western horizon. We'd only seen a few wildebeest, all of which were cows or immature bulls. We pressed on. We didn't find a wildebeest that afternoon, but did come across a baboon.

"It's a big male. Would you like to give him a try?" Ronnie asked.

We saw hundreds of baboons everyday. In many parts of Africa there are way too many. So many that they've become a problem. They steal food from the local villagers, spread disease, kill pets and small livestock like chickens; even a fairly large dog is no match for a couple big baboons. They've even been known to run off with small children on occasion. From tribe to tribe and village to village, baboons are seen in many different lights. Some places they are considered vermin, like rats. In others they are considered a delicacy and are given the status of deity in yet others.

After shooting the baboon, we found out what the local population thought of them. They believed to touch one would bring bad luck. When Ronnie instructed Kadoni and Danger to go pick it up, they almost turned white. They walked toward it, talking quietly to one another for a moment. They took their time. Usually they ran to any downed game that wasn't dangerous; with the baboon it was as if they hoped he would jump up and run away. Halfway there, Kadoni picked up a few long sturdy sticks. He handed one to Danger. They eventually slunk their way over. Kadoni, careful not to get too close, reached out and poked it lightly with a stick. When there was no reaction he jabbed it again, more forcefully. Then, he and Danger worked together to lift the baboon with their sticks. They carried it back, making sure to keep it as far from themselves as possible. The baboon sat way in the back of the truck, Kadoni and Danger almost on our laps. We rode like this all the way back to camp, where Ronnie, chuckling, took care of the big male himself.

Our final morning was mostly uneventful. Everyone was quiet, taking it easy. I took another impala and we saw another nice herd of sable, but the real excitement of the day happened when we spotted a sitatunga by the swamps. In an effort to close the distance, we promptly got stuck and the sitatunga promptly disappeared. We were jinxed by those water-loving ungulates with splayed hooves. If we weren't stuck in the muck, we were probably being charged by an enraged elephant. The constant surprises and the unknown kept us on our toes. At least we saw one.

We dug and pushed ourselves from the mud, leaving us just enough time to take a few photos of sable, crocodile, hippos, waterbucks, impalas and anything else which happened to run in front of our cameras before lunch. We were back to camp by noon for a farewell meal featuring tender roast form the steenbok we'd taken the day before.

Ronnie was the first to leave the table. "I've got to catch up on a ton of paperwork before you head out, so if you will please excuse me."

"Yes," Mary said. She began gathering up dishes. "I have some last-minute packing as well." She waited until he was gone then said, "I sure am going to miss him."

"He really is a nice man, isn't he?"

Ronnie had become more than a man who took us hunting. We considered him a friend. We cared about him, cared what happened to him. In the future, when we thought of Botswana, we'd think of Ronnie Kay and the way he introduced us to the country. We were privileged to have met him, to have hunted with him.

Photo Camp: Mary

From Ronnie's camp we flew to Maun, spending one night on our way to Ngorongoro Crater in Tanzania. We would meet our friends, Bob and Bonnie Delay and Andy and D.J. Andrews, in Nairobi. They would accompany us on our photo safari.

The plane landed just before midnight, but there was a massive blackout and we weren't allowed to deplane for another three hours. When we finally made it to the hotel, we went straight to bed.

Bob joined Dick and I for Mass at the Nairobi Cathedral on Sunday morning. We were pleasantly surprised that the Mass was sung in Latin by the entire congregation. It had been a while since we'd been to a Latin Mass. We missed it. To encounter it halfway across the world was refreshing.

We left Nairobi on Monday, on our way to the Ngorongoro Wildlife Refuge. Our courier, Mike, and driver, Phillip, were at the airport when we landed.

"We need to stop by headquarters before lunch so you can be given a short briefing," Mike said smiling.

We were ushered to what appeared to be a classroom, complete with chalkboard and projection screen. We each took a seat at our desks and waited. Within a few minutes, we were joined by another group of clients. We smiled, said hello, then sat in an uncomfortable silence for the next ten minutes. There were some outstanding wildlife photographs on the walls and a large, old, beaten-down desk in the back corner of the room. It was like our first day of high school, the new teacher invariably late. We weren't sure what to expect.

A big, burly man with thick, white, facial hair finally entered the room stiffly, shutting the door behind him. He strolled in slowly, almost arrogantly and glared at us; he didn't approve. He was all business, no greeting or welcome. His deep, booming voice vibrated off the closed windows in the stuffy room. He made it a point to let us know he was the most important person in the room.

"Our facilities are here for your enjoyment," he said. He didn't smile. "But there are rules you must follow. First and foremost, always listen to your couriers. They have been here much longer than you. If you do not follow their instructions, you could put yourself and others in great danger. This is not a zoo; our animals are wild – some of them are very dangerous. You should never drink the water. It will make you sick. We have bottled water if you are thirsty. Finally, under no circumstances are you to tip anyone other than your courier and driver at the end of your trip. Any further questions can be answered by your courier."

He left the room like he was late for an important meeting. Our courier could've given us the same information without trying to make us feel like first graders who couldn't follow instructions. Some people just need to feel important.

We left headquarters, ate a small lunch and loaded up for the drive to Ngorongoro Wildlife Lodge. Six long hours on some of the most horribly bumpy roads through desolate country left us beat. We were dirty, dusty and in dire need of a restroom. The lack of wildlife on the way to the lodge was disappointing. Hopefully it wasn't a sign of things to come. Dick and I had seen a great abundance of game and scenery while hunting. We were now at an area famous for their animals.

"I promise we will see many animals as we approach the crater," Mike said. "You will be pleased."

Well, it couldn't get any worse.

Over 12 miles wide and 2,000 feet deep, the crater used to be a high reaching mountain. Under intense volcanic pressure, it collapsed, becoming a fertile crater. Its high walls serve as a sanctuary for a multitude of African species, as well as a perfect spot for Masai to graze their cattle.

We rolled down into the crater past a green forest area and the place came alive. Through the forest, the flat bowl of the crater became strikingly dry with little green vegetation, but there were many animals, including rhinoceros, elephant, lions, zebra, wildebeest, and Cape buffalo. They'd become so used to the Land Rovers, there were times we had to drive around them – almost like domesticated livestock. It was a beautiful area and we took some awesome pictures, but...

It just wasn't the same. I had the feeling we were in a drive through zoo much of the time and everything was highly touristy.

Black kite birds kept us in the Land Rover for lunch. They were diving and swooping straight into other safari groups, stealing food right out of their hands, leaving cuts and scrapes on more than a few tourists. We laughed at first, but I doubt this is a natural action for those birds – too many people feeding them had altered their behavior to its present state. It made us think about how our own actions, even seemingly insignificant, can impact wild places we hope to preserve.

The highlight of the day was when our driver, Phillip, a Masai tribesman, invited us to visit his village. Few tourists were actually invited to a village. It was a privilege. Some of Africa's greatest warriors have been Masai. They were one of the most feared tribes on the continent.

We arrived just in time for a ceremonial dance. It had something to do with the young warriors.

"By your western standards, the Masai are very primitive," Mike said. "You may find some of their practices crude, even gruesome, but keep in mind this is the way things have been here for thousands of years."

Several children were present. One woman was nursing a baby, who was covered, tiny head to tiny toes in flies; you couldn't help but feel for the child. In all fairness, he didn't seem to care. An elderly woman in a red dress sat making beads while several graying men wearing brown cloaks and sporting three earrings in each ear leaned against one of the thatch huts smoking strange pipes.

"Women do most of the work around here," Mike said. "They gather wood, make sure the cattle are in every night, take care of the family, cook the meals, tend garden and do just about anything else you can think of."

"What do the men do?" I had to ask.

"Mostly, they sit around smoking, playing cards and drinking beer made from cow urine."

"Cow urine?"

"It's not as bad as you might think." Mike chuckled with raised eyebrows. "The main non-alcoholic drink is goat's milk and cow's blood. Appetizing, no? Wealth consists of the number of cows one has, most of which are stolen from other tribes, but don't tell anyone I said that. The men can have as many wives as they can pay for with cattle, but all children belong to all the women. Huts belong to the women as well."

The hut we saw had two rooms with dirt floors. One had a large leather bed and a fire ring, the other was a small empty room off the bedroom. The entire structure was no more than 15-feet-by-20-feet. It was home to five people. And I thought our children's dorm rooms were too small for two people.

How lucky were we? We had a wonderful family, had lived full lives, had been in the company of some remarkable people, and had visited some truly magnificent places. But these people, the Masai, they were quite something. As I listened to their harmonious singing, with no instrumental accompaniment, and saw determined faces as they performed an ancient dance rooted in spiritual beliefs of people whose very souls were still connected to the land and its many faces, I felt like we'd traveled to a simpler time, when survival was more important than manicured lawns and long lines at the car wash. They knew what it meant to be at peace. We were privileged to have met them, if only briefly.

"As you can see, the Masai continue to dress in their traditional garb," Mike said. "This particular ceremonial dance was to honor the return of a young man entering the ranks of a junior warrior."

"Return from where?"

"It is really interesting, though a bit brutal. While still quite young, a boy is circumcised, dressed in black, his face painted and then he is sent out into the wild with a spear to fend for himself until he heals. When his wounds heal, he returns to a great ceremony where he is proclaimed a junior warrior. When he turns twelve, and has returned from another solo trip in the wilderness, he becomes a full-fledged warrior and can marry if he has enough cattle. Nearly 50 cows are needed to constitute a suitable dowry in this village.

"Most westerners find the treatment of the girls a little less agreeable. At the age of twelve, they are also circumcised. A custom designed, it seems, to keep females from enjoying marital relations. They are only to bear children and work. They are also left in the wilderness to fend for themselves while they heal. Many do not make it back. They bleed to death. It is sad really."

"Most everybody seems content enough."

"For the most part, that is true. By our western standards, some of the Masai traditions may seem harsh, but it is what they know, what they have always known. They know how to take what life throws at them with a smile. I wish I had more of that in me.

"Another custom you might find interesting is the high treatment of Masai warriors," Mike said. "A warrior will travel from village to village and ask admittance. If he is accepted, he can have or do whatever he wishes. If he enters another man's home while the man is away and throws his spear in the ground at the doorway, this means he has taken the hut and everything in it – claiming the woman as his own for that night. When the man of the hut returns and sees the spear, he knows not to return home until the next morning. Strangely, if there is a child born of this union, the warrior will claim it and take it as his own."

"Is that really true?" I asked.

"On my mother's honor."

We left the Masai village at sunset. Dust billowed away behind the Land Rover. The sight of a tall, slender, bald man wearing a red cloth and holding a spear faded into the haze. How long could they hold onto their pasts before the modern world tightened its grip. It was only a matter of time. It saddened me. By our standards, their lives could be better, but what do we lose? Another link in the chain to our past – another reason to forget where we come from?

At the same time, I knew I was fortunate. I don't always realize my blessings, but seeing, first hand, the meager lives others are thankful for everyday gave me pause.

The following morning we were headed for the Seronara Wildlife Lodge for a few more days of wildlife viewing. So far, we'd spent more time uncomfortably bouncing along on maintenance-free roads from camp to camp than viewing game.

The new area was overrun by tourists and game. The overkill of tourists, which we were a part of, made it frustrating. If an elusive animal or one of the Big Five was spotted, a contest of whose vehicle could get the closest was, too often, the result.

The animals had learned to live with vehicles full of gawking humans and somehow seemed less dignified – resigned by the fact their daily lives will be spent surrounded by the incessant pursuit of metal monsters. It would be a lie to say we didn't enjoy ourselves or that we weren't often awestruck by the beauty the animals possessed. But when the trucks form their circles around the beasts, their spirits seem broken – not from the bars of a cage, but from something just as inescapable.

"Look at those idiots," Mike said as we pulled around the bend.

Fifty yards off the road, a leopard rested in the crooked branch of a tree. He was fairly close and in easy sight, but not close enough for two other parties.

"They're going to drive right under the tree. He'll be gone in a second. Idiots."

The two vans closed in. As Mike predicted, the tom rose from his stupor and darted away. Nobody had a chance to get a picture. Not even the passengers in the two vans.

"Some of these drivers believe it's more interesting for their clients if they make the animals more animated. Please excuse me for a moment."

Mike put the van in park and walked off the road. He went over to

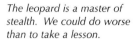

The leopard is a master of stealth. We could do worse than to take a lesson.

the driver's side of the first vehicle, its driver and passengers were all smiles, but only for a moment. We couldn't hear what he said, but the discussion was lively. By the looks on the faces in the vans, the drivers were subjected to a severe tongue lashing.

A little further on, we encountered a year-old leopard cub sleeping in an acacia tree. His mother rested in the tall grass beneath the tree where she could confront any potential danger. When other vehicles started crowding in like vultures, we moved on. It was like we were back in our boat at Lake McConaughy trolling for walleye. No matter what, while you work an area, another boat will join you. The next thing you know, more than a dozen boats are scooting back and forth along the shoreline – it matters little that nobody is catching fish. The mere presence of other anglers must mean walleye are thick in the area.

Later that afternoon, we stumbled upon a pack of wild dogs asleep under a small tree. Wild dogs are hard to come by.

"They are some of the most proficient predators on earth, killing the large majority of the prey they chase," Mike said. "They hunt in sophisticated packs and run their prey down with astounding stamina. Unfortunately, the mortality rate for pups is high and they are quite susceptible to habitat loss. Their numbers are nowhere near what they used to be."

We spent a few hours watching them from a distance. Their coats were blotched with shades of black, reddish brown and white. They

The African wild dog is one of the world's most efficient predators. Working together, a pack can run their prey to exhaustion.

sported large, rounded ears and dark muzzles. The younger canines played while most of the adults lazed around in the shade reserving energy for the hunt.

A National Geographic photo and video crew was at our same lodge. They'd been filming for over two months, having yet to see a wild dog. When we told them we could show them where the dogs were, they became ecstatic and talked about it all night. It was nice to see their enthusiasm, but their exciting questions eventually began to wear on us. We soon excused ourselves for a quick shower before dinner.

The room had no air conditioning. The only way to enjoy a pleasant breeze was to open up the sliding glass door. Pale, thin, peach-colored drapes floated in the breeze like ghosts slipping through the window in the dull evening light.

"Look, Mary. There are a few animals roaming around out there," Dick said. "I'll go get the binoculars and cameras from the car."

The lodge was built high on huge boulders, giving guests a wonderful aerial view of the area. We could see the entire green dale below. When the sun drifted down toward the darkening horizon, we were enchanted by a soft layering of violet, red, orange and yellow. I couldn't remember a more beautiful sunset.

It was a serene moment, but such moments do not last. D.J. and I turned from the sunset for only a brief second, but it was long enough. Long enough for the stunning scene to be replaced by a big, hairy baboon. He pushed away the curtains and entered our room as if he owned the place.

We screamed.

He screeched back at us, revealing his long pointed canines.

We yelled for the guys. Andy heard our screams and was already on his way. Dick was down at the vehicle. He had no idea of our predicament. There was a brief standoff where it appeared the big, beefed-up primate was going to hold his ground. Then, Andy grabbed a chair and shooed him. The baboon shrieked in protest before scampering out the way he'd come. We closed and locked all the doors and windows before bed.

The next morning, a mother cheetah and her two baby cubs were lying in the grass, keeping a close eye on a menacing hyena.

"He's contemplating how best to steal one of those cubs," Mike said. "Mortality rates for cheetah cubs are extremely high. They fall prey to most of the other large predators, such as lions, leopards, wild dogs and as you can see, spotted hyena. Look." Mike pointed. "Over there is our photographer friend."

The situation was unpromising for the cheetah and her cubs. At least the hyena was alone. The cheetah's motherly instincts kept her diligent in her efforts to keep the strong-jawed undertaker of Africa at bay. The hyena tried every possible point of advance, stopping short each time the mother growled at him.

"We should probably leave," Mike said. "These could be some great shots for National Geographic. If we stick around, we might disturb them. The more people, the more nervous they will be."

We left the photographer with the cheetahs and hyena. He stayed several hours, filling us in later.

"The mother cheetah killed a gazelle," he said. "Of course, the hyena tried to steal it. She successfully ran him off again, only to have a lioness charge in to claim her kill. She slapped the lioness across the rear with her claws, but she was well out-matched. Plus, she still had to contend with the hyena trying desperately to take the cubs. She eventually ran the hyena off, but lost her kill to the lioness. I got some wonderful photographs, as well as some great film footage. It would've been something had there been a more intense confrontation."

I couldn't say for sure, but he may've silently been rooting for the hyena.

Before long, we happened upon a lioness on the hunt. She was surreptitious, sneaking through the long grass, crouched low, inching along silently. Her tawny coat blended so well with the grass we almost lost sight of her more than once. She crept along, her target three small warthogs drinking from a waterhole. When they turned, she froze, her

The cheetah is a diligent hunter, but often loses prey to larger, more powerful, predators.

eyes glowing with concentration and murderous intent.

"Death comes from every corner in Africa," Mike said. "There is a crocodile hunting the same warthogs. He just poked his eyes out of the water and is slowly moving into position."

The suspense was as invigorating as any blockbuster thriller.

Opportunity is fleeting. In this case, a reedbuck strolled down for a drink straight into the path of the hidden lioness and spooked. The reedbuck dashed away, the three warthogs darted back into the brush, a dust cloud rising in their wake. The lioness stood up, sauntered over by the water and plopped her rear to the ground. We stuck around for a bit, hoping something else might show up for a drink, but with the crocodile patrolling the shores, only extreme thirst or daring would cause a beast to venture too close to that waterhole.

The drama at the waterhole worked up our own appetite; the lioness wasn't the only one hungry. A cream vegetable soup was pleasant after we added a healthy portion of chili sauce and our main course, a fish fillet, was edible after we pulled off the heavy egg battered breading. The food left much to be desired, but lots of sauces and spices helped us gulp it down.

Though our feeding time is often dictated by the hands of the clock, lions feed when hunger strikes and opportunity knocks. For a certain pride, it was time. Two females, two large males and 18 cubs, most of which were nearly two years or younger, were feeding on a fresh buffalo kill soaking in a stream. Positioned high on the east bank, the pride knew we were there, but they didn't seem to mind. They fought to tear chunks off the mangled, black carcass. Streaks of blood washed away in the current. An hour later, one lion wrestled his way into the buffalo skin – his back end and tail protruded, his body converging with the buffalo's as if they were one. Then a big male lion turned toward us with dark blood stains around his face and a piercing stare. We knew, even from the safety of the vehicle, we were more afraid than he was. He made sure we knew it.

A young leopard cub strutted into the road just as we rounded a corner. It growled at us with all its little might. We stopped to stare at him. He was tough. We were laughing. He held his ground proudly until his mother, sitting on a dead mopane tree called to him. Then he scampered off in all his glory.

Two days later, we left Mike and were off to Kenya for more wildlife viewing. Our new courier, Robert, was a large man with massive hands and a bushy, frazzled, untrimmed beard with matching moustache. Mountain man was the first thought that came to mind. He wore khaki shorts and a khaki button-up shirt. He didn't look as if he'd bathed in at least a week and he spoke down to us in quick phrases.

"Names Robert. Car's over there. Put your bags in the back."

He didn't say much during the drive to camp and didn't offer to help with any of our luggage. D.J. had broken both her arms just prior to our trip and couldn't help with the bags, so we had to make a few trips to and from camp headquarters.

We were in for another treat when we tried to check in at the hotel.

"I'm sorry," the desk clerk said. "We are sold out. We have no more rooms."

"What do you mean you're sold out?"

"I am sorry. The night clerk rented them out without our knowledge. We have erected tents behind the lodge I am sure will be to your satisfaction. They are very comfortable."

Another man hurried over and whispered in the clerk's ear.

He smiled. "I am pleased to announce we have one room available at the lodge."

"You two should take it," we said to D.J. and Andy. With D.J.'s broken arms it would be too much of an inconvenience for them to stay in a tent.

The tents weren't so bad; it was more the principle of the matter that had us perturbed. We had reserved, and paid for, a lodge room with running water and showers. We were offered a tent with an outhouse barely within walking distance. The hike to the bathroom would've been fine if management hadn't fed the birds, baboons, leopards, and crocodiles in the name of ambience. They weren't afraid of people in the least. We guarded our food diligently from birds and baboons that zipped in when we weren't looking to snatch our fruit or pie or whatever was easiest for them to grab before we turned back around.

The camp was crawling with tourists. There were far more two-legged creatures than our four-legged brethren. This was more disappointing than the whole room situation. We had no choice but to make the best of it.

Robert showed up for dinner and put on a good act about a horribly upset stomach. His stumbles and slurred words were indicative of his ailment – the whiskey flu.

"Go to bed," we said. "Try to take care of yourself."

"Thank you," he said. "Be at the car – 6 a.m."

The last we saw of him, he was at the bar with a drink in his hand.

"I think I'll order us a bottle of champagne," Dick said. "It looks like all they have is Chandon for $35 a bottle."

He called the waiter over to point out what we wanted.

A few minutes later, he returned with a bottle of Dom Peringon.

"Are you sure this is only $35?" Dick asked.

"Yes. Our champagne is $35."

"Well then," Dick said. "Keep them coming all night."

I cannot remember how the food was that night, but I don't think any of us have had better $35 "Chandon".

We finally retired at midnight, escorted to our tent by an armed guard. I couldn't decide if I should've been reassured by that or not. I had to wake Dick in the middle of the night so he could stand guard while I used the outhouse. One animal the camp was not in want of was baboon. They shrieked and screamed, making all sorts of racket the entire night. Maybe a leopard was nearby stirring them up. Our thin nylon tent suddenly didn't seem so safe. I slept sparingly throughout the night.

At 5:30 a.m., our tent flap was attacked. It wasn't until I heard a man's voice that I realized it wasn't a wild beast trying to claw his way in. It was time for breakfast.

We searched the camp for Robert, but were unable to locate him. His stomach affliction must've flared back up after the last shot of whiskey. Truth be told, we weren't too disappointed. He wasn't really a people person. He was the type of guy who didn't say much and when he did it was usually about himself and how he was one of Africa's greatest hunters, how he'd saved many a person from the attacking jaws of lions and leopards, the horns of buffalo and the tusks of elephants. With all this, he also made sure to let us know about his current affliction.

"Oh dear, my stomach is not feeling well today, I do not think I shall go with you today. I'll meet you at the bar for dinner."

Lucky for us, he was only the courier and not the driver. John was our driver. He was courteous and did his best to be helpful. Game was scarce, nothing like they advertised or like we encountered elsewhere. The droves of people were a major part of the problem. If they limited the amount of visitors, maybe the animals would have a little room to roam. We did see a few species we hadn't encountered thus far in our African adventure. Like the gerenuk – a strange, but striking, antelope with a long, slender neck like that of a giraffe which enables them to stand on hind legs and nibble leaves high up in the trees. Their color pattern is similar to an impala's; if not for their long neck and tiny looking face, they could almost be mistaken for one.

Then we spotted the rare Grevy zebra. We'd hunted the Burchell's subspecies – the differences between the stripes of each are distinct. The Burchell's have broad stripes, giving them a more black and white look with a beautiful pattern. The Grevys have narrow black stripes with a less noticeable pattern and an all white belly. The hair on their manes is a little shorter and the mane runs from the front of the head all the way to the tail. Unlike the Burchell's, they look more like a striped wild ass than a wild horse.

"I am enjoying myself," Dick said. "But I think I might need to excuse myself behind a bush."

"Again?"

"Me too. It must've been something at breakfast."

"To tell you the truth, my stomach is cramping a little too. I think we should just head back before these Kenya Kraps get the best of us."

We took Pepto and Lomotil like we were addicts. I was on my third trip to the outhouse when I was stopped by an attendant.

"We are pleased to allow you to stay in new room, yes." He smiled at me, nodding his head.

"Can we move in right now?"

"Oh, yes. We will have it ready soon – within the hour."

Within the hour? It was back to the outhouse.

The room was finally ready after lunch. While we were transferring our gear, we saw Robert. He was at the bar with a drink in his hand, telling grand stories about himself. We looked for him again when it was time to head back out, but he was nowhere to be found.

"He has bad stomach," John said.

Robert didn't get a tip.

He was at the bar again when we rolled into camp. We couldn't take it anymore.

"We will not be requiring your services any longer," Andy said.

"Excuse me? You cannot fire me. I've been sick."

The leopard's eyes are focused, and full of conviction – fearless. They are the eyes of a predator.

"You've been drunk," I said.

"How dare you. I need the drink to help settle my stomach."

"Regardless, we'll take our chances without you."

"Well then, if that's how you feel – I'll need money to get back to town. You cannot expect me to pay for it myself."

"Sorry pal," Andy said. "It's not our responsibility."

"How am I supposed to get back to town?"

"That's your problem," Dick said. "You're outta here. You're done baby."

I don't know how or when he left, but we saw him stumbling at the bar again that night.

Our introduction to Africa ended at that camp. It was anticlimactic, but on our last night, while we lay in our beds listening to the wild cacophony outside our window, we knew we'd never be the same.

Africa had taken something from us we could never get back. We took part of her with us as well and left a piece of our soul. It would always beckon our inevitable return. We didn't know how, we didn't know when, but we would return someday – that was a certainty. We would return – only it wouldn't be for the first time.

Majestic elephants (charging or otherwise), lion roars echoing through the darkness, harmonious songs of a remarkable people, the royal gait of a kudu bull, the confident stare of a Masai warrior and the eerie brief silences of the predator's night will sprinkle our dreams with wonder for the rest of our lives.

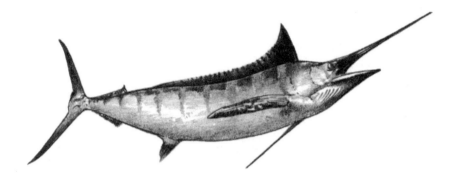

Part Four:
Billfish & Buffalo
in the Land Down Under
1988: November 1 - 24

Island of the Lizards: Dick

One of the best ways to truly understand the culture of an area, to see what a country is really like, is to get beyond the tall buildings and bright lights of cities, as far away from the tourist traps as possible. We found hunting, in any part of the world, could still expose us to people who haven't been influenced by our western values. Even in the United States, when we take a step off the paved highways to venture into our own wilderness, we find adventure is not a thing of the past. There are people who, not unlike early frontiersmen, are most at home when their ceiling is the sky and their recreation room the forests, plains, mountains and woods of our great country.

A city is a city. Most have a few unique characteristics, but beyond those are the constant drum of rolling tires, honking horns, and thousands of strangers too busy to see one another. That may appeal to some people, but for us they are all too similar. Thus, when we discussed a visit to Australia in the fall of 1988, our conversation involved marlin and buffalo. We spent a few days in the cities and found them pleasant, but were interested in a more authentic Land Down Under, with some semblance of its past intact.

The Great Barrier Reef region is famous for its marlin, but I knew little about the hunting opportunities on the island continent, so I called Gregg Severinson, an expert in hunting and fishing destinations, who runs Cabela's Outdoor Adventures for us. Gregg was quick to recommend an outfitter by the name of Bob Penfold for hunting buffalo. He also added the shores off a secluded little place called Lizard Island boasted some of the best marlin fishing in the world.

Lizard Island – white coral beaches run amok with overgrown four-legged creatures of the reptilian order, monitor lizards. We felt like we'd been written into a Michael Crichton novel. The menacing reptiles not only called the beaches their home, they expected to be given quarter. Many was the day Mary and I sat for a nice quiet picnic on a private beach when one or more of these four-foot lizards would barrel in uninvited and attempt to steal our food.

After dinner, in darkness, we took the long way back to our villa. With the moon as our only light we couldn't see much, but the porch lights of each villa were left on. We always kept them in sight. Suddenly, we heard a swoosh no more than a few feet above our heads. After a few seconds, another, and another. A list of nocturnal birds quickly went through my mind, but with the regularity of the aerial attacks, it had to be some kind of flock. The swoops came with more force as we approached the villa. A few times, they were so close we could feel the air as they passed, causing us to duck. A few more yards to the villa steps and it hit me – bats. We hurried in for a flashlight. Sure enough, hundreds of huge fruit bats dove, swooped and soared just above our room. We spent more than one night on the porch, listening to the bats, watching the stars and contemplating how lucky we were.

The lone resort on the secluded island offered a private getaway with little of the touristy atmosphere many tropical destinations tend to share. Sure, we encountered other guests, but could always find a beach back in a small cove we could call our own for the day. We only spent a few days as beach bums – we snorkeled, picnicked and chased giant lizards away from our food. There were, after all, marlins to be caught.

Black marlin fishing near the island is legendary. Anglers from all over the world come to compete in the annual Lizard Island Black Marlin Classic in October. It's a testament to the number of fish the waters hold during the peak marlin migration. As much as we enjoyed secluded beaches, colorful coral and tropical fish in the crystal-clear water, we were ready to go fishing.

There is no fishing experience quite like a giant marlin leaping high into the air above the ocean, thrashing its powerful tail and whipping its sword-like bill as if making a direct challenge to the angler, just try to bring him in. Few fish can excite the soul in such ways, beckoning you to rise to the challenge, pushing you to your physical and mental limits. I admire the marlin. For his strength, his stamina, his explosiveness, but mostly for the way he grabs the angler's will and matches it with his own at each pull, each crank of the reel.

Marlins belong to the billfish family, which include swordfish and sailfish. There are black, blue and striped marlins off the coast of northern Australia, but black are most commonly pulled from the waters. They can reach up to 1,500 pounds. Guides and outfitters who hunt them all their lives may never hook one over 1,000 pounds. Between 100 and 400 lbs. are probably most common.

First days always hold the most promise. Anticipation of giant billfish slapping our bait with its bill, stunning before striking, with the force of a torpedo, had us bright-eyed. We watched the ends of our poles and scanned the glistening water with expectation.

Our captain pulled the chartered fishing vessel away from the island at 8:30 a.m. as the sun rose past the horizon. The cool breeze blew into our faces like a giant, outdoor fan set on low. We closed our eyes to the relaxing wind, letting our imaginations dream of the day's possibilities.

Bait came first. A little tuna called bonito, also referred to as skipjack in some locales. Some captains troll at relatively fast speeds with artificial lures until a school of baitfish is found, but our captain, Captain John, preferred to find bonito or other bait if available, catch 15 or 20, then look for marlin. Captain John was a big man. He stood at least 6'5" and easily weighed over 300 pounds. He had a tattoo of a woman on his lower left leg and the mean look of a bull. He was the kind of man most sane people would be afraid of. We expected a deep penetrating voice, but his tone was light and airy when he spoke.

When we found our first school of baitfish, we needed little skill to catch them. We threw shiny lures in the water, let them flash a couple times and braced for a feisty, little fight. For the most part, we used a pretty heavy setup so we couldn't really play the fish or feel the fight with our short, stiff rods. They would've been a hoot on lighter tackle. Captain John and his deckhand Paul would unhook our new bait and have us cast back in like it was a race to see if Mary or I could catch the most bonito. I'm pretty sure Mary won that race.

After that bit of excitement, it was time for marlin. We were ready. Unfortunately, you can't catch marlin if you can't find them. We couldn't find them. Most of the morning flew by. The non-stop action of the baitfish put time in fast-forward mode.

"We're going to troll at around eight knots for a while, see if we can't make something happen."

Captain John didn't talk much, but when he did it was usually an instruction of some kind, said quickly with a strong and proud Aussie accent. Sometimes he ran his words together and there were times we couldn't understand him at all.

Paul, on the other hand, rarely closed his mouth. He was a tall, thin, friendly young man, but his accent was more pronounced than Captain John's and he rarely let you get a word in. He would ask a question more to talk about himself, it seemed, than to find anything out about us.

"Aye Dick, have you got any young'uns?"

"Yes, we have nine kids –."

"Don't have any myself. Come from a big family though. Boys or girls?"

"Five boys and –."

"I've got three brothers and two sisters. I'm the only fisherman though ya know? You ever been fishing for marlin before?"

"Yes, we've been a few times –."

"Should've been here a couple a weeks ago. There were marlins from arsehole to breakfast time."

We weren't always sure what he was talking about, but we learned not to question him too much. Any question usually started him off on an hour monologue with so much Aussie slang littered throughout we were lost much of the time. He was fun to listen to though – for a while.

"Aye mate, quit your yapping and put a fresh bait on." Captain John could usually shut him up if he gave him something to do, but it never lasted long.

Four hot hours after lunch, we still hadn't found a single marlin. What started out as a day full of so much promise had become a long, tiresome afternoon. We slowly bobbed up and down in what now seemed a tiny boat with no land in sight and no relief from the relentless glare of the sun. The fishing sucked our energy, both physical and mental, without so much as a strike. Our resolve was being tested. By the end of one scorching day, our skin turned lobster red despite sunscreen. The marlin was pushing our limits. Luckily, motion sickness is rarely a problem for us or the constant up and down and up and down rocking over slow, four-foot swells may have broken us.

The following morning the optimism bar was lowered a few notches. Peak marlin fishing was in October and though it was only the beginning of November, we started to wonder if we missed the run. We weren't as gung-ho as we had been the day before, but were still hopeful. If we weren't out on the water with wet lines, our chances were zero. We didn't give in; we prepared ourselves for another long, hot day. Hunting and fishing teach patience and persistence. The sweat, blood and tears we put into Cabela's made it that much more rewarding. The marlin wouldn't win that easily. We weren't quite as enthusiastic, but it couldn't be slower than yesterday.

Over an hour in the morning was spent looking for bait. It was from atop his perch in the captain's seat that Captain John finally spotted a marlin. Within minutes the billfish struck the already dead bonito with its bill and then slammed into it with the force only a marlin can muster.

"Fish On!" Paul yelled.

The fish soared into the air. It splashed and thrashed with power and acrobatic grace as if trying to pierce the sun with his bill. This was what we had come for. Marlin.

Mary was in the seat before the fish's dorsal fin disappeared beneath sparkling blue waves. She cranked and pulled, cranked and pulled. The black marlin ran. This was a battle of wills. It was the marlin's strength and power, its instinct to live, against my dear wife's small, fragile body and gripping determination to bring him in. Mary, my wife, woman I love, sweet, proper and petite has a different side, a side city folk rarely see. She is also tough, gritty, and has the endurance of an African wild dog. You can only see this side of her while following game up mountains, across hot savannas or fighting giant billfish. The marlin hooked on the end of her line thought he would win this battle. His royal instinct to fight would not let him give in. I knew whose will would hold out longest. I could see it in her eyes.

The fish battled valiantly, but with the aid of a seat, a footrest, a pole, a competent captain and a sharp hook, Mary pulled and cranked him beyond his physical limitations. He broke.

"A fine fish," Paul said. He held tight to its bill. "I'd say between 200 and 250 pounds. Mary, come have a look before I release him."

Exhausted, she pulled her feet from the rest and her bare legs from the leather seat before achingly moving to the aft of the fishing boat to peer over.

"He is truly magnificent," she said.

Paul tagged and revived him – he didn't need much. Someday, older, wiser, bigger and stronger, he may again match wills with another. He would live to fight again.

Although she had been pushed around and bruised, Mary was quietly pleased. She was pleased with herself, with Captain John, with Paul, and with the noble fight her black marlin had given. I was pleased too. It's always great to see your loved ones do well in any endeavor. But to see them truly enjoy your passion, your borderline obsession, to witness a transformation where your passion becomes theirs and you share something so deeply words are unnecessary. Our relationship has been one of shared passions, shared experiences, shared lives. We are closer because of these things.

Hopping into the seat, I scanned the water, hoping, expecting, needing to see a marlin. An hour later, I began to lose concentration.

Once again, the ocean, the never-ending expanse of water and the sun with its draining, searing heat were toying with my conviction. I've never been more exhausted in a relatively comfortable leather chair. But I didn't move, didn't head for the escape of the shaded cabin. I had to be ready. I waited. The sun started its migration west, still I waited. We cruised the ocean using mostly artificial pink squid-looking lures. Captain John was focused though he seemed a bit nervous. Paul was quiet. Oh well, there was always tomorrow.

I was drifting in and out of sleep when I was quickly rejuvenated. "Fish on!"

I popped my head up in time to see the marlin shoot from the water like a bullet, sleek and silver. Water glistened from his belly as his tail thrashed in a seeming effort to keep him suspended in the humid air. Then he slammed back into the water and ran. *Zzzzzzzz!*

He was big. The time had dragged. Now it was as if the action had never stopped. *Zzzzzzzz!* He didn't slow down. Then he soared again. Not as high as before and more horizontal than vertical. His bill was the first part of his body to break the surface and the first part back under. He was a scrapper, but he might've used up too much energy with his initial burst of fight.

Captain John backed into him as I grabbed the stiff rod and cranked the reel. At first, we didn't gain ground. Any extra tension on the line caused the marlin to run hard, but he didn't pace himself. Little by little, we wore each other down. He was first to give in to the constant tension pulling him toward the boat. There were a few more short bursts when we brought him in close, but they didn't last long. He quickly ran out of steam.

Sweat dripped off my brow like it was raining directly over my head. The salty perspiration burned my eyes. When we finally got him in, I was as exhausted as the fish. Another quick tag and release and he was gone.

I caught my breath as I looked around. It became apparent I'd fought him longer than I thought. The hot sun was not quite so hot anymore. It was well on its way down for the evening. Its golden-orange reflection made the water look like fire. We reeled in, the sun slowly sank into the water and Captain John sped us back toward Lizard Island. The day's two noble marlin made yesterday's monotonous hours well worth it. We could hardly wait for tomorrow.

The Mako and the Bleeder: Mary

Sleep came fast and hard. The morning popped its head up too quickly, but it was time to fish, so we drug ourselves out of bed and prepared for another day on the water. After yesterday's success, we were confident in ourselves and in Captain John and Paul. They'd found us two eager fish and we'd held up our end of the bargain. However, we did bring some reading material. It was always possible the action might be limited, the dull intervals long. We didn't think so, but we brought along some books anyway, just in case.

Thank goodness we did. It was worse than the first day – we didn't even catch bait. The sun was relentless. Heat and humidity squeezed every ounce of energy we had, dripping it to the deck in the form of sweat. All day long, nothing kept us awake except Paul and his stories – many of which never seemed to end or have a point. It helped break the monotony even though we couldn't understand him much of the time. We caught enough words to follow along for a while and then he'd completely throw us off with something like "he was a dinkum lad who always seemed to be the meat in the sandwich." We made out most of the words when he didn't talk too fast, but we could rarely translate them before he was on to a new story.

It went on like this all day. No fish. Oppressive heat. Paul rambling. Dick and I feebly trying to follow him. Captain John, all alone at the wheel, concentrating hard on an unchanging surface of water. It was exhausting, much more tiresome than reeling in fish. The problem with fishing is there's always a chance you might hook one in the next few seconds. We were hot, tired and finished with our books, but we couldn't quit. We had the boat from dawn till dusk for the next two days. We were determined to make the best of it. The marlin won the day, but we'd be back in the morning, full of anticipation and hope – maybe even a little confidence.

The morning began with rod-bending, line-zipping excitement. I think Captain John was focused on bait. He wouldn't be skunked two days in a row.

Right away we hooked a rainbow runner. It streaked back and forth, giving us an exciting fight. For the next hour and a half, we hooked and fought rainbow runners to the boat. It was non-stop for a while. On more than one occasion, Dick and I had to try to stay out of one another's way as we battled these hard-fighting little scrappers. It was like we had turning torpedoes on the end of our line. It didn't take long for our arms to weaken with pleasurable pain.

By mid-morning, we'd caught 25 rainbow runners, three bonitos, a wahoo, and a mahi-mahi. Each of these fish are hardy fighters. With semi-light tackle, they can be some of the most exciting fish anywhere, not to mention some of the best tasting fish in the world. We'd already enjoyed a great day of fishing. It was still morning.

It didn't take Captain John and Paul long to rig up some live bait and troll them slowly behind the boat. You could see they felt it was going to be a good day. Their confidence rubbed off on us. I think Captain John even smiled a few times, but I can't be sure. Paul was jovial. The excitement emanating from the deck was thicker than the humidity. A marlin struck within the hour. I jumped into the seat like a kindergartener playing musical chairs. My arms were still tired from all those rainbow runners, but it would've taken an army to pry me from that chair.

I worked the rod, cranked the reel, waited for the splendid aerial show only a billfish can put on, but it never came. I fought that big boy for 30 minutes when it suddenly felt as if he'd given up. The line went slack and it came in much easier. There was still something on there giving a little tension.

"I think he might've got off," I said.

"Really?" Paul said. "Reel it in anyway. We'll have a look at the hook. Make sure it doesn't need sharpened or something." He peered over the back of the boat, waiting for me to bring in the line. "Bloody Nora!" He said. "A bloody shark, mate." He held up the head of what would've been a nice black marlin.

"Bloody hell." Captain John yelled back. "Let's get back in the water. This is a good spot."

Paul re-rigged another bait and threw it overboard.

"You can have the next one, Dick," I said.

"That one doesn't count," he said. "You just stay where you are."

"But I fought him for a long time before the shark took him. It's your turn, honey."

"No, you go ahead."

"Are you sure?" I asked.

"Yeah, I caught the last marlin a couple days ago," Dick said.

"Okay, thanks hon." I knew he wasn't going to change his mind.

I sat in that seat until late afternoon, waiting for another strike. All I had to do was head for the restroom. I was through the cabin door when I heard those reinvigorating words.

"Fish on!"

I was back in that chair before he could finish his two-word exclamation.

A medium-sized black marlin shot from the ocean, trying to spit the sharpest bonito he'd ever tasted from his mouth, but the hook held tight. I had him. I knew I'd get this one in.

He fought hard for a few minutes, running and thrashing. Then he seemed to quit. It suddenly felt like a halibut. I was reeling in dead weight. There was a constant tension on the line, but no more running – it just slowly came in. I leaned over to reel then pull back rhythmically like a metronome. It was slow. I gained very little ground with each crank and pull.

"It feels like I'm bringing up a rock," I said.

Paul's expression changed as he pondered the situation for a moment. He pushed on the corner of his lip with his thumb and chewed on the inside of his cheek.

"Is it still coming up?" Captain John asked from his perch.

"Yeah mate, he's still on there, but he ain't budgin' much."

"Shark?"

"Could be. We'll know in a bit."

"You think it's a shark?" I asked.

"Don't know yet, Mary. You just keep working him. We'll find out soon enough."

So, like a rocking horse, I cranked and pulled and cranked and pulled. Thirty minutes later, I began to run out of steam. The spool was filling up so I kept at it.

"Here it comes," Paul yelled. "Well bugger me dead. That's one hell of a shark. Give me a little slack Mary."

He grabbed the line with his gloved right hand and with his knife sliced the steel leader. I didn't even get to see it. Luckily, Dick had crawled up next to Captain John to capture the massive bull shark on video before Paul released it.

The next morning, we were up at the crack of dawn, looking forward to our fifth and final day of marlin fishing. If the pattern held true to form, we wouldn't get a bite. We'd hooked marlin every other day; today was the no marlin day. We were hopeful, but it was tempered. It was the last day. We were running out of time. There's never enough time. That's just the way it is. Time waits for no man. Marlin cared less if we had to leave in a few hours. They feed at their own leisure and sometimes, even if you throw a perfectly delicious live bonito right in front of their long bill, they turn away repulsed at such a disgusting offer.

One more would be nice. One big one. I didn't think that was asking too much. After all, we traveled halfway around the globe for the slight chance to fight one of these legendary game fish in the beautiful waters along the Great Barrier Reef.

The morning crept by with enough action to put a bear into hibernation in July. It began to look as if our schedule of fish one day, zip the next, was holding true. It was the slow times that made us question why. Why did I drag myself out of bed for this? Why would we come all the way to Australia to sit in the hot sun? Why, oh why, aren't the fish biting? You begin to wonder if your eerily quiet captain knows what he's doing.

If you're honest, you realize he most likely knows exactly what he's doing or he wouldn't be doing it. The fish are just plain finicky. You remember the long days on the lake back home. You know there's walleye where you're fishing, but they aren't biting. Or the many hours spent casting into a swirling pool where you just knocked the trout dead the day before only to be skunked a day later. No, Captain John knew what he was doing; the marlin just wouldn't cooperate.

Why? Would I have been there if it was easy? The chance to hook a fish or the distant likelihood a giant buck is just around the next tree. We keep coming back because we don't experience those things every time out – or maybe in an entire lifetime. Just one more cast and that monster will strike. Just one more.

That's how the afternoon went. We sat in the hot sun, sweated, watched the water sparkle – waited and tried to will it to explode with a giant billfish. Waiting and watching – watching and waiting.

Did the tip of the rod jerk or were we seeing things? For a fleeting moment excitement sliced through the thick, sultry air, but it passed by like the wind on its way to the sandy beaches of Lizard Island.

Uncharacteristically silent, Paul popped open his fourth Coke of the day and chugged it. "Ahhh that hits the spot. Would either of you care for something to wet your whistle?"

Before we could answer, he threw his empty can on the deck.

"Fish on!" He shouted.

Paul was wearing a giant grin on his leathery face as he snatched the rod, gave it a stout series of jerks to make sure the hook was set and jammed the butt into the chair's rod holder.

Dick's face was an excited look of wonder as he reached for the rod. I've seen that look many times. It's a look all our children have had at one time or another – a look all children should have all the time. I knew how he felt. I was bouncing up and down. "Oh! Oh! Oh! Fish on! Fish on! Oh! Oh!"

Paul looked at me as if I were crazy.

The big black marlin didn't waste any time bursting from the water with a series of acrobatic displays that could make a rainbow trout walk on to the shore to clap its fins in approval. His display was like watching a ballet performed right before our eyes. It was all there – the struggle, the drama, the grace and the beauty.

I don't recall exactly how long Dick fought that fish, but I wondered if he'd be able to hold out. Sweat poured off him like a thunderstorm. It dripped in a steady stream off the tip of his nose as he battled that fish with pure determination and focus. We knew from the first leap this was the largest marlin we'd hooked into. It was fitting it was during the last few hours of the last day my strong-willed husband struggled against such a gritty fish embodying a strength, power, and beauty which, at that moment, was unsurpassed by any fish in the ocean.

The fight progressed; our excitement dwindled. We watched Dick go through a transformation from a man full of so much wonder and enthusiasm to being so physically drained. I was worried. We poured water over his head, tried to give him some, but he was too engrossed in the moment to drink. I wanted to take over for him, but he refused. How he continued, I do not know, but as I watched the event unfold, I was afraid. I was afraid my husband was overdoing it. The black marlin went on another run, zipping the line with him. I was almost sure the fish would win the contest.

Dick grunted. His glasses had long since slid from his sweat-soaked face and clattered to the deck. I tried to put them back on, but it was useless, they wouldn't stay. His eyes were so blurred and stinging with sweat his glasses wouldn't have helped anyway. All we could do was watch and hope the fish would soon give up. Dick wasn't going to. I looked back. For the first time, I saw a look of concern in Captain John's eyes.

"Dick, let me take over," I said.

"He's coming in good now." He could barely speak between grunts.

I didn't believe him. The marlin had been coming in good numerous times only to take off with renewed vigor, snatching a bit of my hope along with yards and yards of line. I stared at the spool. Dick cranked on the reel. Paul gingerly reached in to adjust the drag. I could see the fish was coming in, but good was too strong a word for it. Each pull, each crank, brought mere inches. Dick made progress, but we'd seen it before. The marlin, as determined as my husband, would allow himself to be pulled in as he regained his strength, but only so far. When Dick pulled him to that point, and we were sure it was almost over, the old scrapper turned and sped away each time. I prayed Dick wouldn't lose this one. I often saw him push himself to the limits, but this went beyond what I was used to, into an extreme I rarely encountered from a man who has never known the meaning of the word quit.

While Dick worked his marlin, the earth's rotation made the sun sweep further across the sky. Sunset was close. Neither man nor fish showed signs of giving in. Dick was nearing the point of collapse. His marlin had to be running out of steam. Dick must've felt the fish give when he cranked it in past that imaginary line the black marlin had, up to this point, refused to cross. With his last ounce of strength, Dick pulled and cranked. If the fish made another run, that would be the end of it. Dick used up everything he had left. He wrenched the rod up, reeling in when he lowered the rod again. He was in a rhythm, but it was obvious he wouldn't last long. Like a fading metronome, his pulls were not as high. Each crank barely made it around.

Dick's marlin gave a valiant fight, but, in the end, had lost too much blood.

Captain John stared hard for any sign of life from the marlin. Paul looked as if he was prepared to catch Dick in case he collapsed. I watched the reel fill up with line, afraid the spool would *zzzzip* again. It never did. Dick hauled him in and Paul leaned over the deck.

"We've got a bleeder." He yelled to Captain John.

"How bad?"

Paul looked up, shaking his head.

"Let's get him in then." Captain John hurried down to help heave the big marlin into the boat.

Dick was slumped down in the chair, barely able to lift his arm to take a bottle of water. He finished it. I handed him another. He drank half in a few swallows. Both Dick and the marlin gave everything they had. Unfortunately, the fish was bleeding profusely. It wouldn't make it. The right thing to do was put it out of its misery and take it to the research station on the other side of the island.

At the end of the day, the calm water inside the reef sparkled orange like a giant prism as the sun was swallowed by the ocean. In the gray haze of twilight, we toasted Dick's marlin, bidding farewell to a breathtaking island where giant lizards roam white coral beaches surrounded by water as clear as air; where beyond the Great Reef, huge black marlin leap from the ocean to taste the humid sky. Paradise may not exist on earth, but we were close.

Buffalo – Aussie Style: Dick

Water buffalo are not indigenous to Australia. They were abandoned in the 1800s when military settlements were disbanded. A large number of feral buffalo roam wild in Australia offering a challenging hunt. The only hunting we'd done which was comparable was for African Cape buffalo.

That hunt had been engrossing. I had high hopes for water buffalo. It was during the Africa trip I started to think I might attempt to hunt buffalo in other parts of the world. I hoped to eventually hunt them all, but one step at a time. We had water buffalo ahead of us. That familiar drop of nervous anticipation was wiggling its way into my gut.

Bob and Kay Penfold picked us up for the drive to camp at Arnhemland. The Aboriginal-owned area allowed a commercial live-harvesting company access. Bob knew their access was highly limited because it was sandy and soft country. To take the buffaloes alive, they had to be able to get trucks in and out. On top of that, it was late in the season and conditions were hot and dry. Buffalo were no longer in peak market condition. The harvesting company was gone. We'd have the entire range to ourselves.

Peter Goli, an outstanding Aboriginal hunter who often hunted buffalo with Bob, spent a few days exploring the area with Bob before we arrived. They were pleased; trophy bulls were plentiful. We couldn't wait to get started. It wasn't until Bob told us the length of the drive that our excitement began to abate.

Now in Australian terms, a five-hour drive is described as "just down the road a bit." It turned out that "not far" was about the equivalent of driving across the state of Nebraska. The long, hot drive over barren ground lasted just beyond forever. We counted road-kill kangaroos about one every few kilometers. That only kept the monotony at bay for so long. After the fourth time Bob said it was "just a bit further," we stopped asking, resigning to spend the rest of our trip listening to the steady hum of tires.

We finally made it to camp late that afternoon. We were beat from the long drive. By the time we could get ready, the day would be over, so we decided to have a relaxing dinner, a few drinks and some of that refreshing conversation found around hunting campfires worldwide. Besides, Bob had some work to do on the truck anyway.

Bob was quite a character. He was both the quintessential, rough-and-tough, outback Australian and, when he had to be, a highly skilled businessman. He was polite and confident, bold and unassuming. He had a way of going from a guide and outfitter to a friend you could've known for years within minutes. Like many Aussies, he loved the sun.

Once the business side of things were taken care of and we were settled in camp, it was rare to see him wearing a shirt. He walked around in a pair of shorts and a smile, soaking up as much sun as the day would hand out.

"Make yourselves at home," Bob said. "There's beer there in the refrigerator. I've got a bit of work to do on the truck. I'll catch up to you at dinner."

We sat around, watching the sun burn out across the horizon. No matter where you are, a beautiful sunset can move you like few things. Nebraska, Tanzania and Australia each have unique sunsets. When conditions are right, they are all breathtaking. It was one of those sunsets – the nearly cloudless sky fading from blue to an amber glimmer before slowly falling into twilight gray.

I finished a Castlemaine and on my way to the refrigerator for another, I saw Bob working on the truck. Sweat dripped off his face in a stream. He looked like he could use a cold one.

"Well thank you, Dick," he said. "This is like being on a hunt with me mate. Shouldn't I be the one getting you a drink?"

"So what's the plan for tomorrow? What should we expect?"

"We'll get you up bright and early and go find ourselves a couple of buffalo. There's quite a few around. We do a lot of spot and stalk from the truck, but when we get to an area that looks like buffalo, we'll do a fair amount of walking. The heat in this area, this time of year, can get quite unbearable so dress accordingly. Don't worry about water; we'll make sure to pack plenty." Bob stood up and slapped me on the shoulder. "Well, mate. What do you say we grab another beer and head over for supper? Kay's probably waiting on us by now."

Kay prepared all the meals and, in general, took care of camp, a couple two-person canvas tents and a larger wall tent used as the kitchen and dining area. Those canvas tents were miserably hot. It was tough to sleep in a pool of sweat. Peter might've had the right idea. He stretched out each night on the hard, dry ground. A never ending stream of oversized creepy crawlers that took over the night made Mary and I think better of it. We chose sweat dripping off our bodies over scampering legs of insects running up and down our arms and who knows where else. Peter, on the other hand, found the ground much more comfortable than a tent.

I woke up in a saltwater lake formed from my own perspiration, but was able to sleep a little. We managed to get through our first night without being snatched up by a bunyip – the Australian version of a sasquatch. Local legend stated that at least one bunyip roamed the nearby billabongs and water holes. Of course, we didn't believe in imaginary monsters, but some of the strange shrieks, howls and cries in the night jolted us from our slumber. We made sure our tent was securely zipped – as if those last few inches actually made us safer.

We decided Mary would take the first buffalo, so I was a spectator for the first day. Bob wanted to check out a nearby swamp. We piled into his truck and raced off, a rising cloud of dust floating in our wake. There were no roads; we just drove through the outback over fields of dying grass, occasionally turning to maneuver around the few thin, gray trees dotting the landscape. Every once in a while, we would come across a kangaroo or two, but the area had a much higher population of wallabies. We stopped to glass a few buffalo. They were mostly females and younger bulls.

We found buffalo easily enough; all we had to do was find water. A mature bull was a different story all together. We hunted, mostly using the classic spot-and-stalk technique. We drove around until one of us – usually Peter or Bob – spotted a buffalo. We glassed a lot. If we came across a herd, we usually took a few hours, stalking closer to see if a good bull was in the bunch. We looked over loads of those big, black, wandering bovines throughout that first day, covering a ton of ground, both on foot and in the vehicle.

It was mid-afternoon when Bob spotted a big bull. Judging horned animals can be tricky, especially if there are no other males around to compare against your prospective trophy. When Bob pointed and said, "There's a good bull." there was no question.

The buffalo stood beside three other bulls. His heavy set of horns made the others look like babies. His grayish horns had thick bases, deep ridges and were over 30 inches long on each side.

They knew we were there. Like many buffalo species, they stared us down defiantly. We inched closer, trying to use thin trees for cover as best we could. A few more steps and the smaller bulls nervously turned their heads back and forth. They trotted a few yards.

"Okay Mary, when he turns, shoot him in the shoulder," Bob said softly.

Mary held on him and waited. He glared at us forever, offering only a chest shot with his nose in the air. We were close enough for her to make the shot. Bob must've thought the same thing.

In a calm, soothing voice he said, "Can you put one in the center of his chest?"

At that moment, the bull turned to join the others in his small band. Once he reached them, he made a brief, yet fatal mistake, stopping broadside and turning his head to look back.

"Now. Take him now."

The herd bolted at the shot. Mary's bull, hit well in the shoulder, went in the opposite direction.

Mary's first try at buffalo was a stubborn old water buffalo that took every bullet from her .375 before going down.

"Give him another, Mary." Bob said. He had his binoculars up.

"And another."

One more bullet from Mary's .375 and the bull staggered before tipping over in a hump.

"Great shooting Mary," Bob said as we approached the buffalo. "Reload and keep on him. These buggers sometimes don't know when to quit."

We approached cautiously from behind. Mary kept her rifle raised and pointed at the motionless bull. He was done. Mary's second and third shots had been unnecessary. The first bullet mangled his heart.

After we field dressed him, the four of us pushed and pulled in a struggle to load him into the truck. The temperature was well over 100 degrees. I was drenched in sweat. Bob, as always, was without a shirt; how his skin took such a beating day in and day out was beyond me.

It was well after dark by the time we left for camp. I don't remember how long the drive back took – I dozed off – but we didn't get back until after 11 p.m. Mary woke me when we pulled up next to the tents.

"I don't know how you can sleep when it's so rough"

My eyes barely open, I shrugged as we headed for our tent. We were too pooped for dinner. Much of the work on the buffalo was left unfinished.

On an African safari there is usually a plethora of bodies to handle the workload, leaving the professional hunter and the client more time for hunting. Our modest camp consisted of just five people, two of which were clients. We were not expected to help out, but we didn't mind. It beat sitting around waiting.

We spent the entire morning finishing up the work left on Mary's buffalo. Peter and Bob did most of it. We tried to help with anything we could, doing our best to stay out of the way when things were under control.

"We need to get this taken care of," Bob said. He and Peter were fleshing out the cape. "Do you mind if we don't head out until after lunch? We should be done by then."

"No problem. What can I do to help?"

"If you could hold him here that would be splendid."

We cleaned up the skin while the sun moved high into the sky, shooting the thermometers well past 100 degrees again. Bob pulled his shirt off. I shook my head as I put a thick layer of sunscreen on my arms, legs and face. I still got burned.

Lunch was understandably late. We scarfed it down, eager to head to the outback. With only a few hours of daylight left, we stayed closer to camp. The temperature was horrendous, but when we spotted buffalo, the misery seemed to rise away with the heat waves. When it was slow and we didn't see anything, it was like walking through smokeless fire. How anyone could live in this inescapable oven was beyond us. I guess that's why the massive majority of Australia's population resides along the coasts. The water is their only reprieve from the relentless sun.

We drove from area to area, hiked around "buffalo-looking" spots and glassed a few borderline bulls. At the end of the day, we'd looked over a dozen bulls, without finding one we wanted. With dry throats, sunburned skin and exhausted muscles, we wandered back to camp. Kay already had a wonderful meal prepared. Our lack of success was quickly forgotten in a bowl of delicious vegetable soup.

"What do you say we do a little exploring tomorrow Dick? The old military map shows a bit of high country a few hours from here. It will take some time to get there, but the area probably has a few good buffalo about."

"Sounds good to me. I always enjoy a good expedition. Besides, I wouldn't mind seeing some different country."

"Okay, then. We'll have to jump out of here pretty early. Four o'clock okay?"

"We better be getting to bed then. Try to get a little rest."

The next morning we awoke to the sound of big raindrops slapping the roof of our tent. The wet season was just around the corner, so a little rain was not entirely unexpected. It wasn't too bad, but Bob was having second thoughts about traveling so far from camp. Mary and I, on the other hand, we were ready to explore.

"Do you think it will get much worse than this?" I asked.

"It's still a bit early for a real heavy rain. But you never know."

Right on cue, the rain died down. Bob and I smiled.

"We can just throw some extra fuel and a tire in back. If the heavy rain does come, this could be our last chance to explore the high country," Bob said.

We loaded up the truck with our gear, some extra fuel and two spare tires before leaving camp. I was just getting comfortable for the long ride when Peter told Bob he forgot his good knife in the village. He didn't want to skin another buffalo without it. Bob was reluctant, but after a bit of discussion with Peter, we took off with a brief stop at Peter's village on the itinerary.

We rolled into Peter's village at the break of dawn. The children were naked as can be and seemed joyful enough. They played some sort of game in the street which involved throwing rocks. As we moved a little further on, they darted away. We saw their target. A sad old woman sprawled out on the ground, her back against her crumbling home, drifting in and out of consciousness. In the slender fingers of her right hand, she barely held on to a half-empty bottle. She raised her head, yelled something inaudible to the children and then took another swig before slumping down with closed eyes.

Mary and I stared in disbelief. Bob and Peter glanced briefly and carried on. A few rotting houses away, a small underfed child stood beside her passed out mother, her mouth wide. She cried loudly and had tears running down her cheeks. She had been weeping a long time. A moment later another bony child, a few years older than the first, appeared sleepy-eyed from the dwelling, walked over, struggled to pick up her wailing sister and carried her inside. Before she disappeared into the dark doorway, she turned to look toward us with empty eyes. Some of the children cheered and chased after the truck. Most of the adults we saw were passed out drunk or caring for someone who was. Trash and empty bottles littered the ground.

It's hard to describe how we felt. Before us was an entire community which had given up on life. The utter destitution was tear-jerking. Unlike some of the dirt-poor villages we visited in Africa, these people were not content. It was like they had lost their will to face the day. They had more in terms of possessions than the few African villages we'd visited. Other than the children, most were clothed and even wore shoes. Most of their possessions lay dirty, battered and broken from years of disregard.

The only smile we saw from an adult was from an old unclothed white-haired man whose face brightened up when Peter hopped down from the truck. The old man was his father. He struggled to his feet and stumbled forward to greet his son. It wasn't 6 a.m. and he was stone drunk. Peter touched his father on the shoulder, said something and then vanished into the house. The old man followed him.

"The dole has ruined these people," Bob said. You could hear the disgust and sorrow in his quiet words. It was impossible not to feel for them. "I only hope that by giving Peter this job I can keep him from this fate. He's a great hunter and a good lad, but the downward spiral of his village seems to feed off itself. We just keep doling out money to them so we can feel better about ourselves, but it has only dragged them further into the ground. There has to be another way, but I guess it's out of sight, out of mind for most people. It's a shame really."

It was a shame. We'd never seen anything like it. We would remember these people and pray someday things would be better for them. Of all the adults we saw that early morning, only a small handful appeared sober. They were either coming or going, overly busy caring for children and the inebriated.

Just before we left the village, an event took place that was both sad and a little embarrassing for Peter. It was also a bit comedic. It could have been taken straight out of a Monty Python episode.

Peter reappeared with his knives and hopped into the truck. We began pulling away when, all of the sudden, his father decided he wanted to come with us. He jogged out on the road behind the truck, naked. He yelled, staggering back and forth across the road. He chased the truck flopping around, somehow keeping his balance, when from out of their home, his sober wife came dashing after him. She was screaming, waving his underpants above her head. I'll never forget that image. The look on her face was of grave concern. The fact he was drunk at such an early hour didn't seem to bother her, but the thought of him leaving without a clean pair of shorts was mortifying.

We pulled away from the village, driving in relative silence for a few miles, but Bob's lighthearted, laid-back demeanor made it impossible not to smile. Both he and Peter knew how to keep the atmosphere not only pleasant, but fun.

"It's just our dinkum Aussie hospitality!" They said with big grins and slaps on the back.

We've met few people who are more genuinely eager to please. All three of them – Kay, Bob and Peter – were so full of energy and enthusiasm. Even when things didn't go well and the situation turned frantic, it was all taken with a grain of salt, greeted head on with a smile.

We drove all morning to reach our destination, stopping for lunch around noon. Shortly after we finished our sandwiches, we moved into a swampy area – perfect for buffalo. The next few hours were spent on a typical spot-and-stalk drive minus the stalk. We glassed a few bulls in the distance, but nothing worth pursuing. There were numerous cows and young males, but the big, mature bulls kept to themselves. The light rain of the early morning was replaced by a high, red-hot, searing sun. It was all we could do to keep cool. We drank so much, our water supply was dwindling, the tiny breeze offering little reprieve.

It's funny how a little change in scenery can make you forget about everything else. Around 3 p.m. we made a right turn, Bob slammed on the brakes and we instantly forgot how hot it was and how dry our throats were. Fifty yards down the dusty trail was a lone, old, gray buffalo with his nose pointed high in our direction. His front legs were spread wide. He was ready to move quickly if need be. But he seemed more defiant than frightened, as if warning us we'd entered into his domain and to proceed would be foolish.

Mary's bull was coal black with a much thicker coat. Most of this old boy's hair had been worn off long ago. What was there was more grayish in color, revealing the many years he'd roamed the outback. The look in his eyes told us he'd stared down many a challenger. We were merely the next in a long line.

I knew right away. "That's a good bull," I said to Bob.

"It sure is." His wide eyes confirmed my first thoughts.

We backed away and parked the truck around the corner. "Take him when you can," Bob said as we stepped away from the truck.

We used the tree line for cover, slowly making our way around the corner. He'd moved a few yards, but was still in the open. I steadied my rifle against a small tree, fired, reloaded, fired again, reloaded and fired again. With buffalo, one shot is rarely enough. The third bullet struck him just behind the shoulder. He staggered and tipped over. I pushed three more bullets into the magazine, but I didn't need them. He didn't move.

We took our photos, loaded the old bull into the truck and with big grins and animated conversation started back for camp. In a few minutes, the rainy season started in earnest. One minute the sun was shining, the next everything was gray and the downpour mind boggling. Visibility went from miles to a few yards. A few billion drops of rain couldn't dampen our spirits, or so we thought.

On the long drive back to camp, one of us started to sing. The cab was suddenly filled with a splendid cacophony of four voices, not entirely in tune with each other, crooning both American and Aussie songs. Poor Peter rode in back. He looked cold, but had a smile on his face and lifted his voice above the pattering rain on the roof. It didn't matter if we didn't know a song. We just followed along, humming until we could join in on the chorus. I think some of the songs Bob and Peter

Bob led Dick to his water buffalo just before the rainy season flooded the area.

just made up as we went. We carried on like this for a good hour until we rolled up to the first creek crossing.

Bob stopped his 4X4. We stared, with a heavy dose of trepidation, at a rushing river, the color of chocolate milk.

"Looks a wee bit deep," Bob said. He stuck his neck out to look over the hood.

"It sure does."

The crossing wasn't too wide, but the swift current was ominous. It crashed against the banks, spitting up murky splashes of sludge in violent anger.

"Oh well. We'll never know unless we try." Bob's hand slipped down to the gearshift. He was laughing. "Hold on there Peter!"

We started at a crawl, barely moving, like a timid swimmer testing out the water's temperature. When half the tires were under the rushing water, Bob slowed down and popped his head out his window into the pelting raindrops.

"No worries." He said. Then the bumper disappeared.

Two more feet to the halfway point. I looked back through the window at Peter. He smiled tepidly, but his tight grip to the side of the truck and his eyes told me he was more concerned than he wanted us to know. When I turned back, the bottom half of the headlights were underwater. Mary held on to my arm with both hands. She didn't say anything. Finally, the headlights came out of the muck, then the bumper.

Soon we climbed out on to more solid ground. I glanced back at what a few hours earlier had been a dry creek bed. It had risen an inch or two since we began to cross.

"Like I said. No worries, mates."

Visibility or no visibility, it was suddenly as if we were in a desperate attempt to catch the leader in the Indy 500.

"We better pack up camp and buzz on out of here before we get stranded for a month. Those creeks get any higher and you'll be spending more time in our country than you bargained for."

When we pulled into camp, Kay already had much of the smaller items packed. She was sure glad to see us. She had dragged the heavy stuff as far out of the puddles as she could.

The first thing we noticed through the blurry waves of rain were the frogs. There were frogs everywhere, thousands of them. They croaked and jumped around, making such a racket. You couldn't walk more than a few feet without half a dozen green frogs hopping out of your way. Where they came from, I don't pretend to know, but it was unbelievable. We'd never seen so many frogs in all our lives. If it wasn't so imperative for us to rush out of there, we probably would've spent a few moments to enjoy their loud coming-out party.

We took down the tents in record time, then loaded Bob's heavy propane refrigerators and the water pump. By the time we piled everything into Bob's two trucks, they were a few inches closer to the ground. We worked so hard and so fast that even if it hadn't been pouring, I still would've been totally drenched in my own perspiration. The campsite had gone from an exceptionally peaceful dry area to a highly dangerous floodplain in a matter of minutes. The nearby river was rising by at least an inch every fifteen or twenty minutes. We had to get out of there.

We were wet to the bones, dead tired and a bit anxious, so we hurried to the trucks, praying the few creeks and rivers we had to cross weren't already too high. The first creek wasn't too bad. The waters were sweeping and deadly fast, but they only came up to the bumper. We pulled through with little difficulty. The last two involved a little more faith. Faith that the 4x4 would pull through. Faith that Bob's assessment of the rushing water's level was accurate. Faith that our time wasn't up.

We made it through without drowning, but fully submersed the headlights and our feet got wet as water seeped in through the doors. There were a few hairy moments when the vehicle seemed to shift. We wondered if we were about to be swept away in the powerful current. If not for the considerable weight of our disassembled camp piled into the back, we most likely would've been washed away.

One thing which almost invariably occurs while on a hunting

expedition is that you find you have collected much more than a few trophies and memories that will last you a lifetime. Friendships are usually formed, especially if a hardship or two must be overcome. You usually don't think about it too much while you're there – you're most likely chasing buffalo, trying to maneuver around more frogs than you knew existed or challenging newly formed rapids during a torrential rainstorm. But when you shake hands for the last time, you realize you're leaving a special place and special people you are lucky to be able to call your friends.

Part Five:
Back to Africa - Ethiopia
1989: February 4 - March 10

Always Remember to Drink Lots of Water: Mary

It was only a matter of time. Two years after our introduction to the Dark Continent, we returned. Two years. In some ways it didn't seem that long ago. But in other ways – ways I didn't entirely understand, and wish I didn't feel, it was almost as if we'd never been there at all. I can't really explain it. I can remember everything. The sights, sounds, smells, everything. Still, I sometimes ask myself – was I really in Africa? When I was young, I thought the few hundred miles from Sidney, Nebraska to Casper, Wyoming was a long way from home. I never imagined I would someday travel as far as Africa. Was I really that adventurous?

Ethiopia was in an entirely different part of Africa than where we'd visited before. I didn't realize how different it would be. I don't know why really. Africa is huge. Ethiopia alone, at over 1 million square kilometers, is nearly twice the size of Texas. I'm sometimes as guilty of it as others, but too often when we speak of Africa, we tend to forget its diversity. The differences in geology and biology in the areas referred to as southern Africa, northern Africa, central Africa, western Africa and eastern Africa are impressive.

Consider just a few of the continent's countries; South Africa's interior plateaus and long coastlines, Cameroon's tropical rain forests, Zimbabwe's granite outcroppings and kopjes, Namibia's great deserts, and Africa's biodiversity becomes more apparent. Even when we break it down into countries or regions, we fail to paint a complete picture. When I say Colorado, you instantly think of high Rocky Mountain peaks, yet much of the state consists of short-grass prairie. One of the first things we assume about Cameroon is the hunt must've taken place in the jungle. Most safaris take place in the more arid areas of the country.

Everything I knew about Ethiopia came from brief glimpses of desolate communities with starving children on the news and in commercials asking for money. I truly believed we were headed for a barren land full of desperate people. Although I am sure these problems existed in Ethiopia, what we found was a rich and fertile land of abundant joy.

We had an overnight stay in Addis Ababa, then on the morning of Wednesday, February 8, we left for camp – a new adventure. Our scheduled time of departure was for 8:30 a.m. Heavy rain and thick fog grounded us until afternoon.

"We cannot take all these bags," the pilot of the twin-engine plane said. The tone of his voice suggested this was non-negotiable. "They are too heavy. We will be overloaded."

Of our six bags, we had to abandon four. Unschooled in the mechanics of flying, we figured better safe than sorry. Gear or no gear, we wouldn't turn back. We'd already traveled too far. Unforeseen minor setbacks such as these are often part of a hunting trip abroad. If there was ever a safari that went completely according to plan, I haven't heard of it.

A few minutes into the flight, I was glad we left those four bags. I have no fear of flying. Rarely have I been afraid while in the air. But our two hour flight to Gurafarda was, at times, terrifying. Although much of the fog had lifted at Addis Ababa, the mountains were shrouded in a heavy mist. Little air separated the plane from the peaks. Pushing through blinding fog made me nervous enough, but throw in one of the bumpiest plane rides of my life and my apprehension often made the leap straight to fear. There were a few times the plane dropped violently slamming us into our seatbelts. If we had overloaded the small plane with our four bags of heavy gear, I'm certain our graves would've been marked under a layer of dense fog, with wreckage and fuselage serving as headstones. I was never so happy to step onto solid ground in all my life.

"I didn't realize we were so popular in Ethiopia," Dick said

"Yeah, I guess this is how a rock star feels getting off the bus," I said.

Two to three hundred natives had gathered at the edge of the dirt runway. Some cheered, but most just stared. Two light-skinned westerners were a rare sight in these parts. It was cause for a gathering. After another three hours via truck, we finally made it to camp.

It was quite lovely. Tents were put up under grass-covered canopies and each bed was covered with netting to keep out the nighttime creepy crawlers. Rock pathways led to our hut where we enjoyed private showers and toilets – all inside. Everything was clean, the climate was cool and the food was tasty and filling.

There had been a rumor flying around that elephant hunting was going to be shut down all across Africa for political reasons. Dick always wanted to hunt elephant. When you grow up reading the exploits of such masterful storytellers as Hemingway and Ruark, some of your greatest passions involve stalking, tracking and shooting and you have a thirst for high adventure, an elephant hunt is only natural. Dick had already successfully hunted lion and Cape buffalo. He confessed that the pursuit of the remaining three of the Big Five captivated him. Of all the game we hunted in Zimbabwe and Botswana, nothing pumped his blood quite like lion and buffalo. Elephant was on the top of his list. He figured if he didn't do it now, he may never get the chance.

I wasn't near as excited about hunting elephant as Dick was. I'd read some of those same stories he had and excitement isn't exactly the word I would use – more like fear. But when he said there was a license for me, I said I would try. I didn't know what I was getting into.

Elephant hunting in Ethiopia couldn't have been more different than our safari in 1987. Instead of flat, open plains dotted with the occasional acacia and mopane forest, we found ourselves in a dense tangle of vines, weeds, trees, shadows, and very limited visibility – we found ourselves in a rain forest. Camp was surrounded by a seemingly impenetrable wall of thick vegetation. It was peaceful, but a bit unnerving as if we were trapped in our little clearing and someone or something was always hiding just within the tree line, in the shadows watching us, waiting for us to try our escape. (Your mind plays funny tricks on you in strange, wild places.)

I was coming to grips with the unknown demons of the forest when we crawled under our bug-netting for the evening. Then the darkness filled with rustles, shrieks, screams, and all other sorts of carrying on. What had I gotten myself into? If the devil were having a celebration with all his ghosts, goblins and ghouls, it would sound frighteningly similar to the Ethiopian forest at night. I wondered if I'd sleep the entire trip. If our first night was any clue, I wouldn't sleep a wink.

Dick, the ever-calm, sleep-anywhere guy, even had some trouble sleeping – although he did his fair share of snoring. Between all the jungle noises and my whispers ("Dick did you hear that? Dick what was that?"), he was kept from an optimal amount of rest. Although I was tired, I was happy to see the sun rise.

We've never been big coffee drinkers, but the tea was so tasty, we came to enjoy a cup every morning by the fire. Breakfast is one of the most important meals – never more true than when hunting – especially when hunting elephant.

Elephant hunting is nothing like the spot-and-stalk method commonly used while pursuing the large variety of animals referred to as plains game. The technique for elephant is tracking. Lots and lots of tracking. Actually, a few highly skilled native tribesmen do most of the tracking. We merely follow behind, marveling at their uncanny abilities. Half the time, I didn't see any tracks at all. There was way too much debris on the ground. It was difficult to tell what kind of elephant we were following when we were on a trail. Like a fingerprint, elephants have distinguishable cracks on the bottom of their feet. The older bulls have huge feet with deeper, wider cracks. But in the jungle with its thick undergrowth and many layers of dead leaves, truly accurate prints were hard to come by. With a high number of elephants in the area, when we found a track from an old bull, there were many crossovers and separate trails obscuring it. It can pull even the best of trackers off the original bull. It was amazing this didn't happen more often.

We caught a track about 9 a.m. and started hiking – okay, hiking sounds much too leisurely. We climbed, crawled, jumped and chopped our way through the thick jungle. After three hours, sweat rained off us. At one point, we briefly crossed paths with a young bull that gave us a snort before crashing away. He created a small pathway, but the foliage was so thick he disappeared within a few feet. The dense vines and trees closed in behind him like he was Moses parting a green sea, uniting the two sides back together at will.

I didn't like being confined in small areas with ancestors of the woolly mammoth. That young bull was only a few yards away when he took off. I hadn't even known he was there until he cracked a tree on his way out. If he'd chosen to run toward us instead of away, we could've been crushed.

The break for lunch was welcome. Corn beef and cheese sandwiches hit the spot, but we couldn't escape the muggy heat. I didn't drink much. I never do. Any woman who spends a considerable amount of time in the bush knows why. I'd later find that small inconveniences are far more tolerable than the consequences of avoiding them.

After lunch, we pushed ourselves from the shade and trekked on. We were still trying to get a read on our professional hunter, Nassos Roussos. It usually takes the first few days for everyone to loosen up. Everything we heard or read on the subject of hunting in Ethiopia left us with the idea the best in Ethiopian hunting starts and ends with Nassos Roussos.

Nassos is a tiny man. What he lacks in size, he more than makes up for in perseverance, endurance and concentration. He had the look of somebody who has seen pain and hardship, someone who has faced things we couldn't fathom; the look of a man who has taken life head on and fought his way through. Such trials would harden most men, but Nassos was kind and gentle, although tough as railroad spikes. He was quiet the first few days, but he was highly considerate and observant. He hardly broke a sweat, as he pushed us and tested us without a word. He seemed to know when we needed a break without as much as a glance back to see how we were doing. He would come to a stop, listen to us pant a few minutes and then carry on like it was him who needed the brief rest. We soon fell in love with the short, quiet man.

Early that afternoon, we took a break beside a cool, shallow stream when a few of the porters huddled closer to Nassos and whispered excitedly. Within moments, our entire group of trackers, porters and skinners were circled around Nassos, pointing every which way. We were surrounded by elephants.

"It's mostly cows and calves," Nassos said. His eyes couldn't hide a little apprehension − cows with calves are often highly aggressive.

Had Dick and I not been along, I don't think he would've been so nervous; he considered our safety his responsibility. He motioned us to fall in behind him quickly. We hurried to find a place to cross the stream and get to higher ground.

The behavior of the most experienced trackers often alludes to the gravity of a given situation in the bush. Thus, when our head tracker zipped past Nassos, not quite at a run, but close, we knew things would turn hairy in a hurry. Suddenly, a cow screamed, rushing at us. The three of us jumped behind a tree, but the way she snapped trees and branches like toothpicks, I doubted we were very safe. It was only a false charge. She waved her ears, shook her head and snorted at us before backing up. It was a warning. Leave or feel my wrath.

It was our every intention to avoid confrontation. With as much haste and as little noise as we could combine we headed for higher ground. It took us a few minutes to catch up to the rest of our group. Most of them smiled and gave animated accounts of their narrow escapes. Nassos grinned and pushed on.

We found the track of another elephant and followed it for an hour. He never slowed down. He led us at least two hours from the truck. With dusk a short time away, we pulled off and headed for home. I was relieved. Sweat clung my shirt to my skin like shrink-wrap. It seemed to get hotter by the minute. I was thirsty and tired. Just a little farther. Just a little farther.

"Are you okay?" Dick asked.

He was breathing heavily. It sounded like his asthma was starting to act up.

Nassos stopped for a break. He looked at me rather peculiarly. He offered me a drink of water and I took a sip. Not even water was palatable at the moment. The sooner we reached the truck the better. I'd be fine once we made it to the truck.

Half an hour later, sweat drained every last ounce of fluid from my body. It stung my eyes as it poured down my forehead. Things began to blur. The three men ahead of me became three sets of twins. I couldn't focus on the ground or the obstacles in my way. Vines seemed to grow thicker. I had to take bigger steps over fallen logs. With their hazy edges I wasn't sure how large they really were. At first, I thought the sweat made everything fuzzy. I rubbed my eyes. Then I began to feel dizzy. I looked up. The jungle spun. Tiny rays of sunlight fought their way through the canopy and, like a twirling prism, spun clockwise. I stumbled once, twice.

"Are you okay? Are you okay?"

I could only make out blurry outlines and forms as the ground spun me like a merry-go-round. I heard Dick's voice – at least I'm pretty sure it was his voice – and somebody helped me to my feet again, but I couldn't make out the words.

Stubbornness got the better of me. I started thinking I could make it if the men could. Don't let them see you fall again. I imagined they'd believe I couldn't handle it because I was a woman. I could handle it. I knew I could. Damn pride got in the way of my common sense. It didn't take long for pride to turn to prayer. I can honestly say I believe God guided my feet. I couldn't make them move and had lost my ability to follow the man in front of me, yet I always took the next step.

I don't know when, I certainly don't know how, but I made it to the jeep. I collapsed in the back seat, took a few small drinks of water as I drifted between reality and some other dark place I can't remember for the entire drive back to the camp. I'd never been so happy to see grass huts and tents. I didn't feel like eating. I thought I should make an appearance though. Besides, I figured I should probably get something into my system. Dinner was superb. I couldn't eat much. I was still feeling the after-effects of my brief spat with what I assumed were the early signs of dehydration. A few bites of hot and spicy Ethiopian chicken, Chinese cabbage, what I think was pork and a glass of red wine was all I could force down.

The lingering symptoms of my ailments evolved through the evening. I began spinning again, was light headed and felt sick to my stomach. But it was Ethiopia's much more explosive version of Montezuma's Revenge that was the real kicker. I was a complete basket case. Dick was kept awake with worry. I finally sacked out, sleeping well until about 3 a.m. when the sky began to explode in a light and sound show that would inspire any fireworks director for the Fourth of July. Then came the rain. Not in a drizzle or sprinkle or even a pour, but an overwhelming surge. I instantly remembered our experience in the Australian outback. I began to worry about flood possibilities.

By morning the rain subsided. It left a thickness in the air that saturated us as we walked. We were on another trail within minutes of leaving the jeep. Even a novice could read these tracks. The ground was extra soft from the overnight deluge. The heavy animals sunk into the mud. There were many different sized tracks, but it was the two big tracks with deep cracks that caused us to give chase.

A little concerned about the high number of overlapping prints and unable to discern accurately how many elephants comprised the herd marching in single file, Nassos sent two of his more fleet-footed trackers to catch up with the herd to count them. We followed the trail for an hour or so when our two runners slipped through the vines and tall undergrowth. They'd run at least a couple miles and didn't even seem to breathe irregularly. Dick and I were sweating profusely and sucking air while moving at a rather leisurely pace. They made me feel old and out of shape. They were used to it – they lived there; they're young and full of energy. No matter how many excuses I made for myself, Nassos, his tracker, the porters, the skinners and most everybody else in camp were impressive in many ways, one of which happened to be their physical stamina.

Their report: At least thirty elephants with a few very young calves. They didn't see any old bulls.

Nassos didn't need to hear any more. It was difficult to approach a large group, especially when there are a number of small calves and nervous cows to contend with. Elephants may not see well, but in this kind of rainforest environment their ears and noses pick up your advance. They have no need to see you. Besides, Nassos said the elephants had been displaying highly aggressive behavior lately. No animal is more formidable than an angry mother protecting her calf. We abandoned the trail, going back to camp for an early lunch.

"I think we should move to fly camp," Nassos said over a cup of tea. He never ate much. No wonder he's so thin. "Herds are too big here. We need solitary bulls."

"How far is it?" We asked.

"A couple of hours." Nassos talked quietly with a Greek accent. We often had to lean forward in order to hear everything he said.

Soon five young men began singing an upbeat tune. Their work kept in step with the beat of their song. They smiled, they sang, they loaded. *Him Bu Haum Bay, Him Bu Haum Bay.* Smiling, singing, loading. One man stood on the back of the jeep, catching gear as another threw it up to him. Equipment was tossed from one man to another until it finally ended up in the hands of the man in the jeep. He swayed back and forth, every once in a while adding a brief solo – *Alee At, Alee At* – in a high pitch. This common, everyday occurrence was a show we would've paid top dollar to see. Some of today's pop stars would do well to take voice lessons from a few of our Ethiopian friends.

"I'm afraid our departure must be delayed," Nassos said. "The other truck has been taken to town to make an arrest for the theft of a mule."

We didn't press for more information and Nassos didn't offer. He merely placed his hands on his hips and, with a lowered head, walked away.

A hunting trip rarely goes as smoothly as planned no matter how prepared you may be. If you do not take the small setbacks in stride, you'll never enjoy yourself and should take up another lifestyle before it's too late. We have yet to meet an outfitter or professional hunter who looks upon these minor details as more than part of a normal day – they wouldn't be in the profession if they did. One of the allures of hunting for a living is knowing every day will be a new experience, challenging a hunter's skills, resolve and patience. More than anything, they do it because they love it – all of it.

Not long after our lunch of toast, potatoes, spaghetti and some kind of roasted game meat (I don't know what it was, but it was tasty), the crew pulled back into camp. Apparently the arrest had gone smoothly. They were all in a jovial mood even though they returned with news that the truck was in need of repair. So we sat around a little longer. We chatted and waited. What else could we do?

We left for Camp Samarta late that afternoon. After a two hour drive, we arrived at our new base of operations. Nassos and his crew had fly camp set up in record time. Busy bodies were everywhere. One tent up. Two. The kitchen tent and then staff quarters all before dark. *Fo Ma Qua Fo Ma Qua Laay.* Maybe we should sing a little more when we work back in the States. Camp Samarta was not as elegant as the main camp, but it was comfortable. That's all we needed anyway. Some people would disagree with me, but I know what I like. As much fun as roughing it can be, a little comfort never hurt anybody.

Saturday morning arrived too quickly. We were ready to go anyway. It's always easier to get up for hunting. We sped through a breakfast of oatmeal and tea before taking off. Camp was in an optimal spot; we left on foot directly from the big, white, canvas dining tent.

Great hunting areas rarely come without trade-offs. Dense jungle with visibility reduced to feet; steep inclines to climb; an infinite number of swat-resistant insects of every size (some as big as your palm and some too small to see with the naked eye); an oppressive tangle of vines maliciously gripping at your ankles, knees, arms and throat, are all a part of the deal. The trade off: tougher hunting equals more elephants.

I'm glad the morning was only warm instead of hotter than the devil's lair and the humidity was only 99% instead of 100% and there were plenty of tripping vines to grab onto to pull myself up an incline which at least turned flat once every hour or so. Most of all, I'm glad Nassos stopped a lot.

Hot and exhausted, our break for lunch was welcome. I didn't feel particularly well, so I only had a boiled potato and a Coke. While everyone else finished lunch, I took a nap. A few miles further, I found myself in a spinning jungle. My stomach was upset and I shook uncontrollably. I thought it would pass. I didn't say anything. We continued on. It wasn't the first mistake I've ever made. It certainly wouldn't be the last, but it was one of the more serious.

Half an hour later, I was feeling nauseous and started hyperventilating. Now I was worried. The consensus among trackers, bearers, Nassos and Dick was I was terribly dehydrated. The situation, although none of them told me to my face, was serious. I didn't see any doctors in our group, but Nassos said he'd seen it many times before. Instead of scolding me for not drinking enough water as he had instructed, he turned his attention to helping me. That little man who had fiery determination in his eyes at the outset of each morning now had an expression that mirrored my husband's – concern. We were hours from camp, but there was a nearby village we would head to after a brief rest.

I barely had the strength to lift a canteen to dump its contents over my head. It was freezing at first. The water splashed over my scalp, slipped under my shirt and slid down my back. I shivered. But I let it pour. When the canteen's cool stream finally became a tiny trickle, I handed it back to Nassos.

"I will mix you medicine," Nassos said. His quiet Greek accent was soothing.

I tried to watch him, but my eyes were blurry, the dizziness overwhelming, like I was on an out-of-control merry-go-round that wouldn't stop. Fear began wrapping its twisting grip around my stomach. What I wouldn't give to trade that fear for the crashing, tree-snapping, get-the-heck-out-of-the-way fear of a charging elephant. An elephant charge is one of the most terrifying encounters in all of Africa, but it's also quick. You have no time for cognitive thought (not that I was thinking too clearly). There is only reaction and the right reaction makes all the difference. A charge is like an abrupt thunderstorm roaring down on you. This fear was different. It was the lightning show before the storm, the thunder and the light rain – a taste of what's to come; inescapable nonetheless. I was helpless, black clouds approaching from every

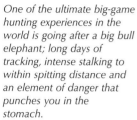

One of the ultimate big-game hunting experiences in the world is going after a big bull elephant; long days of tracking, intense stalking to within spitting distance and an element of danger that punches you in the stomach.

direction. There was no escape from this storm, of that I was certain.

Somehow, I made it to the village. Once there, I forced down Nassos' concoction. We found some shade where I slumped to the ground and leaned against a wide tree. The village kept coming in and out of focus. My eyes opened and closed with the speed of a sloth while the rest of my body did its own high-speed version of the jitterbug. I had to be a pitiful sight. When my eyes opened, the hazy vision of a native village whirled by. When they closed, even the darkness was fuzzy and spinning. My eyes creaked open. I saw Nassos speaking with a group of women, pointing and waving their arms in the air. I could feel Dick holding my hand. My eyes closed.

I don't know if I slept or how long I was out of it, but when my eyelids lifted the darkness Nassos was crouched beside me, talking with Dick.

"The women say they heard elephants nearby a few moments ago. There are big tracks. I have sent trackers to investigate. We will stay here and rest until they return." He glanced in my direction, but said this as if he needed the rest as much as I did.

I knew we only rested because of my condition. I was too weak and queasy to protest. Heck, I was too weak to sleep. I'm quite certain anything I said was mostly incoherent. I was aware – I think, but my thought process was jumbled like a thousand separate pieces of a puzzle.

By the time the trackers returned, my shaking had subsided substantially, but not entirely. I felt a little better, the rest helped, but I didn't know if I was ready to continue hunting. I leaned forward, trying to make out what was developing between Nassos and the trackers. One tall, slender man in particular seemed to hold our PH's attention with his quick talk and lively hand gestures. Like a statue, Nassos stood, listening with his hands on his hips. He let the tracker finish his entire five minute briefing, then shook his head in agreement once, held up his right hand and said something which must've been equivalent to okay. Nassos always had an expression which was difficult, if not impossible, to read. With an almost stoic look, he strolled back toward us, his hands still on his hips, and crouched before Dick. Déjà vu.

"They did find the elephants," he said.

From the corner of my eye, I saw Dick perk up. Nassos quelled his building excitement just as quick.

"But we do not want any part of them. There are close to 100 in the herd and they said they didn't see any huge bulls."

To hunt a single bull in a herd nearing 100 head would be highly difficult, if not suicidal.

"We are still nearly four hours from camp. We should not try to pick up another track."

Although Nassos gave a good reason to return, I think my condition had something to do with it. We took the quickest route back to camp. Four hours.

After a few miles, my symptoms returned like a rotating storm. First the dizziness and nausea, then the blurred vision and outright spinning. I held on to vines and trees for balance, doing my best to appear fine. But my ruse wouldn't last long. It was when the darkness slapped me across the face I knew (as well as everybody else) I couldn't make it any further. I don't know how long I was out after I fainted. I remember reaching for a low-hanging branch then waking up on the ground with Dick and Nassos staring down at me. It was only a split second to me. It must've been longer. Most of the trackers and bearers who had been walking in a single file line, were now in small groups, some of them sitting with their backs against trees.

Nassos had me force down more of his medicine as we rested a few minutes. Then, as if I had just fallen into an icy pond in Antarctica, I began to shake uncontrollably. What was wrong with me? I was sweating an ocean, yet under the shakes, I felt chills. I knew I couldn't proceed on my own. It hurt just to breathe. Getting the right words out of my mouth was like trying to solve mathematical equations. A strange white lady quivering non-stop with a blank stare on her face. What a sight.

Nassos assessed the situation quickly. Without a word from me, he instructed a litter to be built. I wish I could've protested. I could barely think straight, let alone move. They had a sturdy litter constructed in less time than it took me to finish off the medication. All without a tool or piece of rope within miles. Near death or not, I was impressed. They gently placed me on the new bed and two men began dragging me along. Within 100 yards, we knew it wouldn't work. The terrain was too bumpy, the undergrowth too dense.

I felt sorry for those who had to drag me, but the other option was for me to ride on their backs. What a pain I was. They took turns carrying me. It was amazing how far some of these men, many of which were smaller and thinner than I, could go with me on their backs. It was embarrassing to have to be carried back to camp. My pride was flung into the air like a clay pigeon and demolished by thousands of pellets from a scattergun. It was my own fault. I should've had more water. So what if women's hunting clothing was nearly non-existent and I had to make the men turn their backs before finding a secluded bush in the dark shadows of the jungle. Those small inconveniences are better than the alternative.

Half an hour from camp, the rain rolled in like a gang of marauding thieves, stealing away any joy we imagined to have. I don't remember what time I was carried into camp, but we all looked as if we'd been swimming in the river. I was a mess. Shaking, shivering and unable to move myself, they set me by the fire, handed me a Coke, took off my wet shoes, pulled my sopping socks from my feet and carried me to our tent. Dick struggled to get me out of my soggy clothes and into something dry. I'm a mother. I know how frustrating it can be trying to get a child, unable or unwilling to cooperate, dressed. My limp limbs and incoherence couldn't have made things simple.

Dick brought me a bowl of lentil soup. I could only get a couple of spoonfuls down before I fell asleep. I woke up when Dick returned from supper. I could tell he was both tired and anxious for tomorrow's hunt. I could see it on his face. Outside his deep concern for me, he was having the time of his life. Three decades of marriage allow you to read a man in a mere glance. Just before I drifted off to sleep, I saw Dick chug down water from a canteen. I guess he didn't want to suffer my fate.

Shoot Him If He Charges: Dick

Mary was in no shape to hunt. I wasn't sure if I should leave without her.

"Go ahead, Dick. I'll be fine. We came here to hunt and spent too much money to sit around in camp. I just need some rest. I'm fine really. Have a wonderful time."

So I left, but not without reservations. I know guys who bring their wives halfway around the world to go on safari only to leave them in camp everyday. Now some of the fault lies with the women who refuse to enjoy anything uncomfortable like mosquitoes, tsetse flies, vines, perspiration and charging elephants. They don't know what they're missing. There are also many who are just waiting to be invited along. Then there are the few, like Mary, who refuse to be left behind. Like their husbands, they thirst for adventure. At times they need it more. Yes, I knew she'd be fine in camp – as fine as one could be while recovering from dehydration, knowing one's husband is out after elephant. I guess she might be a bit restless, maybe even a little jealous sitting in camp.

We started out half an hour later than usual – after 9:00. Within another half an hour, we picked up two elephant tracks traveling north. At least I think it was north. Sometimes it's hard to tell. The dense undergrowth forced us to turn every few yards and the thick canopy of interlocking branches dense with leaves blocked out the sun. I suppose the tracks could've been going south. Nassos and the trackers hadn't steered us wrong yet. I didn't worry about it.

We gave new meaning to hunting hard. Back home, in Nebraska, we hunt hard, but seasons usually take place when the prairie is cooling down or downright frozen. True it was February in Ethiopia, but we were only north of the equator by a short distance. Although the mornings were pleasantly cool, I cannot overstate the excessive heat and oppressive humidity of our midday jungle surroundings. We scaled steep inclines, ducked under low branches, climbed over fallen trees while pesky little flying menaces of every sort bombarded our eyes and ears. I swam in my own sweat. The trackers chopped and slashed a trail – sort of – but the forest seemed to close back in, covering our tracks almost immediately. Only big herds of elephants left clear paths. They could leave the rainforest looking as if bulldozers had just plowed through.

We stayed on the tracks. I huffed and puffed. Everyone else perspired a little, but otherwise cruised along like they were out for a Sunday afternoon stroll in the park. It was hard to believe we could hunt in this stuff. Visibility was measured in feet and the way we crashed through there, you'd think an elephant, with its huge ears, could hear us coming for miles. But we pressed on. I tripped and staggered more often than I'd like to admit, but kept up well enough.

Shortly after 2 p.m., we stumbled upon our elephants, causing them to crash off downwind. We could pretty much forget about giving chase. Nassos peered up, wiped his forehead with his arm, looked down at his watch and put his hands on his hips.

"It is too late to keep going. We will head back for camp now, okay?"

I nodded, too tired to talk. My muscles felt like gelatin. I'd be sore in the morning. Pain never felt so good.

At one point during the long hike back, the lead tracker stopped and tiptoed to Nassos. He whispered something. I knew from his demeanor we had come upon an elephant. Nassos and I left the others behind, dodging thick vines, trying not to rustle too loudly as we moved into position for a judging session. I snapped a small twig with my boot. We froze, listening. The elephant never stopped feeding; we hadn't blown our cover.

When I was a boy, I dreamed I'd stalk quietly through a dark damp jungle with a rifle in front of me like a soldier. I dreamed about what it would be like to step into the shadows, into the unknown. I used to dream about man-eating tigers in India, killer lions in Kenya and rogue elephants. Those were just boyhood dreams. This was real. I once believed those dreams were intense. I don't believe that anymore. No story, no unlimited imagination, no picture show, could ever prepare me for what it meant to fulfill those childhood fantasies. I was a young boy again. My heart raced, my mind focused, my palms sweat, and we inched closer. We'd been mock charged already. Anyone whose stomach doesn't tremble when an elephant's bearing down on them is a liar or a fool. The ground shakes like an earthquake, the infuriating scream is like something out of a horror show and outrunning an enraged elephant is at very best impossible. Man learns fear quickly when he has an elephant barreling down on him.

Nassos had stalked this close to elephants thousands of times. He was cool, calm and collected. He knew the signs, he'd let me know when we were in danger. He reached out with his left hand, pulled down a leafy branch to reveal our boy. The bull had his rear to us – a massive, stinky, gray wall a few yards away. He tore bark off a tree like it was string cheese. We could hear him chewing on it – *crunch, crunch, crunch.* I wondered if I could stick my rifle barrel out there and poke him in the butt. I think it may have been possible. I wasn't going to find out. He turned his head slightly, revealing his right tusk – a young bull. It didn't matter; I felt alive.

We backed out as slowly and quietly as we'd gone in. There was no need to goad him into a tirade. We'd go around this youngster. I couldn't believe how many elephants were in the area. With all the cover, an air count couldn't scratch the surface. Poaching and the ivory trade had taken its toll on the elephant population, but it appeared as if the steep, deep jungle of Ethiopia offered some refuge for this magnificent animal.

We strolled into camp around 5:00. I hurried to tell Mary about our close encounter. She smiled meekly through my recitation.

"I wish I could've been there," she said.

"How are you feeling?"

"I had a shower then lounged around the rest of the morning. I tried to eat lunch, but started sweating and shaking all over before I could get anything down. Asarat and the staff took really good care of me. They are so thoughtful and helpful and always so darn happy. I'm starting to feel a little better now, but I'm still weak. Maybe after another night's rest, I'll feel better. I'm surprised you guys are back so early."

"Yeah, it just got too late to go deeper into the forest," I said. "You know how fast it gets dark."

And it did. Not just dark, but black. The moon and the stars are blocked out by the roof of trees. Wandering around in that kind of darkness is just asking for trouble.

Sadly, Mary was still too ill to join us again the next morning. She hoped she'd be able to go the next day. She wished me luck and I kissed her goodbye. We took off in the same direction as yesterday, sloshing our way through the forest for over two hours before finding a fresh track. The rain and wind had kept us up most of the night, but the soft ground made for better tracking.

We stopped in a small village along the way where another tracker who knew the area better than anyone else joined us. We followed a single track until around noon when we made a brief stop for lunch. I recalled what happened to Mary and made sure to drink plenty of water. I emptied my canteen at least twice a day and re-filled it each time we ventured upon a river or stream. I just happened to have a filter I was testing out for possible inclusion in our catalog. We gave that thing a workout. By the end of each day, the filter was black and filthy, but it worked like a charm. The water was clean and even tasted good. One drawback was its size. If it weren't for the long line of bearers Nassos employed, I wouldn't have carried the filter everyday. I would've had to ration my water more carefully. As it was, an entire canteen never lasted long with me chugging on it all day.

We caught up to a bull early that afternoon. He looked big. One thing true the world over in hunting is that big is big. Whether you're hunting for whitetail in Texas, black bears in Alberta, elk in Montana or elephants in Ethiopia, big is big. You can see it right away. He stood there like an immovable boulder, his tusks hidden in a verdant bush. I had a shot, but we needed to make sure he had teeth.

Nassos looked at me with wide eyes. "He's big," he said. He raised his shoulders and lifted his arms in front of him, fists closed, like a muscle man.

Blood raced through my veins. This was it. I was sure of it. I raised my .500 and held steady, waiting for the go signal. We were close. I felt good. Just pull your head from the bush. Just once. I swear his tail didn't even twitch. There wasn't a quiver from his thick, wrinkled gray skin. For a full minute, he stood there motionless – egging me on.

CAW EEEEEET! CAW EEEEEET!

That elephant completely flattened the bush as he stomped over it. Some excited bird screeched like there was no tomorrow. The bull was gone before we understood what happened. We never saw his tusks. Must have been some bird to be able to terrify a big bull elephant like that. Stupid bird. I bet 500 grains of lead would shut him up.

Nassos and I looked at each other blankly. I wondered if he was upset. I'm sure he thought I'd be mad the rest of the day – an opportunity like that, blown by a feathered fiend. The corner of his lips started to rise. We both busted out laughing. What else could we do? Anyone who can't handle these kinds of setbacks probably shouldn't be hunting. We debated as to whether or not we should follow him, but one of the trackers alleged he was sure one of the tusks was broken.

Rain started to sprinkle through the leaves lightly. We wiped the setback from our hands and marched on in single file. I followed in Nassos' footsteps listening to the swooping, slicing and cracking of machetes clearing a more traversable path. We ended up on what appeared to have once been a road and caught another track. Two elephants had walked along the old road. It was the path of least resistance. That suited us just fine. We'd busted our backs for five days following these beasts through some of the thickest, most irritating, trip-you, smack-you-in-the-face ground. We were ready for something easier.

I don't know if comfort breeds complacency, but I rather enjoyed my lackadaisical stroll. I think everyone had their guards down. The trackers ahead of us and the bearers behind us were no longer walking in single file and talked amongst themselves, as always, smiling. That kind of utter content in what was a simple hard life was inspiring. It tends to rub off on you. I'm pretty sure I was smiling too.

The sun broke through when the rain subsided. It turned the wet jungle into a sauna. I guzzled from the canteen. I heard a crash. The rifle was thrust into my other hand. As if by some kind of silent magic, Nassos was by my side. The band of bearers had disappeared.

In their place was a bull that had just exploded into the clearing. In my right hand – my shooting hand – I held my canteen up to my lips. In my left, I held my rifle loosely and vertically. An elephant with 50- or 60-pound tusks was coming right at us. It was another five-step false charge, his ears flapping, his eyes a dangerous mix of fear and rage. He lifted his head high, tilting it slightly to the right, his dark pupils contrasted sharply against the white part of his eyes at the top of his sockets. I was frozen like an ice sculpture with the canteen stuck to my mouth. My left arm trembled with the weight of my rifle and my knees took their cue from my arm. What a predicament.

"If he charges again, it will be for real," Nassos whispered in my ear. "You must shoot him if he comes."

Shoot him if he comes?

He was only fifteen yards away. He'd be on top of us before I could drop the canteen. By its strap, I deliberately lowered the canteen to the ground, never taking my eyes from the colossus mammal. His thick, gray, cracked and wrinkled hide gave him the look of an old warrior sizing up his adversary – us.

He came forward a few more steps, but they were without conviction. At twenty yards he turned and trotted off. His fluid mobility was something to watch, strange, yet perfectly natural at the same time. With an animal of that size, you'd expect something more awkward, but nature has a way with perfection.

He was a small tusker. We were after something with a tad more substance. The ivory's weight would have meant very little had I been forced to deliver a fatal bullet to a 10,000-pound mass of rampage approaching at over 20 miles per hour, hell bent for delivering a fatal blow of his own. No, I would've just been happy to have won a collision of that proportion.

When my knees solidified from their gelatin state, I finished my drink. Something stronger than water would've been nice. We gathered our crew from behind trees, under logs, sliced up in the middle of thorn bushes, 30 feet up trees a leopard couldn't climb and pressed on. Picking up two more tracks within the hour, we followed them deep into a high, thick, wall of elephant grass. Our sight greatly limited, we moved like sloths, our senses of smell and hearing thrust into high gear.

Nassos was the epitome of intense concentration as our lead tracker pushed aside blades of green grass and pointed at sign with his other hand, more for himself, I think, than for anyone else. Through this entire process, I never saw the tracker look down, yet he pointed directly at the tracks and stayed right on course. His movements were as graceful as the elephant's. His light steps gave him the appearance of a cat sneaking in for the kill. Though he carried no weapon, he was a master hunter.

The tracker stopped. He seemed to blend with the grass, becoming a part of it. My heart stopped with him. Silence and stillness was a sign an elephant was near. I don't pretend to understand how he knew. Visibility was limited to a few feet in most places and I hadn't heard a thing, but an elephant walks surprisingly silent. I listened, intently staring at the grass, as if to force the appearance of an elephant by will alone. Nothing. I glanced to Nassos, but his deep focus would not be bothered by the likes of me in such a situation. I looked back to our tracker for some sort of sign, but he was gone.

My heartbeat grew louder, like distant thunder from an approaching storm. Silence spread like a prairie fire on the horizon. The weight of oppressive air began closing in on me. I wanted to see the elephant, needed to see it. At the same time, I desired to escape from the claustrophobic confines of the grass. We didn't move.

My sweaty palms slipped on the gun's stock as I braced myself for a stampede. We waited. My eyes darted from Nassos' small but unyielding frame to the endless barrier of vegetation. I could hear each bead of sweat tumble from my brow. Then, as if he'd never been gone, our tracker materialized in his original position, slowly backing up until he was beside Nassos.

They whispered a few words. Nassos turned to motion we were moving out with a wave of his hand. I never saw the elephant. Disappointment and relief swirled in my wake. It turned out the elephants in tall grass were a bit small. Triggering a showdown with a pair of young tuskers was not at the top of our priority list.

A rainstorm pelted us with the fury of a meteor shower during our long trek back to camp. Dark clouds spit their wrath upon us and stole away what little light we enjoyed. Three hours later we sloshed into camp, the wet weight of our clothes dragging us down. I thought we'd never make it back. All in all, I'd say we walked ten hours in sweltering heat or monsoon conditions. Who says hard work isn't fun or fun isn't hard work?

"You're finally back." Mary said when I shlurped into our tent, rain pattering on the roof like relentless machine-gun fire.

I collapsed onto the single bed, my legs burned, my clothes inundated with a mixture of perspiration and rain. I didn't have to tell her we hadn't been successful. That dead-giveaway gleam in the eyes of all successful hunters failed to make a presence. My muscles ached, my garments dripped, and my mind was mush, but I related the events of our day. She could see through my exhaustion I wasn't going to give an elaborate account, but she listened with interest anyway and asked few questions. As I prepared for dinner, I asked how her day transpired.

"Nothing too exciting. After my shower, I was drying my hair and one of the boys ran over to that bush behind our tent. You know, the one between us and the bathroom. Anyway, he ran over there with this big grin and jabbed his spear into it, ran over to the other side and stabbed at it again. I have no idea what was in there, but I can tell you I didn't go to the bathroom all day. You're going to have to go over there with me. Then after lunch, around 20 natives came by and just stared at me for a long time. It made me uncomfortable so I went back in the tent even though it was like a sauna.

"You've got to be hurting," she said. "I went for a five-minute walk in that heat and was exhausted by the time I got back to the tent. Just before dark I was sitting outside when something started moving in that bush again." Mary pointed in the direction of the bush, though we couldn't see it from inside the tent. "I stared for a while, scared out of my wits as it rustled around in there. It ended up being a damn little dog. He came out, looked at me and scampered away. I think I scared it as much as it scared me."

That's the way a hunt should always be. The way Ethiopia was. Non-stop adventure on the trail and if for some unforeseen reason you cannot make it out of camp, the little adventures are always there to keep you company. I had a quick bite to eat, more than one cocktail and the addictive kiss of my wife before drifting off. I dreamed a strange combination of charging elephants and bush-rustling puppies.

Mama Goes Elephant Hunting: Mary

In all my young girl dreams and fantasies, I never imagined spending Valentine's Day hiking behind an Ethiopian tracker in a dense jungle after an elephant, hoping to get a shot at him with a big rifle. I never even dreamed I would see an elephant, save in a circus or a zoo. But here I was, February 14, with Dick and Nassos, surrounded by jungle and swimming in sweltering heat. Instead of being the princess I envisioned in my girlish thoughts, I was endearingly referred to as Mama, both at home and in Ethiopia. I'll take that over princess every time.

I had to stop for a drink of water after we'd trekked up a high hill for half an hour. I felt pretty good, but it occurred to me that we moved at a much slower pace than the day I was ill.

"Are you taking it easy on me?" I asked Nassos as he held up a branch for me to duck under.

"Shh." He held his finger up to his lip. "We're hunting elephant. Big ears."

Before he turned to lead on, I saw a smirk sneak away with him. I became more enamored with Nassos every day, although sometimes it was difficult to figure out when he was serious or when he was joking. Once I discovered it was mostly the latter, I smiled a lot.

We stopped to the sound of cracking wood. Not the sound a snapped twig makes. This was more like the crack of a bat striking a baseball at 100 mph multiplied by 1000. The sanity of traipsing after an animal which could snap an entire tree like it was a pencil must not have occurred to any of us. It sure occurred to me at that moment. We couldn't see them, but the splitting echoes were coming from just beyond the dark shadows of dense forest. We moved back to a tiny patch of ground Nassos referred to as an opening and sat down against one of those trees the elephants seemed to be so fond of.

We waited, and waited, and waited. Not another peep. Nassos sent two of the boys in one direction and two more in another to see what they could find. While they were away, we waited. It didn't take long for Dick to drift off. Nassos sat by himself staring into the edge of the shadows. I wasn't tired. Too many tree-snapping elephants in the area. I spied on a big, black ant struggling with a leaf ten times his size and listened to Ethiopia. If you listen long enough and hard enough to a wild place, it will speak to your soul. You'll find yourself at peace, until an elephant cracks another tree in half, reminding you your peace doesn't come without a catch. The unforgiving side of a feral land demanded respect. But if you listen even longer and harder, you'll discover the violent side of nature can sometimes be peaceful too.

Eventually, the big, black ant disappeared and the distant elephants lost their interest in clear cutting, but my education continued. Two of the spotters came back with negative reports, so we moved the last few hundred yards to the top of the hill. We could see the entire valley from up there. If an elephant decided to saunter into one of the few openings, we could get a good look at him. We left a couple of the boys so they would be there to greet the other two trackers when they returned.

Nassos had his binoculars welded to his eyes while Dick and I stared out across a small part of the world that hadn't been changed in thousands of years. When God changes something, He takes his time, making sure everything is perfect, giving it a chance to perfect itself. Some places are worth saving.

Pretty soon, some of the boys gathered into a circle. I nudged Dick with my elbow and pointed. Two were crouched down doing something on the ground. I couldn't see what; they were surrounded by five porters, who seemed to be waiting. Then I noticed it. One of the porters turned. He was holding a hand-rolled cigarette. They all held unlit smoke sticks. I guess even without the Marlboro Man some people choose to light up. When the poster boy for Phillip Morris' untapped Ethiopian market took another step, I could see our two trackers were busy starting a small fire by continuously striking two sticks together. Their diminutive blaze had but one purpose – to set alight gum leaf cigarettes. With little more than a bit of nature and some ingenuity, an addiction is born. They procured all their necessities from the land and also enjoyed some of Mother Nature's small pleasures. There was no local convenience store to purchase another pack. When our Ethiopian friends wanted a puff or two, they simply made it.

We had lunch while waiting for our other two trackers to return. In terms of heat, the day reached its peak in the early afternoon. Pushing it during this time is usually more detrimental than productive. We reclined for an after-lunch nap in the shade. I couldn't help but notice the day had been overly easy – too much so. He never said as much or hinted at it, but I'm sure Nassos took it easy on me my first day back. I was embarrassed. I guess if the roles were reversed, I'd have been cautious too.

The only sign of elephant activity the trackers reported was a small band of cows and calves we wanted no part of. Many of the elephants in the area had shown signs of aggression and nobody wants to mess with protective mothers. It was too late to find and track another elephant, so we started for camp.

Why is it that, invariably, the return trip always seems to take so much longer than the initial journey? I have no answer, but was amazed, if not dismayed, at how far we were from camp. Maybe it was the sun, or the fact we were no longer hunting, only hiking, but the morning's trek had been much more enjoyable. I was hot, tired and my clothes looked as if I'd just jumped in a river. Because I don't perspire much, I appeared relatively dry compared to Dick. Though everyone walked into camp on their own, I felt a sense of accomplishment as we approached our tent. I'd been incapacitated the previous couple days. My confidence was rising. With a full supply of water and newfound conviction, I was ready to prove the difficulties of the last couple of days were nothing but a fluke.

That day, Valentine's Day, 1989, wasn't marked by a dozen roses, heart-shaped boxes of chocolate or your traditional romance, but it was filled with love and adventure. We even managed a glass of champagne by the fire that evening. To my recollection, I've never had a better Valentine's Day. Dick and I were together, still deeply in love after all these years, and I can think of few activities more enjoyable and fulfilling than pushing ourselves to the limits behind the world's largest, most intimidating animal.

Sleep was rough that night. I think the lack of rain actually kept me up. I was used to the constant pattering upon our tent. It tends to drown out the night's screams, howls and snapping trees. Yes, after many nights of cursing the rain, I missed it. Its constant drum, I found, could be soothing.

"Today, we drive," Nassos said the following morning.

Good clients that we were, we gathered our gear to wait by the Land Rover.

"How far?" Dick asked.

"Forty-five minutes." You could detect the hint of a smirk on his lips. "Maybe two days. Depends on the condition of the road. Didn't rain last night, so maybe we'll be okay."

I let a nervous giggle slip, but my eyes were glued to the road for what turned out to be exactly 45 minutes. I soon discovered a non-stop, two-day ride would've been a piece of cake compared to the next three hours we spent traipsing through a jungle so thick Mowgli himself would have trouble traversing it with the aid of all his animal pals. I was sure I'd feel a great sense of relief coming out of that dark jungle, but our prey led us right into some of the densest, highest elephant grass I never cared to be in.

I think I disliked the tall grass more than the rain forest. At least in the forest you could usually see five or six feet in front of you and there were small clearings every now and again. In the long grass, two feet was good visibility. The silence can tickle your crazy nerve until it shoves you over the edge. The wind even failed to whisper. Movement slowed to a crawl. The trackers seemed to glide more than walk, insects ceased to buzz and the elephants, out there in the blades, waited in intense silence. The little man, Nassos, whom we'd put our trust in, brushed away his grin like it was a pesky tsetse fly, replacing it with serious concentration that dare not be interrupted.

The grass whooshed as something ran, paused, ran again. My heart was a pinball in my stomach. I glanced around, soon realizing concern was etched in my face alone. What it was, I don't know. Since only I cared, it must not have been an elephant or some other fierce, creature lurking in the long grass waiting to gore, stomp or eat me. No, I do not care for elephant grass.

We came out unscathed and approached a trickling creek where I had to cover my mouth.

"What's that stench?" I asked Dick, almost vomiting.

"I don't know." He had the look of someone who just stumbled upon a feedlot for the first time. "Smells like something died."

Fifteen yards further we discovered what.

"No more than a few days old," Nassos said.

Before us was the decomposing carcass of a baby elephant, proof of nature's unforgiving side. The natives walked by, seemingly unmoved. An everyday occurrence in their world. I found the image poignant. I couldn't take my eyes off the poor thing. The vision of its decaying, putrid body covered with shadows, its little trunk extended toward the creek as if its last effort was to reach for a drink it would never consume, was haunting. I can still see it.

We continued on to a nearby village. Nassos hoped to employ the services of an old man known as a tracker with near supernatural abilities, but the deadliest creature in all of Africa, and the world for that matter, had incapacitated him with malaria. Mosquitoes – the diminutive killers of the world, through malaria and other diseases, have claimed more Africans than all other creatures combined. Though our prospective tracker would live, he was deathly sick. He smiled at Nassos as he sent for his brother and son, assuring us they would find elephants.

We saw nothing before lunch. During an hour lunch break, I noticed our two new trackers had disappeared. Had they deserted us? Maybe they just wanted to be alone for lunch. Where they went, I don't know, but within moments after we finished our peanut butter and jelly sandwiches, they re-appeared. We took off at about one o'clock, tracking a band of four bulls. Our vanishing duo were merely being diligent, locating fresh tracks while we enjoyed a relaxing meal.

We heard the crashing, trumpeting, splashing, spine-tingling racket of an elephant party – a party I cared not to attend. Yet Nassos waved me forward. Overcome with fear, I couldn't move. I also lost my verbal abilities. I couldn't see any elephants, but from the sound of their commotion, I knew we were too close.

Nassos and the sick tracker's brother were 10 feet ahead crouched in bushes. They pointed forward, having a private conversation.

Nassos turned back and looked at me. "Come here Mary. Shoot this elephant."

He waved me forward again. His voice was calm and quiet, but his eyes said now.

Against my better judgment, despite a stomach full of butterflies, I took a step forward. I couldn't hear the elephants cavorting around anymore – I couldn't hear anything. No elephants. No calling birds. Not even my own footsteps. I slid into position, trembling. Had I lost my mind?

"My life's in your hands," I said softly.

Nassos smirked and pointed. "Shoot that one," he said.

What the heck was he pointing at? Thick bush, tall trees and hanging vines as thick as pythons presented a collage of colors, from a faded deer-brown to a verdant brush of leafy greens with a touch of the sun's bright golden rays sneaking through the forest roof. The Realtree people ought to see what I saw: camouflage that could hide an elephant less than 30 steps away. In the perfect blend of shadows and foliage, I finally picked out a patch of gray. I raised my rifle. Then, through the 1x scope, I was startled to see a single, fiery eyeball in a mass of wrinkled gray staring back at me.

"Shoot," Nassos said.

But the trembling.

I refocused. The butt of my rifle kicked me like an enraged mule. I didn't feel a thing. The blast set off a brief, intense stampede. Nassos added a bullet from his massive rifle to the confused melee. Then all was

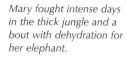

Mary fought intense days in the thick jungle and a bout with dehydration for her elephant.

silent. Nobody moved. The elephants had disappeared, swallowed by nature.

Crack! Crack! Thud!

He was down. Excited whispers grew in volume and number in a language I didn't understand. But, like a pat on the back, the meaning of those murmurs were crystal clear. Mama had killed an elephant.

His tusks weren't huge. I didn't care. I'd just accomplished something few hunters, and fewer women had done. An elephant is an unbelievable animal. Hunting them will test the limits of your endurance, patience, resolve, marksmanship, and most definitely, your sanity. I congratulated myself for following through with it, immediately telling myself I'd never do it again.

I tell myself lots of things I don't really mean.

Godfather of the Jungle: Dick

I awoke to the smell of rain less than an hour old. I couldn't wait to get out. The aftereffects of Mary's success left camp in a groggy mood – a mood I didn't share. I toasted Mary and her elephant along with everyone else; however, the possibilities of the day were more than enough to make me anxious. In the cool morning, light glistened off tiny droplets of water slipping from the dense greenery surrounding us.

We happened upon a sizeable elephant track within minutes. My enthusiasm reached a feverish pitch. This was the one; I just knew it. Our trackers chopped through dense forest crowded with hanging vines and stabbing thorns that snagged, tripped and grabbed with each step. Our bare arms were covered with bloody scratches, our ankles sore from the gripping undergrowth. The big bruiser's massive, cracked footprints were soon joined by another set of tracks, similar in size to his own. Within the hour, two more elephants became part of the growing gang, as if they were gathering for a showdown.

I imagined them as Johnny the Trunk, Toothless Guido, Harry Pachyderm, and the Godfather. Uprooted trees and flattened ground were their trademark. The quartet's tracks soon diverged into two double sets, all four big and menacing. The two traveling north were monster-sized, but the old man was all we were interested in. We followed cautiously. Then, as if attempting to throw us off, they split up.

Nassos studied each trail. He chose to follow the tracks leading into the darkest, thickest most tangled mess of terrain I'd ever seen. Thorns and vines, thorns and vines. Duck, vines. Watch your feet, roots. Ouch, thorns. What a mess.

Wet foliage added moisture to the sweaty fear emanating through my pores. The great thing about fear while stalking game that can and will turn you into the prey, is it fires up the senses. You become more alert than at any other time in your life. The subtle whisper of the wind – you feel. The dung you can't see – you smell. The slightest movement of a shadow – you see. The rustling of a hard-working beetle – you hear. The coppery fear – you taste. Very little compares to the path hunters experience and a few men, men like Nassos, choose to live.

When we stopped, when we abruptly stopped, I knew it was time to focus. The feral part of me took over, learned from generations of ancestral instincts. I slipped behind Nassos, and peered through miniscule openings in a collage of vegetation, both alive and withered.

We'd been duped. This fellow, Toothless Guido, so named because his tusks were no longer than my arms, stood so still he could've been mistaken for a granite statue. He couldn't see us, but he knew we were there. His tail didn't even flick.

No sense in agitating him. The local population seemed quick to rush you and ask questions later. By his actions, or lack thereof, he was already tense. We inched away, careful to move with silence and deliberation. The old kingpin had pulled a fast one on us, getting us to follow his big-footed cohort. We weren't going to let him get away with it. The trackers picked up his trail within moments of hiking back to the point of separation.

We heard him before we saw him, tearing away at the bark of a tree, chomping on its nutrients. Nassos motioned with his hands that he wanted to check the tusks. Fluid, soundless and languid, Nassos moved like a leopard melting into the shadows. I concentrated, trying to will him to reappear. The tiny pauses, the miniscule seconds of waiting, are the authors of insanity. Where did he go? How long will he be? How long has he been? What does he see? What am I missing? Am I really this impatient? Then, just as lithely as he disappeared, he glided out of the false darkness.

Without a sound he'd told me what I'd waited days to hear. We'd found the shooter, the dominant, old bull. Far past his prime, wise and wary, if not a little on edge, the elephant I'd worked so hard for was just beyond the brush – maybe. I stepped quietly in line behind Nassos, attempting to quell the butter churn in my belly.

"I've only seen one tusk," Nassos whispered. "But it is a good, old bull. If his other tusk is good, we will take him."

We sized him up from behind a tree, discovering he wasn't a monster, but still a respectable, mature bull. What little wind there was must've changed. Without warning, the bull made the decision for us. He turned. This was it. Bearing down on us, he shaved 30 yards to less than 10 in about the same amount of time it took me to yank the .500 Nitro to my shoulder. I remember those milliseconds in a blurred, slow, almost dreamlike state.

The ground trembled. Okay, it could've just been my legs, but in those fleeting seconds, the whole world shook. The jungle absorbed his deafening crashes. He was on us – even in slow motion – instantly. I don't specifically recall squeezing the trigger, but I sure remember the sound of the bullet as it struck the charging bull between his eyes. It was a dull pop, the sound of a bare-knuckled Ali landing a solid right on an unsuspecting, double-chinned challenger – multiplied by 1,000. The big bullet was enough to slow him and turn him slightly, but it didn't stop him, not even close.

If my next bullet didn't stop his charge, I would have had to throw that expensive double rifle at him. I could hit him with ease. At the same time I squeezed off my second round, Nassos sent his own lead into the 12,000-pound semi-truck barreling down on us. It took Nassos' first shot and my second bullet to finally turn him. He was seven steps from our feet. Nassos fired once more before the big, aggressive bull disappeared, echoing crashes following him through the forest.

Only then, after the brief moment passed, did I realize how close I had come to being crushed. Seven of my steps – two for the elephant. Nassos was smiling and a little wide-eyed. I trembled like a teenager on his first date.

"What took you so long to shoot?"

My guide's – my friend's – grin was contagious. I turned back to see if Mary witnessed this, the most intense hunting experience of my life. I was initially surprised when I realized Nassos and I were completely alone. Every tracker, porter and game guard within 20 miles had bolted for their lives. We found Mary, her back to us, tangled in a mess of vines, feebly struggling to free herself and join the natives who had sprinted by her, terrified the angel of death in the form of an enraged elephant was surely on their heels.

She was petrified almost to the point of tears. There is a hint of comfort in holding a rifle, but she was unable to enjoy that thin ray of hope. The boy who'd been holding it, carried it with him on his Olympic sprint for safety.

Emotional dissonance bombards your senses at such moments – brief instances in time. It is overwhelming. With the snap of a finger, it can whisk away your mental and physical energy. Allowing your guard to subside in even the least degree can be fatal.

Although confident, we couldn't be sure how severe the wounds we'd inflicted on the rogue bull were. My palms were slick with sweat, my head spinning, but we had a responsibility to finish what we started. Some folks would call it machismo, others may refer to it as crazy, or bold, or adventurous, or just plain foolish, following a wounded elephant into the thick Ethiopian rain forest. I think of it as duty. I chose to begin this quest which has so little to do with machismo and is so much more than just adventure. I, the hunter, had an obligation to finish it.

I was afraid. Excitement and suspense kept me alert even though I was drained to the point of falling over. I cannot fully explain what it is like, stepping light-footed, but with a heavy-heart, after any wounded beast; let alone one that would just as soon stamp you into pancake batter than run from something he deems inferior to himself. An adult elephant has only one natural predator – humans, but that doesn't always keep him from looking down on us as mere ants which are no match for his speed, strength and power.

Every shadow threatened to strike out in furor. Every dark spot was studied with caution. We moved slowly as we followed giant footprints laced intermittently with blood. Thoughts of your own mortality, rarely considered before this point, inundate you like the perspiration soaking your clothes.

We pressed forward – two unarmed trackers and Mary following close behind. Nassos and I held our loaded rifles, fingers on safeties, ready to point and fire if need be. I recalled traipsing through a corn field in Nebraska or South Dakota, waiting for a rooster to explode from beneath my feet. Only we hoped for nothing to flush, prayed our quarry required nothing but cleaning and the reverence a creature of such

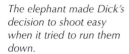

The elephant made Dick's decision to shoot easy when it tried to run them down.

majesty demands.

A few hundred yards later, we cautiously approached a patch of gray color we saw through the soft wall of vines and leaves. We studied it for a minute or two. It didn't move. We moved forward a step, then another. Nassos slowly reached out with his right hand to pull down a thick-leafed limb. Lying there motionless, tiny beams of light piercing the natural canopy above dancing on his giant body, was the bull elephant.

We all breathed a sigh of relief, thankful for many things, but mostly for the shared experience. I was hooked forever.

Our trackers and bearers whooped and shouted for joy, patted me on the back and shook my hand with vigor. Nassos was as excited as we'd seen him. I was far above cloud nine.

Mary smiled weakly, still shaken. "I'm glad this is over," she said.

"Wasn't that exciting?"

She looked at me blankly.

"You have done very well, Dick," Nassos said. "I have been in such a situation before and most men turn and run. Very few hold their ground the way you did. I would say at least seven of ten hunters flee when they should shoot."

"Where am I going to run?" I had a much better chance to stop him with a bullet than outrun him.

"I never do this, but for you, Dick, I will skin for full mount."

"I will put him in our new retail store for everyone to enjoy."

"Will you tell them you shot it?"

"Only if they ask."

Many people cannot understand why someone would want to hunt an elephant. It is not in my power to sufficiently explain. I can say from experience, the dead, soulless existence of city living shields most of us from truly knowing what we're made of. In our daily grind, we have largely forgotten where we come from, ignoring the things which connect us to the land. All I can say is there have been few days in my life when I've felt more alive.

John the Doctor: Mary

I looked down at my watch when Dick was sneaking into firing position. We'd been tracking for over six hours. I was in the process of mentally preparing myself for the long trek when we stepped into a familiar clearing. Thatch-roofed huts, rock lined walkways and a few busy-bodied Ethiopians carrying supplies back and forth on their heads. Camp. We drove for 45 minutes this morning, walked and tracked for over six hours only to have Dick shoot his elephant a mere 30 minutes from camp. I knew there would be celebration upon our return, but this pleasantly short hike was cause for a full-blown gala. And then...

"What kind of operation are you running here Russos?"

A surgeon from the States charged toward Nassos like an enraged buffalo as soon as we stepped from the forest. He'd just returned from a five-day backpack hunt with mules in search of a tusker that would tip the scales at over 100 pounds. He'd known another hunter who had been there the month before and taken one as big. He expected, no, demanded, he be put in a position to shoot one bigger. Now hundred-pound elephants are not completely impossible, but they are extremely rare. It's like demanding a deer scoring over 200 inches. It occasionally happens, but only to the most dedicated and luckiest. Anyone who knows anything about elephants realizes the implausibility of such a demand. It just doesn't happen that way. Even two first-time elephant hunters like us knew as much.

"Five days of hiking all over hell and the biggest thing we see is a measly eighty-pounder. Can you believe this crap?" He looked to us for support.

"Dick just shot a very nice 70-pound bull," Nassos said.

"Mmph."

Nassos started toward the kitchen hut with John the Doctor hissing at his heels like a snake.

"I thought you were supposed to have the best elephants in Ethiopia.

What a shoddy operation. I've seen better elephants in a zoo. I should've gone to Zimbabwe where they have real elephants."

Nassos slipped over to our hut during a break in this tirade. "I am sorry for this." His eyes, showing frustration, were apologetic.

"You have nothing to apologize for."

"We did very good today," he said smiling. "I must go to fetch the truck. I will be back for dinner. Congratulations on your elephant Dick."

John the Doctor screamed at Nassos as he drove away with one of the other PHs. Then, to our amazement, he took a few steps after the truck and threw not one, but two, beer bottles at them. He glanced our way, seemed ready to come over, but when we slipped into our hut he must've decided not to disturb us. Other than this unnecessary outburst, he seemed like a nice enough fellow. Hunting is not a guaranteed endeavor. When things do not go your way, venting your frustrations on those breaking their backs to help you succeed rarely makes things better.

In any case, what should've been a night full of jubilation and camaraderie was quiet evening with eye contact held to a minimum. I felt sorry for Dick, though it was apparent nothing could bring him down. The air was strangled by tension, and there was a feeling a tiny spark could set off a barrage of explosions, especially by John the Doctor, who still had steam coming out his ears. Nassos, his other PHs, Alex and Johannes, all the trackers and bearers were all terribly insulted. They had gone to the edge in an attempt to fulfill an impossible request.

Later that evening, Nassos excused himself to check on the cooks. John the Doctor was on his heels instantly. Though they were away from the group gathered around the fire, we couldn't help but hear their conversation.

"We'll be going out in the morning and I want you personally to take me. You know where the hundred pounders are. [Anonymous] got one and told me he saw one bigger. I insist you take me to it."

In as calm a voice as he could contain himself to, Nassos reminded John the Doctor he was told before booking the trip that an elephant of such proportions was highly unlikely, but they would do their best to find him a trophy bull.

"I cannot hunt with you tomorrow," Nassos said.

"And why not? Am I not as important as the Cabelas?"

"The Cabelas have contracted for me. I intend to honor the contract."

"This is preposterous. I paid good money for this hunt. I better get my bull. That is all I have to say." With that, John the Doctor returned to his quarters.

He did join us for dinner and was quite cordial. But his tantrum had already sullied the mood.

We would've understood had Nassos felt obligated to succumb to John the Doctor's insistences that he personally guide him after his quest for the Holy Grail, but were pleased to hear him say he would stay with us. There was nothing one angry little surgeon could say that would tarnish Nassos' impeccable reputation, achieved from years of quality hunting and outstanding service in the industry.

Like I said, nothing could bring Dick down from the clouds. He toasted his guide and his charging elephant with a couple beers of the local variety on that night. How else could he calm his nerves? I know I'll never be able to get back those beats my heart skipped.

I was exhausted, but knew a restless night with visions of giant beasts would force me to keep one eye open. Every snap of a twig, every peep, every creek, every howl provided a jolt of adrenaline. I'd seen firsthand – far too close – the kind of destruction an elephant was capable of without the least degree of strain. Our thatch-roofed hut offered little solace for my weary anxiety.

When I was a youngster, I used to love going to the zoo to see the elephants, so docile and seemingly apathetic, separated by a wall and large canal. I can't remember why they so fascinated my adolescent mind, but many years later, in the jungle without fences or concrete, in the hour of twilight, a feverish hope there were no elephants within 100 miles dominated my thoughts.

To my surprise, I slept like a hibernating bear. After midnight, the darkness fell silent. It allowed my nerves to calm just long enough to drift away. Early the following morning, we awoke to an entire camp busting their tails in preparation for John the Doctor's departure on an overnight backpack hunt in another cold attempt to claim his great prize. The endeavor had blinded him to the privilege and blessings he was surrounded with. Just look around.

We dressed, packed up our gear for our journey back to the main camp and went for breakfast. Two eggs over hard, wheat toast and juice. During a cup of tea by the fire, we wished John the Doctor good luck before he and his entourage disappeared into the forest. He turned and smiled at us before he gave himself to the shadows. That was the last we saw of John the Doctor. Nassos never brought his name up again. I sometimes wonder if he ever got his 100-pound elephant. I suppose we would have heard if he had.

We arrived at the main camp in time for a lunch of Ethiopian chicken. Talk about spicy. I ate a ton of sponge bread and mashed potatoes, but my mouth was still on fire for an hour. Perfect ingredients for another round of the Ethiopia Enema. Nassos was ill from a tick bite which had swelled his ankle to the size of his calf. He opted for a nap after lunch. He didn't say as much, but I think he was a little embarrassed, not to mention insulted, by his other client's outburst the night before. A few hours to spare, Dick cleaned our guns as we prepared ourselves for a pursuit of slightly smaller game – bushbuck.

All of Africa seemed on fire that evening. The hot, orange glow of burning grass, surrounding us on nearly every side, turned the evening into dark with its black cloud of smoke. Our eyes burned as our lungs quarreled with the corrupted air. Twilight never lasts long. Add a thick layer of brush smoke and the millions of stars were all that kept the sky from pitch blackness. The land, on the other hand, was aglow. Flames dancing silhouettes on the horizon gave the appearance of incandescent ocean waves splashing sparks into the air. Though at times frustrating, the burning radiation, both destructive and fascinatingly beneficial, was nonetheless a magnificent sight to behold in Ethiopia's otherwise charcoal night.

Dinner was late that evening. Everything was fried. Fried cauliflower, fried cheese, fried potato puffs and, for the main dish, fried meat, of what kind I do not pretend to know. It was certainly not beef, but was quite tasty. The night was capped off with tea by the fire and an agreement for an early morning hunt. The bush fires, so far in the distance now, appeared as large cities, their electric output keeping the sky alight.

Asarat, the camp attendant, woke us at 4:30 a.m. In a bumbling, hurried effort, we dressed and set off. Right away we spotted a genet. With one quick shot, Dick put it down. Though often referred to as genet cats, genets are not really cats. They are more closely related to mongoose and are part of the *Viverridae* family. Omnivorous creatures, genets feed on fruit, frogs, insects, small rodents, lizards and some birds, including domesticated chickens, a thieving practice which in some areas of rural Africa has caused them to be considered pests. Genets are usually solitary, nocturnal and mostly arboreal, making them one difficult animal to hunt. Add to that their uncanny ability to blend with their sur-roundings via a spotted coat, and merely catching a glimpse of one in the bush is a rare occurrence. Mongoose-like in shape with long, slender bodies, short legs and large ears compared to the sizes of their heads, genets are highly capable predators. Some subspecies were once even used domestically in homes to help keep local rodent populations in check before house cats became the rat-control specialist of choice. They are remarkable animals with dark spots on a brownish fur, long ringed tails and distinctive mask-like marking on their faces.

The early morning was full of sightings: waterbuck, duikers (all female), bushbucks (all female and one small male), an awesome bug-eyed bush baby, and a civet, which is closely related to the genet. We mostly only caught short glimpses of these creatures as they dashed for cover upon our approach. Except for the young male bushbuck, which stood there staring at us, seemingly fascinated by the bipedal animals making their way through the forest.

On our way back to camp to repack for tomorrow's early morning flight to the Omo, one of the trackers spotted a porcupine ambling into the bush. He disappeared, but Nassos and Dick went after him anyway. I heard him shoot. I could hardly believe it when they returned a few moments later empty handed.

Dick shrugged his shoulders. "I missed."

They both climbed into the truck and we were on our way to camp like we hadn't even stopped.

"Those fat little things can run like the wind when they're startled. There's no way I could've fired twice."

Never a day without excitement. Never a day without a lesson learned. Such is a typical day of hunting anywhere the world over, especially in Africa, where diversity is king.

In the Omo: Dick

The entire afternoon on Saturday, February 18, the day I shot my first genet, was spent packing and loafing around. I'd rather have been hunting, but we had to prepare for our trip to the Omo. I'd forgotten how much gear we had until we started gathering it up – and we'd left a few bags in Addis.

Late in the afternoon, we were hunting again. We encountered a lot of game, but not desiring to shoot any young animals, passed on everything we saw. Nassos thought it would be fun to show us what came out in the night, so we took in a bit of spotlighting. We weren't hunting, but saw more game than you could shake a stick at. Nighttime in the bush belongs to all sorts of creeping, crawling creatures. Even with our flashlights, we were the most out-of-place animals under the starry sky. Those beasts that only show themselves under the cover of darkness held our interest until nearly midnight. By then we were tired and rest dominated our thoughts.

I hadn't been asleep for more than a few minutes when I awoke to a familiar sound.

"Dick, wake up."

After a few tries, Mary's excited whisper finally accomplished its objective.

"Huh? What? I'm awake." I sat up, resting on my elbows.

"Do you hear that?"

"What?"

CRACK! CRASH!

"That."

It sounded like the forest was falling down on us. But, I must confess, had Mary not awakened me, I probably would've slept right through the ruckus. I am a notoriously deep sleeper. When I'm tired, earthquakes, tornadoes and nearby explosions are not even stir-worthy. A ten-foot section of our ceiling back home crashed down one evening, but was I awoken by the crashing clatter? Well, not until Mary chimed in with her agitated whispering.

CRACK! CRACK! CRASH!

There were no bulldozers around for hundreds of miles. It was the elephant's destructive affinity for some of the local trees telling us more than one was feeding disturbingly close to our tent.

"If there were any cause for concern, I'm sure Nassos or one of the others would inform us," I said in an effort to console my light-sleeping wife's nerves.

Of course, there was always the possibility Nassos was a heavy sleeper and hadn't been roused by the ensuing commotion. I was snoring soundly again within moments. Between the elephants and me, Mary didn't sleep much. She told me as much the following morning. It seems the elephants didn't stop feeding for over an hour. I sounded off all night long.

Nassos would only spend two days with us in the Omo. He had other clients coming in which he must accommodate. Alex, more than an adequate hunter and an all-around good guy, would become our full-time PH. Fun would continue unabated. It was sad to see Nassos go. We had grown close to the small, soft spoken man, proud to be able to now call him friend.

The short jaunt by plane to the Omo culminated in a stark change of scenery. The rolling forest gave way to a scorching plain where shorts, as opposed to safari slacks, would dominate the daily attire.

The two pilots joined us for a lunch of spaghetti and fresh fried potatoes at camp – a mere five minute drive from the makeshift dirt runway we arrived on. We bid them farewell after lunch. We were tired, but the sun was pelting the earth too intensely for us to sleep. Mary spent the time interrogating Nassos about the ostrich roaming the camp like one of the chickens.

"Her name is Madeline. We've had her since she was very small. Her inquisitive nature is a constant source of entertainment. This one over here is tougher to get a handle on." Nassos pointed to a civet loafing in the shadows beside the kitchen.

Mary thought it looked a lot like a raccoon with its mask, black and tan markings, short legs and rotund body. Just to be ornery, I told her that I thought it looked more like a civet than anything else.

While we were entertained by one of Africa's small predators, Nassos disappeared for a moment. During his brief absence, we heard a shotgun blast from within the trees nearby. When he finally appeared he held an old side-by-side and a dead pigeon.

"Civet cats will often de-feather their winged prey. Our civet here has not been taught to do this by its mother. It will be interesting to see how it reacts to a freshly killed bird."

We watched her carry the dead bird around in her mouth for more than a few minutes before deciding she didn't know what to do with it. After preparing for the evening's hunt, we came back to learn she had not only eaten the bird but de-feathered it as well. I guess she just didn't like having an audience.

The entire afternoon was spent in pursuit of a specific Beisa oryx. He was the best trophy in a group of eight. Oryx are some of the most strikingly beautiful antelope in all of Africa. Their long, rapier-like horns can be ultra-deadly. They've been known to attack hunters when threatened or wounded and there are instances in which they have used the weapons on their heads to inflict mortal wounds on attacking lions. The most seasoned PHs know to approach a downed oryx without caution is foolhardy. These grayish antelope of the desert have highly distinguishable mask-like markings on there face, making them easy to identify. Discerning males from females and trophies from sub-par animals can be much more difficult. Females carry the long straight horns same as the males. The females horns are often longer, though usually more slender. Judging a trophy oryx from the distances required to successfully hunt one of the wary animals is an art form in itself. Becoming proficient is only attainable through many hours in the field. We left the judging strictly to Nassos.

One of the inherent qualities which makes hunting oryx so challenging is they have unrivaled long-range vision and often live in wide-open areas. In most instances, they've spotted you long before you see them. Hunting a single oryx is tough, but a herd of eight will have you pegged before you even know they're in the area. It only takes one to become skittish in order for the entire group to charge off. This group had us from the beginning. We'd blown a few stalks before they were joined by two nervous tiang. We'd come too far to give up now.

Our patience and perseverance eventually won out. One final stalk just before dark provided me with a 300+ yard shot I miraculously pulled off.

The day had been long, difficult and fulfilling. I could think of nothing better than a hot meal, a shower and a tiny bed covered with mosquito netting. Our pesky, malaria-carrying friends went to great

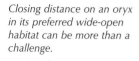

Closing distance on an oryx in its preferred wide-open habitat can be more than a challenge.

lengths to jab us with their stingers. The netting was only one line of defense. We also used smoke coils and drenched ourselves in bug repellant. The insects were relentless though, eventually managing to find a weakness in our defenses. They attacked at the most inopportune times. Like just before we were about to squeeze of a shot on a great animal or during soothing dreams of charging elephants and roaring lions. These tiny flying devils are no longer the mere pests we used to view them as. They are pure evil. That buzzing you can sometimes hear when they approach your ear are their taunts. These maggots of the air can drive a man insane. I am convinced the world would be better off without them. But, of course, these are the ravings of a madman driven to his unstable state by creatures escaped from the underworld, so take them however you please.

A little over dramatic you think? A few days spent with hordes of mosquitoes and tsetse flies may have you singing a different tune.

Before I drifted off to sleep that evening, I could hear them. They hovered just outside the netting, conspiring to systematically drive me over the edge. In defiance, I slumbered off into a refreshing, deep sleep. I awoke the next morning with nary a thought of stings or bug bites. A new day of hunting was upon us.

Camp was alive with activity. Staffers hauled water, the cooks filled the air with the aroma of breakfast, a few of the men – our trackers – lethargically smoked beside the truck and in the river, a large native party bathed, giving little thought to the many crocodiles poking their curious eyes above the surface. It was the unseen reptiles lurking beneath the ripples that would've concerned me.

If not for the truck, we could've been greeting the morning in a time warp, a place where the conveniences and burdens of the modern world did not exist. Surrounded by thatch-roofed huts and a rustic people unblinkingly content with what they have, we could not help but question many of the trivial matters we all too often concern ourselves with. Though some of the staff donned T-shirts and shorts, most of the people in the area sported traditional garb. For the men, that meant a little wrap around the waist and sometimes decorative paint – especially during a celebration. The women wore no clothing, instead covering themselves with ornamental beads, bracelets, and colorful breastplates which hung from their necks. I'm sure pants that covered our legs down to our ankles and long-sleeve shirts seemed a bit odd to them. What should they expect from a couple crazy Americans who traveled halfway across the world just to play in their backyard?

We rushed through a couple eggs, toast, tea and juice. The eggs, fresh from chickens in camp, tasted better than any store-bought eggs we'd ever had. It was Monday, February 20th. We were in pursuit of lesser kudu. The lesser kudu, more slender and sleek looking than its larger cousin the greater kudu, also lacks the latter's beard, instead sporting two distinct white patches on its throat. Hunting the lesser is just as challenging as the greater and in some aspects even more so. They are as wary as their larger brethren, but since they occur in a more limited area, are more difficult to come by. Like much of the hunting in Africa, one of the most widely used methods of hunting lesser kudu involves a classic spot and stalk.

You know your own favorite hunting spot like the back of your hand. Likewise, Nassos knew right where our best chance of finding lesser kudu was. There were a few subtle changes in the topography which made for perfect habitat. We constantly raised and lowered our binoculars. It could've been misconstrued as some sort of ritual to an unknowing bystander. Like a machine on an assembly line, Nassos lifted his optics to his eyes once again. This time he left them there.

"That is a nice Grant's gazelle. Would you like to try for him Mary?"

As often is the case on safari, you'll be looking for or even on the trail of a certain animal when an opportunity for another species presents itself. Great chances come along only so often. When one arises, you pass at your own thoughts of regret. We deemed him good enough to abandon the pursuit of a lesser kudu we had not yet seen.

A short stalk and one shot later, Mary had taken a beautiful, long-horned Grant's gazelle. I smiled at her smile, silently giving thanks for

Smiles and laughter are rarely missing from an African village.

the opportunity to intimately share one of my favorite activities with my favorite person. She'd done well. Her bright beaming face was more than proof she was enjoying herself as much as I was.

Everyone has one of those days when nothing seems to go right; when you make mistake after mistake, botching the opportunities you're given. Today was one of those days. Shortly after Mary displayed her exceptional shooting skills on her Grant's gazelle, one of the trackers spotted the glint of a black, spiral horn. I hadn't seen him yet, but I've learned to trust the people who've spent their lives tracking and hunting the animals of their homeland.

We made a quick plan before starting our stalk. We hadn't gone more than a few yards when I stumbled on a rock or a stick or a weed or maybe just plain air, but I stumbled nonetheless. I grabbed for a tree limb on my way down. *Snap. Crack. Crash.* I hit the ground with a thud, feeling my knee give a little. Not a lot, but enough for me to feel it. I had a bit of a limp the rest of the day. The initial look from those ahead of me began as a stern *shhh*, quickly turning to concern. I gathered myself as fast as possible, my cheeks burning red, and signaled I was fine. My knee had taken a hit, but it was my ego that was bruised. I tried not to let on, but I could see in all their faces they thought the commotion – my commotion – had blown our chance at a successful stalk. I felt like a bonehead, but desired no sympathy. If I screwed it up, I screwed it up. We'd move on. We'd never know for sure if we didn't continue. Besides, we had the wind in our favor.

A little further on, a branch snatched my hat right from my head. As I turned to retrieve it, a nearby bush snagged my arm with the staples it called thorns. I pulled back instinctively, but only managed to tangle myself further. I finally ripped myself free, grabbed my hat and tried to catch up with Nassos. It wasn't hard. He and one of the trackers were crouched over, tip-toeing carefully to a small tree; a brother to the one which tried to steal my cap. I suddenly wished I had an ax. Inching forward, I crouched beside them, steadying myself on the tree. Neither said anything. They just pointed.

We were at the edge of a small clearing. The surrounding vegetation was thick and green, dark and shadowy. Less than 100 yards beyond the clearing, stood a lesser kudu, sleek and mysterious. It was standing broadside, everything but his horns half hidden in the shade. When he moved, he floated like a ghost, his legs hidden, his form silently gliding in and out of the shadows. I had an easy shot when he paused to browse. Steady against the tree, I squeezed one off. The shot echoed. The kudu glanced toward us before slowly vanishing as if he was never there at all. I couldn't believe it.

"You missed," Nassos said.

I still couldn't believe it. An easy shot in easy range and I missed. No one to blame. I briefly wondered if the tree, out to get me and my hat, purposely moved just as I fired. I looked blankly at Nassos. I offered no excuse and he didn't need one. It happens to everybody at one time or another; you just hope it happens when you're hunting alone, without an audience to witness your fallibility. For piece of mind and just in case, we followed his trail a ways, checking for blood, but we all knew.

"We will get him next time Dick," Nassos said.

We headed back for the truck in silence. I tried not to lower my head, but...

They say when you get knocked down you should get right back up, jump back into the fire, if at first you don't succeed, try, try again and all that. Less than an hour after the kudu fiasco, we happened upon a gerenuk. Now gerenuks are a beautiful, yet somewhat strange, antelope. A female and a nice male were making their way along the edge of the thorn bush, offering me a brief opportunity. With the crosshairs steady on his shoulder, I fired. He was gone in an instant.

I missed again.

I'd like to say he'd been on the move, over 300 yards away and I was shooting off-hand when I squeezed, but I cannot. He was within 80 yards standing broadside, perfectly still and I had a rock-solid rest. Nassos just stared ahead in disbelief. Everyone has bad days, but this was getting out of hand. I was well beyond frustration. As much as I hate

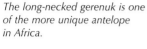

The long-necked gerenuk is one of the more unique antelope in Africa.

to admit it, I began looking for excuses.

I don't pretend to have never missed and yes, like anyone who has hunted for any extended period of time, I have unfortunately wounded an animal, but two complete misses in good field conditions with more than adequate rests needed further exploration.

Nassos must have been thinking along the same lines. "I think we should check you're rifle. Make sure it is still sighted in correctly," he said.

It was a good idea. If the scope had somehow been knocked out of whack, we could rectify the problem easily enough. If it proved to be dead-on, a few shots fired into the bull's-eye would boost my confidence. We were over an hour from camp with no targets in the technical sense, so we used a termite mound. Leaning across the hood of the truck, I rested my rifle on my hunting bag and fired a round from 100 paces. I missed the entire mound. I shot again, just to make sure. A tiny puff of dirt flew up from the very right side of the hill. I was way off. Now that we'd identified the problem, we could concentrate on correcting it.

As morning drifted into afternoon, we headed for camp where we could re-sight my rifle properly and grab a bite to eat. It took over an hour to zero my 7mm. I have no idea how it suffered such a drastic change, but I felt confident the bullet would fly where I directed it in the future. We have forever since made it a point to sight in our guns upon every new arrival to camp. We've had fewer and fewer problems with our rifles through the years as scopes have become more durable and cases sturdier. It is still highly advisable to check the zero of your scope after travel – before you head to the field. It would be a shame if you were to miss a lesser kudu or other trophy of a lifetime because you were not sighted in properly.

Nassos, ever optimistic, said we would try for the same kudu again tomorrow. "He is the biggest bull I have ever seen," he said.

Trophy animals of that caliber the world over do not grow to such proportions by making the same mistake twice. I was disappointed, a little hopeful for another chance, but in the end, grateful just to have seen such a magnificent animal in its natural habitat.

That afternoon we hunted hard for lesser kudu. We didn't even spot a cow. I was still feeling a bit sorry for myself from the morning mishaps and might not have been fully into the afternoon hunt. It was just as well we only came upon spoor and not the real deal. Nassos, I think, could sense the weariness in my step.

"Let's go get dinner." he said as we marched back to the truck.

From behind the back seat, Nassos pulled an old side-by-side shotgun from a case and handed it to me. It looked as if it would crumble in my hands. The stock was cracked, the barrel scratched and I'm not certain, but I could swear I heard a bit of inner clanking when I pulled it to my shoulder. I guess it hadn't found itself in such condition from under use. Nassos pulled out a box that looked older than the gun. A few paper-wrapped shells were all that were in the box. He handed one to me. Talk about pressure. I was supposed to procure dinner with an old shotgun I'd never fired and one delicate looking shell that might not even ignite.

The method of shooting guinea fowl was not exactly sporting by our western standards, but it was a highly successful way to obtain a meal for the entire group. With the old scatter gun, the lack of ammunition for said firearm and the condition of said shell, I would've been more comfortable using the gun as a club to chase chickens. However, we were after dinner for many mouths; a single chicken would not suffice. Soon I learned I was to fire this single shot into a flock of guinea. If I killed less than three, it would be unacceptable. It wouldn't necessarily mean we would starve, but it wouldn't make me much of a provider, would it?

In order to succeed in such a venture, many variables must be in place at once – not to mention the luck involved in not encountering a misfire. First, we had to find guineas and they had to be bunched up. A successful, one-shot, guinea fowl hunt normally takes place in the heat of the day when the birds all gather under a shade tree. A traditional big-game tactic is then employed – spot and stalk. I'd never hunted birds in such a manner and am certain there are some die-hard wing-shooters who would consider shooting any game bird in any other method than flushing with the help of a faithful four-legged companion quite unacceptable. I'm from Nebraska. I wouldn't think of hunting pheasants back home any other way, but I wasn't in Nebraska and we didn't have a good dog. We were blessed with only one old shell and a quest to obtain food, plain and simple. If we were so lucky as to have a little fun at the same time, all the better.

We found a bunch of birds right away, but blew the stalk when the wind changed directions. Nassos and his trackers had an uncanny ability to locate game. Nassos and I soon found ourselves making another sneak on a larger flock of nervous guineas huddled together under a small acacia. To advance upon upland game in the grass and weeds and thicket and corn back home is one thing – they often sit tight, waiting until you nearly step on them before they explode into the air and zip away in such haste as to make all but the most accomplished wing-shooters miss more often than not. But these guineas were often out in the open, where you could see them. And they could see you.

We used what cover we could – a small thorn bush, a few thin trees, the shadows and, of course, the wind. A downwind approach was essential. Like in all spot-and-stalk hunting for anything from squirrels to elephants, your greatest ally and your most feared enemy is wind direction. Nothing ends a stalk as quickly as shifting winds alerting your quarry of your presence long before you are in a position for a shot. Most stalks end in failure, but if you can use the wind, your chances of bagging your prey will multiply.

The light breeze was in our favor. If it didn't change within the final few yards, I'd find out soon enough if the shotgun and shell I carried would perform as flawlessly as Nassos seemed to believe. The two of us inched closer, crouched as low as possible and made good use of broken shadows cast by a tall thorn bush. Nassos looked back with the slightest smile, motioning me to a knee. He was my guide. But he'd become much more in the time we chased game through the forests and fields. He'd become my hunting pal. He was my friend.

We crawled a few more feet and, as was his way, Nassos effortlessly glided from view. It allowed me sole concentration on the winged game twenty yards before us. Without conscious thought, I shouldered the shotgun – an instinctive action I've carried out too many times to count, as far back as I can recall. After rabbits or upland birds or deer or bear, the same fluid motion of lifting the barrel and pressing the butt against your shoulder is the starting point for every shot. It must become second nature, for field situations most often do not allow for this action

Guinea fowl like to bunch together under a shade tree during the heat of the day.

to be deliberate. Pulling the trigger must always be deliberate. When only an instant is available, it is the only thing you have time to think about. Even then, the thought process had better be immediate.

I had ample time. The guineas, unaware of our presence, were in no hurry to scurry from the shadows. Knowing I only had one shot, I waited for a few of them to line up their heads to allow for the scattering pellets to achieve optimum results. I had my eye on four birds in particular which seemed more prone to gather together. When they positioned themselves in a tight group just in front of the main body of birds, I fired.

Frightened and confused, the birds created a dust-cloud the grandest of whirlwinds would be proud of. Before the dust could settle, three trackers rushed by me. I could barely make them out in the commotion and fog-like cloud of red dirt hanging in the air. At one point, I could just see the outline of one man, only a shadow. I watched him grab a struggling bird frantically flapping its wings, twisting its head until the convulsions became a mere shudder and then a limp still-life dangling from his hand. The scene was almost surreal. When all was said and done, the three men returned with a total of six dead guineas and three massive grins.

"The record is eleven, but I guess this will do," Nassos said with the ribbing you could only expect from a good friend.

The old gun and single paper shell performed superbly and we ate well. Guinea is darker than chicken with no hint of gamey taste. The meat fell away from the bone as we devoured the day's kill among good conversation and even better people. I reflected on how fortunate we were. Simple moments – often overlooked and forgotten – are much more gratifying than we give them credit for.

Alex's Turn: Mary

By Tuesday, February 21, we'd been hunting almost two weeks. Some of the wonder of a new adventure had worn off, as it always does, but monotony and boredom are not possible in the bush. You can be in Ethiopia, Botswana, Wyoming or Nebraska, hunting anything from doves to elephants, and day two will always be unique from day one. These things could only bore the deadest of souls. Now they may not be your cup of tea and you may not find them especially enjoyable, but boring they can never be. To be awed by a prairie sunset, feel small under a snow-capped mountain, stand in a cool-flowing stream, or know the gratifying pleasure of pushing yourself to the limit under a bright sky, hoping, knowing, just over the next ridge, you will find the old ram, buck, bull, or stag you've worked so hard for. These things make the hunt great, make it worth the pain. I wish everyone could feel, just once, what I feel at that moment when you know your quarry is close. That tense instant when your heart begins to beat a little faster, your breath starts to burn a little and the good, sharp taste of fear creeps up from your belly. When you know your next actions, along with many variables beyond your control, will determine the outcome of the stalk. There is so much beauty in the hunt, all you have to do is let yourself feel it.

Even on the thirteenth day, I couldn't wait to begin.

"I think we shall find your kudu today," Nassos said. His eyes smiled.

The way Nassos spoke of the kudu Dick had missed, told us it had been a superb trophy – world-record proportions. Our chances of even spotting the cagey old bull, which had been fired upon once, were much worse than slim. Mature bulls of trophy quality in any species tend to disappear for entire seasons once they figure out they're being pursued. Bullets whizzing by could leave no doubts for the one we were after. If Nassos shared our doubt, he didn't let on. He was in a cheerful mood at the beginning of his last morning with us. He'd be flying to Addis in the afternoon to meet his new clients, leaving us in the capable hands of his trusted PH, Alex, who was quite friendly, but particularly quiet. Nassos assured us he would open up when his boss left the scene.

We drove around, glassing for more than two hours before Nassos perked us from our lethargic state.

"There's a kudu," he said. He was peering through his binoculars at a distant mountainside. "It's a cow."

We watched her for 30 minutes. If a bull was with her, he was clever enough to stay hidden in the thicket. To get to where she was would take the better part of the day and the plane was to pick up Nassos at 10:30 a.m. Had a big bull been present, we would've given chase and let the pilot wait.

What started out as a pleasantly cool morning had become an oven. The lack of game added to our weariness. I dozed off once or twice.

Soon we were forced to return and await the plane's arrival.

"I wish to thank you for the hunt we enjoyed together. I had great fun."

I thought we were supposed to be the ones thanking Nassos. His hospitality and undeniable effort were of such high quality, we have rarely experienced their equal.

"No, thank you. You have given us so much. We will miss you."

"Would you like tea?" He disappeared for a moment, returning with a pitcher of tea and some glasses.

We thanked him, sipping tea in awkward silence before Nassos continued with his goodbye.

"You know, I was only scheduled to be with you through the elephant hunt, but I was having so much fun I decided to stay until I absolutely must go for new clients. It is rare to encounter such down-to-earth people who make my job such a joy."

It was a compliment we did not deserve.

"To tell the truth, when you stepped off the plane I thought I was in for a real challenge," he said to me. "It did not take long to discover you were tougher than many of the men I've taken hunting and you are willing to listen to what I have to say about my own country. It has been a pleasure."

"You're not quite what I expected either," I said. "I like you much better than the man I envisioned before we met. We will miss you."

He'd truly become a super friend, part of the family.

"We will meet again," he said. "I would like to come back and hunt with you before you return to the States, or if you finish here, you can meet me at another camp."

So, in this case, goodbye hopefully meant see you later.

The plane was scheduled to arrive at 10:30. At noon it still hadn't appeared. It was a good thing we came in to meet it.

"I hope it does not come." At times it was difficult to ascertain when Nassos was joking, but his nervous eyes were genuine enough. "I do not like to fly," he said, looking to the sky for an airplane that wasn't there.

I couldn't fault him for not wanting to fly over mountains in a small, single-engine flying machine, yet I couldn't help but see a hint of humor in the situation. Here was this renowned elephant hunter who'd shown no fear with a big bull crashing down on him. The mere thought of stepping into a plane had him as nervous as warthog approaching a waterhole guarded by lions. I don't pretend to know, but I think his trepidation stemmed from a loss of control. At least with a charging elephant, he could count on his own marksmanship and nerves if needed. Unless you are a pilot, you have to give your full trust to the person at the controls. If his reflexes were not good or worse, he was incompetent, a prayer or two for divine intervention couldn't hurt.

The gerenuk for lunch was superb, but after only a few short minutes in the dining tent, we decided it was far too hot and scampered out into the fresh air. The heat was inescapable. All we could do was hope for a breeze that would never come and try to keep our whining to a minimum. We finished lunch to the buzz of an incoming plane. Nassos' ride had finally arrived – a mere four hours late.

Flight delays at home have nothing on the Third World. In sparsely inhabited regions, if your flight arrived or departed on the same day scheduled, you could consider yourself lucky. Despite these minor annoyances, the sometimes unbearable weather and any other number of hardships, sportsmen and women always return. I guess we can't help it. I don't know that we would even if we could.

Nassos gave us a nervous smile and a slight wave. He boarded the airplane and was gone. We didn't know for sure if we'd see him again, but we knew we'd always miss him and hoped our paths would one day cross again.

Later that afternoon, with Alex, I took a nice 35-inch oryx and a jackal, while Dick shot a super Grant's gazelle and a second genet, which looked different than the one we shot earlier. It was a good afternoon, but we were all a bit down following Nassos' departure. When we arrived at camp that evening I told Dick I hoped Alex didn't feel we were unhappy to be hunting with him, because he was an excellent hunter and a delightful man.

"What do you mean? We had a great time this afternoon," Dick said.

"Well, it's just that I think we both seemed a little sad. That's all."

"I wouldn't worry about it. I'm sure he didn't think anything. Tomorrow will be better; you'll see."

Of course, he was right. The new day found us much more comfortable together. The sadness of seeing Nassos off had abated somewhat. It was another early morning; we were away by 4:45 without breakfast. We'd return for a bite to eat, but there were Nile buffalo to hunt. There are few endeavors which find me in an excited mode before 5:00 a.m., but when you have so much to look forward to, dark, chilly mornings are welcome. We were able to see the sun rise and set everyday. Plus, the chances of encountering wildlife are greater when animals are on the move and most sane folks are still dreaming.

We found no fresh buffalo sign that morning, nor did we encounter any of those creatures that were supposed to be on the move at such times, other than a few birds and two female lesser kudu. By 8:30 a.m., our stomachs were growling and we returned to a feast back at camp. I cannot recall ever eating such a breakfast in all my life. It was good, just too much. I am partly to blame for my overindulgence, but I didn't want to be rude and refuse such a delectable meal after so much work had obviously been put into it. An eight-ounce Grant's gazelle steak, two eggs, toast, fruit, tea and juice put me straight back to bed. We weren't going back out for a while anyway. It was okay; I was stuffed to the point of misery.

I awoke a few hours later, took a shower and dressed. When I went to the kitchen tent for a Coke, Alex was loading a cooler.

"We hunting at 4:30 if is okay." Alex said in his broken English.

"That's fine with us," I said. It left us just under two hours to relax and get ready. "It seems a little cooler this afternoon."

"Yes, maybe rain tonight."

A rain would be a welcome reprieve in the undying heat.

"I get you cream for bites. Very painful." He pointed to my ankles, swollen red from tick bites and my lack of will power to refrain from scratching.

They appeared on both Dick and I two mornings before. I was convinced that if the malaria or elephants didn't kill me, the itch-induced insanity certainly would. They didn't bother me too much when we were moving around, hunting. But if we were idle, the ruthless itch of tiny vermin we couldn't even see nearly drove me over the edge. Somewhere, somebody has probably come up with a theory as to how these miniature blood-suckers are ecologically important. Whatever it is, it's not worth it. I am wholly convinced the world would be a better place without ticks of any kind. Trying not to be too harsh, they seem to me to be little devils reaping delight from my pain. I know this because they always attack me with much more furor than anyone else. Dick had a few bites on his ankles, but everyone else seemed to be bite free. The cream Alex provided helped, but only if I didn't think about it.

"You want put on long pants today, Mary," Alex said. "We will walk very much. Many thorns. Will stick you."

I was glad for the warning. We went to an area we hadn't yet hunted, looking for kudu for over two hours. The thicket was dense. I cannot recall how many times the bushes and undergrowth would reach out to grab my pant legs. Even with the protection of khakis, we still suffered a number of scratches on our legs. They went quite well with the tick bites.

When Alex finally decided we'd walked far enough, we turned back for the truck. Because we were two hours from the vehicle and entering prime hunting time, we took a slightly different course back, hunting all the way. It was a slow, hard afternoon. We pushed ourselves. It's at these weary times that diligence comes in most handy. Our eyes began drifting to the ground and it took much of our concentration just to take the next step. When your efforts are diminished, you will invariably miss something. That something could be spectacular.

It was a good thing Alex was with us.

When our single-file march stopped, I almost ran into my husband.

"Dick," Alex whispered. "Come shoot. Very good gerenuk." He waved his hand, almost frantically, motioning Dick forward.

From my position, I couldn't see anything, but I was no longer tired. I leaned to the right and stretched my neck, catching a glimpse of tawny fur on the far edge of a clearing. Dick went to one knee, positioning himself for the shot, clearing my view. A beautiful, slender, long-necked, long-horned gerenuk was 100 yards away, walking right to left, straight for a thick line of brush. We waited for the ram to pause; Dick held on him. He lightly touched the trigger with his finger. Then, for reasons unbeknownst to us, the ram started to trot. In a few more yards he would disappear into the brush and we'd most likely never see him again.

"You shoot now," Alex said. "Very good gerenuk."

The gerenuk drifted dangerously close to the brush. In my peripheral vision, I could see Dick's barrel move in unison with the ram. Why didn't he fire? If he didn't shoot soon, he wouldn't get a shot. The instant before the gerenuk disappeared, he squeezed one off. The surprise of the shot caused me to jerk. The gerenuk reared up, nearly did a back flip, landed on its side, shuddered for a brief instant and then lay motionless.

"Good shot!" Alex said as the trackers clapped and cheered.

Dick smiled graciously, but his eyes had the look of surprise. "Just dumb luck, I guess."

I think it was more than that. We spend a lot of time at the shooting range before a hunt. Dick practices these kinds of shots when possible. I would never take that shot, but Dick's always been more of a risk taker than I. At least that's what I tell myself.

Two trackers ran ahead of us and were the first to reach Dick's trophy. They didn't bend down to inspect the ram or start preparing it for pictures as was their habit. They stood there wide-eyed and open-mouthed. One of them put his hand on his head. The other started searching the nearby grass as if he'd lost something.

We approached to discover Dick had shot one of the horns completely off at the base. The bullet had penetrated the brain, but on its way removed the gerenuk's left horn.

"I guess I led him a bit too much."

"We must find horn," Alex said. "It is big horn. Monster."

A search party formed. Within moments a tracker found the prize.

"You know, it takes a lot of skill to shoot a gerenuk in its tiny brain from 150 yards, while it's running, I must admit," Dick said. "Even the gerenuk thought it was amazing. Did you see? He was doing back flips."

Alex translated for the trackers and porters and all had a good laugh, but Dick really did feel terrible about shooting the horn off. He confided to me later that if he had more time to think about it, he probably would've passed on the running shot. Practice at the range is a far cry from the real thing. He didn't have the confidence to take such risks on a regular basis. Sometimes, however, the heat of the moment gets to us and we overstep our honed skills. We usually aren't as lucky as we'd like to be.

I was becoming concerned about the lesser kudu. We hadn't seen a bull in a few days and the females we'd seen were usually far off, disappearing long before we were in range. A lesser kudu really would be a great trophy, but hunting wouldn't be any fun if you knew you'd be successful before going out. The day ended without sighting another kudu.

The rain never came nor did the heat subside with the onset of darkness. Our critical mosquito nets served two purposes, protecting us from itchy bites and adding to the sticky night. Sleep didn't come easy for a couple of westerners who were accustomed to air conditioning.

Morning arrived a few hours too soon. After I said my prayers and Dick did a few morning exercises, we were raring to go.

Alex met us at breakfast. "We shoot kudu today, yes?"

"Yes," Dick answered. "If we can find them."

We were gone from camp for just over an hour when Alex pulled the truck over and led us into the bush.

"Good dik-dik here," he said as he looked back smiling. "Run that way." He pointed into a dense group of bushes and started walking toward them.

Dik-dik are one of Africa's many small antelope, often taken when the opportunity arises while hunting for other species. Veteran hunters who have made numerous trips to Africa will sometimes return specifically to hunt the small antelope. Some consider these diminutive and wily creatures among their most prized trophies. To take an opportunity when it comes is one thing. To specifically try for these species is quite another. Hunting the dwarf antelope of Africa is more than challenging. Their size and considerable quickness makes for difficult spotting and shooting. If you find one standing still, a quick shot is in order. Dwarf antelope wait for no hunter.

We followed Alex into the brush, thorns be damned. We moved slowly, cautiously. As we approached the edge of a thick bush, Alex motioned us down, peering over the thicket for a brief moment before quickly joining us on one knee. He pointed to Dick, to himself and then to the thicket and began to crawl. Soon they were into the shadows. When a thorny branch snagged Dick's sleeve, he methodically reached back with his left hand and pulled himself free. I could make them out for a long time, but not very well – an arm here, a head there. When they finally stopped they were almost invisible. If I hadn't known they were there, I wouldn't have believed it. I guess to kill a dik-dik, Dick had to become a dik-dik.

I didn't have to wait long to hear the report of the rifle and afterward, a bit of muffled, but unmistakably excited mumbling from within the thicket. A few moments later, Dick and Alex crawled back from the bushes.

"Did you get him?"

"Yeah, we got him, but the brush gets to thick so we have to go around. Alex says he's really good."

"How did you shoot through it if it's so thick?"

I just found a tiny hole and hoped the bullet wouldn't hit any branches. We were pretty close. Neither of us saw him at first, but when Alex spotted a female less than 30 yards away, he knew the male had to be close by. He was closer than the female, just off to the right a ways and hidden in some grass. We would've had a little better shot if he would've moved two or three feet to the left, but the female started acting nervous, sniffing the air so it was one of those now or never opportunities. We chose now."

"We go find now," Alex said as we hurried off. What took us 15 minutes would've taken less than five had we been able to push right through, but the location of the animal had us zigzagging and chopping our way through thicket.

We ducked under a low branch, slipped around another bush, stepped over a fallen tree before finding the slender, gray form of the cordeaux dik-dik. From the looks of it, he'd dropped in his tracks. His face was the color of rust and his horns shot right past the dark tuft of hair on his head.

"He's so little," I said.

"No, Mary. Very big." Alex's eyes were wide. He was genuinely surprised. "Never see bigger. This is great trophy."

We didn't know much about cordeaux dik-dik, but Alex sure thought we had something special. We believed him. We didn't realize until later, how right he was. Each horn measured 3 inches and had 2-inch circumferences, placing it in the top ten cordeaux dik-diks of all time in the Safari Club International record book. I remember thinking how little its horns were when, in fact, they were huge. I guess what they say is true. Good things do sometimes come in small packages.

Alex, the quiet PH, was still quiet. His limited English and our non-existent Greek at times made communication confusing if not difficult, but we were opening up to each other. With a little more time we'd be telling jokes around the campfire. After all, laughter translates into any language.

After many moments of admiration, congratulations and picture taking, Alex grabbed the dik-dik without field-dressing it and led us from the tangle. The truck was there to greet us when we pushed through. The two trackers cut our walking distance to nothing and oddly had picked up another passenger out in the middle of nowhere. He was a short, thin man, his hair was graying just a little on the sides, but the wrinkled skin all over his body revealed his age. He wore a single loincloth. It didn't cover anything. The single spear he carried was accompanied by a huge smile. His stench, though, was something awful.

One tracker sat in the shade upwind of the vehicle; the other snoozed in the driver's seat. The old man had a piece of golden grass and was tickling the driver's ear. He placed his finger on his lips when we arrived, his eyes were wide as he giggled silently. Alex shook his head and carried the dik-dik to the back of the truck. He took a sudden step back as he passed the old man downwind and then hurried on by, an incredulous look on his face. We let the old man have his fun. When the driver soon woke up scratching his ear, he wasn't amused. His thanks for offering the old man a ride was torment.

If the old man wanted a ride, he would have to sit in back. Alex called the other tracker over from his shady resting place. The tracker shook his head no. Alex told him to come or risk being left. The tracker shook his head again and blurted something out. Alex laughed, the driver, who was now in the back with the old man (upwind), laughed and the old man's smile disappeared.

Alex translated, "Hussein say he not ride with old man cause old man smell like rotting buffalo carcass."

"Oh my!"

Dick laughed. "He's smarter than we are."

"Yes, he might be," Alex said before yelling back to the tracker who promptly replied in his native tongue.

Everyone was laughing again, save the old man.

"I tell Hussein to stay up wind of him and he say you can never get far enough upwind of a warthog's butt." Alex shrugged his shoulders. "Smell get better when we're moving." With that he started driving away.

As if he suddenly realized how far camp was, the tracker started yelling "Stop, stop!" as he ran to catch us. When he tried to climb into the back of the Land Cruiser, the old man started poking him with the butt end of his spear, impeding his ascent. Not paying attention to the goings on in the back of the vehicle and thinking Hussein had plenty of time to jump in, Alex started to pull away again.

"Stop, stop!"

The old man's smile returned.

When everyone was finally in the truck, the old man had most of the back to himself. The two trackers scrunched as close to the forward part of the bed as humanly possible. The dead dik-dik, which Hussein said smelled much better than the old man, was the only creature near him.

The day was mostly done so we hunted our way back to camp, which the old man said was on the way to his destination. Alex said the old man probably didn't care where he was going; he just liked to ride in the car. It was almost dark when the old man told us to pull up by the river. As if on cue, a couple of natives appeared on the other side and rowed their dugout over to meet us. They were dressed in much the same garb as the old man, which wasn't much at all.

Once across the river, the two men came up the bank to greet the old man like they were long-time friends. They were seemingly oblivious to his pungent stench. We went with Alex to say hello, finding they smelled only a little better than the old man. Hussein refused to leave the truck. They'd been fishing and had caught themselves a nice selection of fresh fish with what appeared to be a seining net. The entire bow of the boat was a pile of fish.

"Would you like fresh fish tonight?" Alex offered.

"Sure," we said, nodding.

Then the bartering ensued. Alex and the two fishermen seemed to argue heatedly. The old man smiled, shaking his head up and down while looking back and forth between the two parties. After a few minutes with seemingly little headway, the old man offered some sort of suggestion and pointed at Dick.

"May I see eyepieces please, Dick?" Alex said, indicating the binoculars around his neck.

Dick shrugged his shoulders and handed them over.

The fishermen's faces beamed as they greedily handled Dick's very expensive pair of Zeiss binos. They spent ten minutes lifting them to their eyes, pointing across the river, smiling and laughing. We didn't think Alex would trade a high-quality pair of optics for a few fish, but the fishermen didn't appear too eager to hand them back. Nobody went for fish either.

With the fishermen enraptured by our optics, Alex slipped up to the vehicle, returning a moment later with our Polaroid camera. When they saw this, the fishermen passed back the binoculars. They posed for photographs, first together and then separately. We took one for the old man as well, but Hussein said it would probably melt from the smell. For the price of four photographs we received ten fish – not a bad deal, I should think. I don't recall what the fish was, but I do remember it was light and tasty.

The old man was the main topic of limited discussion around the campfire that night. The shadowy glow of a hunting campfire is a place where much can be said and even more learned with few words. We laughed into the night. When we ambled off to bed, we felt we'd crossed the line from clients to friends.

Swiss Army Knife: Dick

Searching for that ever-elusive lesser kudu again, we encountered another gerenuk Alex said would rival the one I de-horned. It was another long shot, but I thought I was on him good. I fired. The gerenuk ran.

"Good shot."

It didn't feel good. I knew before we went to the brush line where he disappeared, it was going to be a long morning. Within moments, we realized we needed to circle back to where he was when I fired. We found two tiny drops of blood.

"You hit good?"

"I don't think so."

"Okay, boys will find."

A blood trail was nonexistent, the tracks unreadable, but Hussein and the other trackers had uncanny natural abilities. It was meticulous, but somehow through the layers of intermingling tracks, we followed the right ones. I'd like to say I know this because we walked up on a gerenuk lying still in the grass, but I can't. I know we were behind the right tracks because a few yards into the brush was a speck of blood drying on a single thorn.

We followed the trail for nearly two hours, only finding one other minuscule drop of blood. It was enough to keep us searching until the trail faded into the rocks.

"Flesh wound," Alex said.

Maybe.

Superficial or not, it was still difficult to bear. The day was ruined. I replayed everything in my head, trying to discern what went wrong. In the end, I had nothing and no one to blame but myself.

It happens to everybody. Wild animals are resilient. It was just a scratch. He never broke stride for miles. If it was worse, predators will take him down by nightfall.

I tried to rationalize, but it didn't help. I felt sick and I brought everyone else down with me.

Like any good guide, Alex tried to get our minds off my mistake. He grabbed the old clanky shotgun, thrusting it into my hand with a single shell.

"Come, we get birds for boys."

To tell the truth, I don't remember thinking about the gerenuk once while we stalked guineas. A leisurely walk. A quiet stalk. And this time, a wild flush – well, that might be stretching it a bit. The birds busted us, started to scamper and I blasted into them. With that rusted old shotgun and a shell that had no business igniting, I somehow dropped six again. Nothing like a six-for-one to boost your confidence. But sit around long enough and you begin to think.

The clutch went out on the land rover at 10 a.m., forcing us to return to camp. Alex would spend the greater part of the afternoon working on it. I tried to keep my mind off the gerenuk by reading, taking a nap, doing a few exercises, and showering, but they were merely short-term solutions. I kept coming back to the misplaced shot.

It was nearly 5:00 p.m. when the clutch was repaired and we were headed back out. Mary and the others spotted a kudu right away. Since I never saw it, I think we should only call it a half. That brought the count up to one and a half bulls spotted with time running out. Time was right on hope's heels.

Evening in the bush is not quiet time, but in the dark with the sounds of the night, you're left with your own thoughts, good or bad. The shrieks, roars, screams, rustles, clicks, growls, and barks when it's too dark to see beyond the dancing shadows of a campfire can be more than a little frightening, though mostly harmless. As part of the human race, we depend on our sense of sight. When that is taken away by the earth's rotation, our mind sometimes attaches claws and fangs to the night's voices. Once you realize your fear is mostly unwarranted, you begin to welcome the voices, eventually finding them soothing. It is then, when your mind is no longer engrossed with what's out there and what it's doing, does it begin to drift to other contemplations.

What am I doing here? What's my purpose? Have I truly lived? Where am I headed? Will I know it when I get there? I eventually realized, in time, these questions answer themselves. Whether we understand it or not is an entirely different question. Those not-so-quiet evenings keep it all in perspective – or push me precariously close to the edge of sanity. It can, at times, be a gray line as difficult to navigate as night's pitch-black shadows.

The following morning, Mary shot a tiang, a slender, reddish antelope related to the topi and the tsessebe. The tiang has well developed shoulders which allow it to run quite swiftly, making it one of the more speedy antelope in Africa. One interesting fact about the tiang is it is one of the only antelope known to form breeding leks in which a female in estrus will visit small territories a dominant male has claimed to breed.

We drove around for about an hour before we spotted the tiang. Glassing it from many yards away, we decided it was a good bull. After a relatively short, easy stalk, Mary shot it from a bit more than 200 yards. On the brief walk back to the truck, I realized the old days of the foot safari were mostly over. While certain species sometimes require days and days of foot travel, most hunts for plains game have evolved into a spot and stalk from a vehicle. This, I think, is a good thing. It has made Africa more accessible to all and allowed for a shorter safari, which is both good and bad. Now, to say it has made the safari more accessible and more brief is not to say it has made it easier. Professional hunters are now able to get their clients to good areas more quickly, but this is nothing new. Vehicles were in use on safari long before Hemingway's time. The average traveler does not have two to six months to spare like Roosevelt did. The hunting safari is not like a photo safari where one rarely leaves the vehicle and the animals act more domestic than wild, having come to tolerate the close presence of people, a behavior which had to be learned as most animals have evolved with man as a natural predator.

With a better understanding of conservation, a more competitive field of highly skilled professional hunters, a creeping western culture, and advances in medicine, the safari has become less dangerous. Although some of the same hazards exist as they did 70 years ago, the outfitters have gone to great lengths to ensure both a high level of safety and comfort. The safari industry was still going through major changes in the late 1980s and probably always will be, but there are some things that will never change: the trepidation of a close encounter with an irritated elephant; the chills a lion's roar in the night sends up your spine; the defiant stare of the buffalo before he decides whether to charge or flee; the ghost-like appearance and disappearance of the leopard slipping in and out of the shadows; the congregation of life around a water hole; and the wonder it all inspires. There is a hope at the beginning of each safari, an anticipation unrivaled in any other endeavor, and unlike most, the end of the safari proves to satisfy that hope and anticipation, leaving you with a yearning desire to return – to hope again.

I wanted a kudu, but their survival skills proved better than our hunting skills. We hiked to the point of exhaustion for many days in pursuit of kudu. Our reward was aching muscles and sweat-drenched clothes. Another morning, another kudu slipped beyond our grasp.

"It seems like all we do is eat since we left the elephant camp," Mary said.

We sat before the table with a bowl of spaghetti and meatballs, salad, guinea fowl, cabbage, onions, carrots and bananas. I wondered if we really looked like we needed so much food.

"It's not as if they were starving us in elephant camp either," I said.

"Well, I'd hate to offend the cook. Besides it looks so good. We might as well dig in."

We went on safari expecting to lose weight. Invariably, and not so mysteriously, we returned a few pounds heavier or at least without having lost any weight at all. The endless hiking obviously is not a match for the endless eating.

"Tonight, we find buffalo." Alex said before he left to prepare the truck for our afternoon hunt.

The Nile buffalo, the northern species of the African buffalo, is a little lighter in color and slightly smaller than the Cape buffalo with shorter horns, but a buffalo nonetheless. As such, they should be given the greatest respect. There is very little that compares to buffalo hunting. The danger, the stalk, the emotional and physical strain; these things make any buffalo a formidable challenge. A quarry worthy of its reputation.

We glassed a few herds, but didn't encounter a big, old bull until late in the afternoon. The waning daylight wasn't in our favor. We went after him anyway. True to old dugga-boy form, he stuck his nose up at us upon our approach, staring with that look of insolence. That look that says "just try it, bub." It's a stare that can pierce your conviction and make you question your own sanity. When enough time had passed for us to get his message, he turned to march off.

"I can't get steady and he's moving. I'm not comfortable with this shot," Mary said. "You take him Dick."

I looked to Alex. "Yes, good bull," he said.

We were close, but he wasn't planning to hang around long. He didn't move fast, but it was too much for Mary to feel confident in shooting. I decided it was a shot I could make. He was close enough and wasn't in a hurry, but it would still have to be a quick shot. I took the shooting sticks and found my mark just in time to see him slip behind a small bush and stop. We waited. He didn't move. The light was fading.

I cranked the power up on my scope, giving myself a clear view of the right side of his head. He stood perfectly still. We could pass, we could try to make him move or I could take the shot I had. I held steady, convincing myself I was comfortable making the shot. We were less than 100 yards and he was still as a stone. The best point of entry appeared to be behind the ear. Alex agreed.

I squeezed.

The bull went ballistic. He should have dropped dead. Instead he began thrashing his head around, slamming into the nearest tree. He took it out like it was a twig.

"Shoot!" Alex was well past whispering.

I emptied my rifle into the old bull, diverting his attention straight at us. He'd been pushed too far.

I reloaded. Alex grabbed Mary's gun. He emptied it into the advancing buffalo. By the time I re-shouldered my rifle, the buffalo was staggering. He turned no more than fifty yards away. My next bullet finally put him on the ground, but a finishing round was necessary.

The bullet I put behind his ear had struck within two inches of where I aimed. Of course, two inches high meant I missed the brain and sent an expanding piece of lead into the base of his horn. It had given him a headache, but wasn't fatal. Luckily, his irritated tantrum allowed us to whack him a few more times. The old bull's power and toughness were something to behold. More than a couple of our shots were lethal. I doubt he would have lasted long, but he took what we threw at him and kept coming for more.

The potential danger, the intensity and the overall cacophony of emotions buffalo hunting brings forth make it one of the greatest hunts there is. Any of the African buffalo are worthy of this distinction. Pursuing them will give the hunter an entirely new sense of himself or herself. They will never be the same again. Of Africa's dangerous game, the buffalo is the most widespread, its populations allowing for better accessibility. If a buffalo is available on safari, the hunter should not pass on this grand adventure. It's the hunter, his skills and conviction against one of the most tenacious, exciting beasts on earth. It's a thrill I will never forget, one I will never grow tired of.

We stared down at him; the trembling beginning to abate. Then two skinners showed up. They stood above the bull for a moment before one of them mumbled something. A heated debate ensued between the two. Alex soon joined in the exchange. We couldn't understand, but could tell he wasn't happy. One of the skinners appeared to take the brunt from Alex and the other skinner.

Disgustedly, Alex turned to us. "They forget blades."

I wasn't sure what he meant at first, but when he sliced the air with

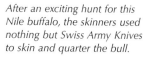
After an exciting hunt for this Nile buffalo, the skinners used nothing but Swiss Army Knives to skin and quarter the bull.

a fake knife, my eyes grew wide. Over an hour from camp at a few minutes to dark without a knife to skin and quarter a buffalo. We were in a pickle. With a little more manpower than we had, we might be able to fit the entire bull into the back of the Land Rover, but that would even be a stretch.

Without another option, I reached into my pocket. "I've got this."

Alex peered down at the small object in my hand. Then he shrugged his shoulders and pulled a similar Swiss Army Knife from his front pocket. "No choice," he said.

We handed our tiny tools to the skinners. Their eyes nearly popped from their heads. They looked at the little red pocket knives, looked back up at us, then shrugged their shoulders in much the same way Alex had. Without a word they began work on the buffalo while Alex ran back for the truck. It was going to be a long night. We'd need the illumination from the truck's headlights.

By the time Alex returned with the truck, the boys had gained much more ground than I expected. I tried to help by pulling on a leg while they worked under it and Mary shined a flashlight on the carcass. The longer they worked, the slower it went. Both blades were dulling. We wouldn't get back to camp anytime soon.

There were no complaints. As in most African life, you take what you have and work with it. So it was a little more work and would take a little longer. It was just another obstacle to overcome. Alex and the people who lived here dealt with much greater challenges everyday. We've struggled in our lives – by the American sense of the word. But few Americans truly know what it means to struggle. Everyday life in Africa was a struggle. And these remarkable people faced each new day head-on with a smile. It almost made you feel guilty. Their challenge was survival, but they never let it get them down. It was a refreshing way to look at life.

It was nearing 2 a.m. when we rolled into camp. A skinning job which would usually take less than an hour with two skilled blades took all night. On the drive back, all but Alex dozed off intermittently between the bumps of a road made from tire tracks only. We did finish the job though, with better than adequate results. Alex and I came to the conclusion that if a Swiss Army Knife was enough to skin a buffalo, it must be good for anything. I knew I'd never be caught without one again.

Four-Day Trigger Itch: Mary

"You need to eat something," I said to Dick before we sat down to breakfast.

He'd spent much of the night dry-heaving. Our late arrival back at camp found us too tired to eat much. Dick's stomach began acting up shortly after heading for bed. I guess if I were to put a positive spin on the whole episode, I didn't hear him snoring.

"I'll just have a couple pieces of toast and maybe some orange juice."

It was better than nothing.

When Alex came to tell us it was time to go, we knew what his plans for the day were. Kudu.

I knew it wasn't supposed to be easy, but I started to wonder if the time we spent kudu hunting could be better spent after something else. I'd pretty much conceded we weren't going to get a kudu. I started to look past it. In the back of my mind, I still wanted to find one, I was just frustrated. The lesser kudu helped me better understand the satisfaction of knowing you've hunted hard, whether you bag your quarry or not.

"Who's that?" I asked as we pulled away from camp.

"Camera safari. Should not be here. Are too close."

They'd set up camp right next to us. Hundreds and hundreds of miles of prime habitat and they choose to come to our spot. We later found out there were two Germans, two Italians and two non-native, but local, guides. They all frowned upon hunting. They chose this spot, not because it was the best spot, but because we were there. Oh well.

I smiled and waved as we went by. All I saw in return were glares. Dick said I was paranoid, but the lady's eyes were fireballs. It didn't matter. We wouldn't bother them and would try to keep out of their way so they could enjoy their vacation. We had every intention to continue enjoying ours.

"Are we going to the Denakil tomorrow?"

"No, sorry. I radio Nassos. We wait for Friday. We all go!"

He was pleased to be accompanying us to the next camp. We were pleased to have him. Overcoming language barriers hadn't been simple, but with a few key words and a few more key gestures, we found we could get by fine. Each day was easier.

Part of me was ready to move on, but the extra time would give us better opportunity to find a kudu or two. The kudu hunting was discouraging, but I never grew tired of the beauty surrounding us at all times. Everything was so green and alive. The forest was thick, the undergrowth oftentimes impenetrable and the flat clearings sometimes went on without end. And the sunsets. Oh, the sunsets could make you cry. When the sky went from blue to a mixture of lavender, orange, pink and gray with no clear lines silhouetting a horizon of umbrella-shaped trees, it was as if a drop of the divine fell from heaven and painted the world. Yes, part of me was ready to move on, but another part – a more primal part – could spend the rest of my life in such paradise.

"Over the hill is water hole. We hunt there."

We climbed the small hill and peered over the top. We didn't see anything right away, but decided it was a likely area. A bit of intense glassing might be beneficial.

"There," I said, pointing at a small bush where I was sure I saw movement a moment before.

"Where?"

"Behind that small bush over to the left."

"Which small bush?" Dick asked.

The ensuing conversation is highly recognizable, with slight variations, by all hunters who have spent time glassing in the company of others.

"Do you see those three trees straight away?"

"The closer ones or the ones way out there?"

"The closer ones."

"Okay."

"Go 200 yards past them and another 100 yards to the left."

"Yes, dik-dik." This from Alex.

"I'm still not sure where you're looking."

"Right there." I pointed.

"Right where?"

"Okay, he's moving now. See this other tree to the left of the three and closer to us?

"The one all by itself?"

"Yes. Now look straight past it way out there and to the right of it just a little. You see that little dark spot?

"Yeah."

"Ten yards past that, standing in front of the bush."

"Okay, I got it. Great spotting Mary."

"Come, we go after." Alex pulled on Dick's sleeve.

We were a long way from the dik-dik. We backtracked a few steps, using the periphery of the trees to conceal our movement. We zipped right through. Keeping up with Alex took about everything we had. After a couple hundred yards, we slowed to a creep. When Alex ducked, we followed suit.

When he moved out of the way, pushed on Dick's shoulder and whispered "shoot," Dick didn't waste any time.

The small antelope heard us. He was on full alert less than 75 yards away, ready to bolt.

Dick made a great off-hand shot, dropping the little guy right in his tracks. Alex sprinted over to Dick's second dik-dik. We caught up to Alex in a moment. He shook Dick's hand with vigor.

"Good shot. Good shot."

Then he put his hand on his hips, shook his head and smiled. This one wasn't quite as good as the first, but it was close. With such tiny horns, it's hard to tell anyway.

Sometimes fate is kind enough to smile upon you, then callous enough to laugh in your face. We were subjected to fortune's mocking sense of humor upon arrival at the Land Rover. We were carrying on, talking loudly, laughing and joking as we stepped onto the trail. Lo and behold, a lesser kudu bull. Stunned, none of us moved, except for Hussein who ducked back into the shadows.

The bull took one quick look at us before disappearing like he was never there at all. He was gone. We didn't know whether to laugh or cry. Inside, I think we all did a bit of both.

Alex's eyes were wide. He had a grave look on his face. Serious, yet astonished. He didn't say anything, just waved us forward, leading us after the bull, pure determination in his step. In less than twenty minutes, we lost the track. The denseness of the brush he led us into gave little leeway for us to follow. He had us beat from the beginning.

A line from Hemingway's "Green Hills of Africa" came to mind:

Now it is pleasant to hunt something that you want very much over a long period of time, being outwitted, out-maneuvered, and failing at the end of each day, but having the hunt and knowing every time you are out that, sooner or later, your luck will change and that you will get

*the chance that you are seeking. But it is not pleasant to have a time
limit by which you must get your kudu or perhaps never get it, nor even
see one.*

Amen Ernest. Amen.

We were restricted by a time limit and our kudu was proving smarter
than us. Just deal with it. Hunt the good hunt. And when the day is done,
when the kudu is yours or you are his, knowing you left it all out there,
in the forest, on the plain, will be satisfaction enough. Tip your hat to
the kudu, his wiliness, his stealth, his majesty. Tip your hat to him and
let him know you will return. And you will. And he knows you will. And
he will be ready.

We had lunch at the truck. Afterwards, Dick tried to nap while I had
a Coke and relaxed with a book. We were beginning to feel the effects
of the long days and short nights. Our feet started to drag and we just
felt droopy. If we were looking to place blame for our weariness, we'd
be pointing fingers at Mr. Kudu. We could never stoop to such levels. So
what if he wore us out during the day? So what if he made us toss and
turn at night with his derisive stare, dancing around in our dreams?
Maybe it's our own fault – but we won't go that far either. Maybe, just
maybe, we'd get another crack at him during the afternoon hunt. We'd
give it another try. Well, maybe a few more.

We hunted hard all afternoon without as much as a glimpse. By the
time we arrived back at the vehicle, we were swallowed by darkness.
Finding the trail suddenly became more than a trivial matter. The sheer
silence was uncomfortable. Alex had a tracker walk in front of the
headlights to ensure we didn't drive into a hole, plummet down a ravine,
or slide down a river's embankment. It was a tedious affair. In the
darkness, we never knew what we might disturb. Better to be careful
and not have to abandon the truck, than to hike back to camp on foot
in total darkness. Although I should have helped Alex and the others
look out for bottomless pits and black holes, I was more concerned with
the shadowy figures that seemed to silently follow us through the night.
I just knew there were elephants out there waiting for the perfect
moment to run us down. Darkness can do strange things to an
imagination, especially after being charged by an enraged elephant just
days before.

My fears proved unfounded. Once the trail was found, it was smooth
sailing back to camp. The fire roared, dinner was ready and although the
kudu had eluded us again, the day was another success.

At times, I couldn't help but wonder if Alex had forgotten about me.
I was hunting too. I'm sure he was more comfortable with Dick. He'd

probably rarely guided a woman, if ever, and I couldn't blame him. No matter how much enjoyment I received from being with my husband and experiencing his successes and failures, I wanted to succeed and fail a little too. I don't know if I would be so bold without Dick's support. We've shared our lives together. Raised nine children. Created a business. Deepened our love. Strengthened our faith. These things would've been difficult alone and far less rewarding.

I know husbands who absolutely refuse to take their wives hunting and wives who absolutely refuse to hunt with their husbands. They do not realize what they're missing. Dick and I hunted as we did most things, together. I wouldn't want it any other way.

I refrained from mentioning it, but I couldn't help but wonder when it would be my turn again.

I awoke that evening to a horrifying noise. A guttural gurgle, followed by a deep loud cough. I was a little frightened. When I realized the sound was coming from Dick, I became alarmed for different reasons.

"What's the matter?" I asked.

He was just outside our hut. I could barely make out his bent shape in the moonlight. His right arm held steady to a post. He answered with another raspy spew.

"Dick, are you okay?"

"Yes," he said. He struggled to get it out. "Stomach's just a little upset, that's all."

His vomiting continued long into the night and went on for a few more days. He couldn't keep anything down. My concern grew by the day, but anyone who knows my husband well, knows he can sometimes be obstinate. For him to postpone hunting because of an upset stomach would be a crime. It's frustrating at times, but it's one of the reasons I love him so.

The following day was long and difficult. We found a kudu cow with a decent bull right away, but they scented us in the twirling wind. They were gone in a flash.

"We should track?" Alex pointed to the ground, then to where the bull disappeared.

Dick shrugged his shoulders. "Sure."

I was becoming more cynical by the hour. At least we'd get some exercise, maybe walk up on some wildlife during our stroll. Fat chance at a kudu.

We tracked for more than three hours through thorny bushes and searing heat all the while being pestered by another of the most evil insects on earth – the tsetse fly. We found some shade for lunch. Though we could sometimes escape the sun and avoid the thorns, the tsetse fly would not relent. I found myself using a word I often scolded our children for using. Hate. These indestructible vermin are impervious to any repellant and, in fact, seem to enjoy the smell. I was convinced their needle-like proboscis was capable of penetrating a suit of armor. That buzzing sound they make is actually laughter and if we could see their nasty little faces, I'm sure they'd be grinning.

All anthropomorphizing aside, I suppose it is a fair trade-off. Presence of tsetse flies is indicative of wildness. Domestic livestock cannot withstand the wrath of the tsetse fly (we could barely stand it ourselves) and as a result, this little pest may, in fact, be the savior of Africa's wildlife and natural habitat. I will take its constant torment over the alternative.

I don't know how far we tracked that kudu, I only know how long. Long enough to make my feet scream. Long enough to turn my skin the color of a radish. Long enough to see the river dry up. Well, the river bed may have been dry before, but as we followed the kudu's tracks further upstream, or was it downstream, so hard to tell without water, I was convinced he was heading for the watering hole up ahead. I wonder if lesser kudu see mirages like we do.

Some time before dark, the bull sauntered beyond the waterless river's bank and we lost the track. About that same time, Dick started to vomit again. Was this quest for lesser kudu really worth it? I posed this question to my husband. I knew the reply before it left his mouth.

"I'm fine. It's just a little sour stomach."

We all know such people. I just happened to marry this one.

Alex had a look of grave concern in his eyes. When Dick was ready, our army-camo clad professional hunter and his trusty trackers led us back to the truck. We'd followed that kudu for many hours. The walk back took only one. We were thankful for that. Despite his rotten illness, Dick didn't want to quit; the word has never held meaning for him.

As a compromise, we agreed to slowly hunt our way back to camp. I was beat. I know Dick was beat. Even Alex and the trackers seemed more sluggish than usual.

This kudu was winning and it was beginning to show on our faces. No first day excitement or anticipation left. We knew the drill and the drill was wearing us down, day by day, hour by hour, minute by minute. One thing allowed us to face each new day, take one more step with drive. Hope. If the day begins with hope, the day begins well. If it ends with the hope of tomorrow, then pushing yourself further is really no major task at all. When you lose hope, you lose so much more.

I hardly understood it, the way my pessimism and optimism sparred like two rutting bucks. As long as there was a chance, hope would continue the battle.

The next day was more of the same, except in addition to the scorching sun, the ruthless tsetse flies, Dick's vomiting, miles of kudu-less tracks and the uncomfortable lack of conversation, every time we took off in the truck, tiny gnat-like bugs would zip their way right into my left eye. I didn't know what kind of bugs they were, and to tell the truth, I really didn't care, but the nameless little bugs were working their way up there with the tsetse fly and the tick on my list of vile creatures whose sole purpose seems to be to annoy me to the point of madness.

I would dig one out of my inflamed eye and it would just start to become bearable when *whack* another kamikaze would dive bomb into my pupil. What the...

There were six of us in the open vehicle. Why was I the only one subjected to this form of insect cruelty? I guess I'm just an easy target. I put on a pair of sunglasses and one of those nasty little buggers still managed to find its way into my already pinched-shut eye. Had I only brought eye-drops along with every other over-the-counter/prescription/witch doctor medicine in our train case, I may have found some respite that evening, while I lay in bed, willing myself not to itch, listening to Dick snore, while a leopard attacked a whole troop of baboons right outside our hut.

"Dick. Dick. Wake up!"

"Wha... What?"

"Quit snoring."

"I don't know what you mean."

"It sounds like a lion. I'm afraid you may call one in... Dick. Wake up!"

"Uh... I'm uh, awake."

"You were snoring again."

"Well stop snoring then."

"I'm not snoring. You're snoring. Dick. Dick. Wake up!"

I tried in vain, most of the night to thwart his thunderous, raspy snores, which he followed up with a piercing nasal screech, sounding eerily similar to a wounded rabbit. At least when the baboons were screaming at the leopard, I knew the cat wasn't stalking Dick's *wheeze-grunt-squeal*. About the time the alarm-clock knock on the door came, I felt as if I could get some sleep. Throughout the course of the sleepless night, the eyelids on my left eye somehow managed to get themselves welded together. Prying them apart brought on a new batch of tears. Damn gnats.

That morning we hiked up a mountain to gain a better vantage point on kudu and buffalo. I honestly didn't see the point. Even if we did spot something from way up there, it would be gone before we could get down to it. On the way up, I was thinking it was a nice little hike, but if I wanted a nice little hike, I could do that at home. I thought it was a waste of time. Pessimism was once again gaining a foothold, but as we struggled to the top, I was glad for the spectacular view. It was as if we could see to the ends of the world. I wondered if God created mountains just so we could have a tiny glimpse of what he sees to keep us awestruck. I wondered what the kids were doing, wished they could see what I saw. And for the brief moment I was on top of that Ethiopian mountain, I felt completely at peace. There was no tsetse fly on earth that could take that away from me. What a wonderful waste of time.

We never saw a kudu or a buffalo from that mountaintop. I'm not sure that's why Alex took us up there. He must've been up that mountain 100 times, but I saw the look on his face. He was as captivated as we were. I think he took us up on that peak to remind us. To put things back in perspective.

We descended the mountain with renewed spirit. We'd hunt hard the last few days knowing we pushed ourselves to the physical and mental limits and in the process learned more about ourselves than we knew before.

We spent more time in camp for lunch than usual. Some government official from the wildlife department was supposed to arrive today to check on the operation, see how the hunting season had progressed thus far. We waited until after 5:00 p.m. He never showed. We never found out why.

"Come. We go hunt." Alex looked irritated. I guess government dependability and accountability are universal long shots.

Alex's demeanor transformed before our eyes shortly after we pulled away from camp. He had a smile on his dark, weathered face. Hunting will do that to you – along with the many other things it tends to do.

"Camp needs meat."

We'd been eating Dick's gerenuk, lunch and dinner for the last couple days. Fresh table fare sounded mighty tempting. There are only so many ways to cook gerenuk in a secluded, mostly archaic camp. We'd tried them all. Meat happens to come from game in this part of the world. Our success in finding and bringing game to the table had not been too stellar the last few days, but Alex beamed with confidence. It rubbed off on the whole truck. For fifteen minutes, we joked and laughed – sometimes at stories there was no way we could understand; it refreshed the entire group.

It was while Alex recanted one of these tales, told in a sort of broken English, half Greek and Native tongue, that our, specifically my, luck changed. Alex had his head turned toward us, telling a certain story we were struggling to follow. The smile on his face was contagious. We listened attentively, managed to catch a few words, laughing when such a response seemed appropriate. Suddenly, a lone hand came from behind us to tap Alex on his shoulder. He hit the brakes and followed the finger's aim. Under the shade of an acacia was a small herd of Grant's gazelle. They were a good distance off. Dick and I needed our binoculars to locate them. The single male in the herd had thick horns reaching far above those of my earlier Grant's.

Alex pulled the truck into some brush, handed me my rifle and led me crouching through waist-high grass. I hadn't fired a shot in four days. My fingers trembled. We crept to within 200 yards without detection when Alex indicated I should shoot from one knee. I was uncomfortable with the idea. I hadn't practiced such a firing position. I knelt and aimed anyway. The big male milled around behind a couple females for a few long moments before he slipped away from the group. I put the crosshairs on his shoulder.

One English word Alex and Professional Hunters the world over have mastered is "shoot". After he calmly instructed me in this one-word phrase for the third time, I did the only thing I could think of. I kept trying to steady the crosshairs.

"Shoot." This time with more force.

Then, to Alex's amazement, I lowered the barrel.

He sported a quizzical look. I animated with an exaggerated wobble of the gun that I couldn't get steady. For a moment I thought he might argue, but despite the pressing look in his eyes, he quietly said "closer." We maneuvered our way to a small tree less than 150 yards from our quarry.

In my attempt to keep pace with Alex during our short stalk, I didn't allow myself to look up at the gazelles and risk falling behind, or worse, falling on my behind. I left the animals to my guide. When Alex steered me into position at the tree, I distinctly heard the word "shoot." When I found the herd in my scope and no longer saw a few languid antelope milling about, I understood the haste.

All eyes were locked on us, the muscles of each animal tense, preparing to flee. One female trotted a few paces. The male briefly looked her way, then back at us. It was now or never. I had the gun in the fork of the trunk and a branch. Just before I squeezed off, a little voice in my head reminded me I shouldn't be so steady. You haven't shot in four days, it said. Like an idiot, I listened to that voice of un-reason. In my moment of unsteadiness, I fired over the heavy-horned gazelle's back.

"Shoot!"

At the command, instinct took over. I jacked another bullet into the chamber and found the bull charging after his harem for the safety of distance. I kept on him, my hope blowing away with the dust-cloud he left in his trail. Then, he made the fatal mistake of a younger bull. He stopped to glance back. The window would be brief, I knew, and though I have never been one to take quick shots, it just felt right. I cannot explain it better than that. Every hunter knows the feeling. Like at the birth of a new day, the sun not yet up, but giving breath to the morning, when its cool whisper refreshes your body and zebras glide into the shadows of dawn, you know it can't get any better. You understand you are lucky, blessed. And the desire to follow them into the shadows of the sunless morning is the only choice. It just feels right.

I knew without a doubt, in that split second before the squeeze springs the trigger, that the gazelle was mine. I left my rational training with the first shot, letting instinct take over. If Alex said "shoot" yet again, I didn't hear. It didn't matter. The bullet was on its way before I had time to think about it. The gazelle was down.

I've made shots that were technically better than that. Longer shots. Shots at moving targets. Shots at much smaller targets. However, that was one of my more rewarding shots. I've always been the type of hunter who needs everything beyond perfect before I pull the trigger. In many cases, I've allowed an animal, even a superb trophy, to escape because I wasn't comfortable with the situation – it just didn't feel right. To have everything so perfect, so right, in circumstances in which my nerves would never allow me to dream of firing, and to stay calm in such a situation was something I was proud of. It was one of the few times I didn't care that I missed the first shot. One of the few times I nearly forgot I did. I've never been in a situation in which I was charged by an animal I was hunting (Thank God.) and I don't know how I'd react, but given my disposition when faced with charging elephants I was not hunting, I doubt I could hit the broad side of a barn.

That evening our dinner of bread, vegetable soup, homemade potato chips, cabbage and onion salad was completed with fresh, succulent Grant's gazelle steaks and a woman beaming under Africa's moonlight. She knew, with certainty, the memories of this hunt with the person she loved most in this world would not fade. It just felt right.

Persistence: Dick

Every hunter has his favorite hunting partner. The one to whom he cannot wait to relate each day's adventures. The one whose successes are more satisfying than his own; whose failures are more painful. My favorite hunting partner is Mary. She's the one person with whom I can confide. Her smile lifts my heart. Frustration and disappointment are shot away by her success. So what if I didn't get a kudu, a return to Ethiopia was not out of the question. It was, in fact, a likely possibility.

Ethiopia brought forth a rare awakening in Mary. Her face shined bright with smiles and her eyes were wonder-filled every morning. She was in a constant state of contentment few people ever experience. At least until happenstance found us near an elephant. Then her eyes filled with fear and her fingers trembled. It was, at times, endearing. I wondered if my eyes ever revealed, in such a striking fashion, what my heart felt.

"Are you having breakfast today?" Mary asked.

"Yes, last day here and all. I expect we'll hunt hard. Probably need the energy."

"I think I'll just have juice and toast. I'm beat this morning. Yesterday was so hot and I forgot the sunscreen. My face, neck and legs are burned. I'm stiff, sore and it's all tender to the touch."

It was a few minutes before we realized Alex wasn't joining us for breakfast.

"What's he doing?" Mary asked.

I shrugged my shoulders in the middle of a yolk-soaked bite of toast. Alex had been back and forth from his tent to the truck at least four times in five minutes. When he carried an item, it was small and we couldn't make it out. He seemed determined. Not quite frenetic, it was more contemplative and a little eager. We later found he'd been packing for the Denakil and in his excitement, kept forgetting small items he'd need for the trip. Later that evening, we saw him back at the truck retrieving items he needed for the night. I think he was more excited about a change of scenery than we were. It was comforting to see we wouldn't be headed for an area he found dull.

Alex's manner didn't waver during our morning hunt. In our effort to locate game, specifically kudu, he drove the truck with focused resolve. We pointed out gerenuk, Grant's gazelle, warthog and even a lion pride, where he briefly slowed the vehicle before concluding there was no male. We were off again. An hour later, a tracker pointed ahead, mumbling. Alex slammed on the brakes, nearly sending every occupant onto the hood.

We composed ourselves just in time to watch a kudu cow disappear into the bush.

"No bull," Alex said, slamming us back into our seats as he hit the gas.

Our only other excitement for the day came when one of the natives spotted two kudu way off in the distance. We had to climb up into the back just to see them. Even then, it took us a while to find them in our optics. Time was quickly running out. This appeared to be our last reasonable chance at a lesser kudu. We spent nearly 30 minutes glassing, but the two females wandering up the hill apparently were alone. Alex, Mary, and I slumped back down into our seats – defeated.

However, a feeling of excitement rose from the trackers behind us like the smoke in their freshly rolled cigarettes. We were headed back to camp. For some reason this lifted their spirits. Something was up, but we refrained from delving deeper into the reasons. We had more pressing inquiries.

"Alex," I said. "Are there kudu at the Denakil camp?"

His answer was a wide-eyed smile and an affirmative nod of the head. For different reasons, my disposition joined the trackers. We were down, but not out.

Emerging from our temporary home after refreshing showers, we discovered why our native friends seemed to be on cloud nine during the ride back to camp. A celebration.

The entire camp was in a festive mood. Most of the men had painted their bodies with some sort of chalk-like white substance. The designs were varied and elaborate. Some were painted in horizontal stripes from their ankles to their necks. Others in vertical or more artistic patterns, such as a mountain, river or thousands of little white dots which reminded us of guinea fowl. One man's body was adorned with handprints, as if the means for cleaning their hands after making themselves up was to slap this man's chest, back and legs with their palms. Even a small, pot-bellied boy joined in the fun, painting himself from face to ankle.

The moon and stars had taken the place of the retreating sun, turning the world silent. At dinner, Alex had a knowing smile on his face. A group of seven decorated men and the young boy lined up by the campfire and stood like soldiers awaiting their orders. A sudden cry from the group of camp staff to the side erupted the area in song and dance. One by one, the painted dancers began a kind of straight up and down hopping dance in unison with the singing and clapping. It was a dance to remember. If their athleticism wasn't apparent during the laborious efforts of the safari, the spring in some of the men's vertical leaps would strike Michael Jordan with envy.

It was a celebration fit for a king and the feast was not disappointing. Fresh warthog shish kabob, beef broth and noodle soup, potatoes and flan made for a filling, fitting end to a grand farewell. We were touched deeply, but did not deserve such an honor. Rest came easy for me that evening, but, as I discovered the following morning, my deep slumber was the cause of Mary's restless night.

"Did you hear the leopard again last night?" she said as we dressed.

"No, did you?"

"For a little bit, but it was hard to hear over your lion snores."

The camp staff threw a grand farewell celebration, painting themselves and dancing and singing throughout the night.

I laughed. "That bad, huh?"

"Worse. I was up all night trying to get you to stop. I swear, one of these days you're going to call a lion right into our tent."

"I wouldn't get carried away now."

"I'm serious. Last night, the leopard kept getting closer and then, when there was a pause in your snores, it suddenly went quiet. Like it was moving in for the final stalk."

"I'll try to do better next time," I said smiling.

Alex was waiting for us at the breakfast table. "Nassos not come after lunch. You want hunt?"

"Let's go."

"No, no. Eat, eat. Then go."

On cue, our eggs, toast, juice and tea arrived and we scarfed it down. We had but a few hours to hunt before moving on.

An hour into the morning, Alex stopped the truck at the trackers behest. They said they just saw a kudu, but it was gone. We wondered if he was worth tracking, but apparently gone meant gone. So, without spotting another kudu, we went back for lunch and to wait for Nassos to arrive.

The plane landed shortly after lunch. Nassos was pale as a ghost when he greeted us. "I do not like airplanes. Very rough flight. You have no idea. Up, down, up down. And my stomach was even worse. Grab your things and we'll get back in that crazy machine."

We would spend one night in Addis, and have four days to hunt the Denakil. Four days. Not very long to find a lesser kudu. Not very long at all.

We would miss the Omo, but the possibilities of a new land, a new adventure, lifted our spirits. Whenever you travel to a region for the first time, you never know what to expect. It's rarely the way you see it in your mind. If you're lucky, like we have been, the reality will far surpass your expectations.

Nassos said very little during the flight. His death-grip on the arms of his seat, his clenched teeth and his wide eyes spoke for him. It was a rare look for our courageous, elephant-hunting friend. It was comforting to see he didn't pretend to be completely fearless – those kinds of people make me nervous. Like they've got something to prove. While trying to prove it, they might just get you killed.

Quiet as he was, Nassos couldn't conceal his excitement that his wife, Susan, and their twelve-year old son, Jason, would join us for the next few days. We couldn't wait to meet them.

"The camp we're going to, what's it like?" Mary asked on our way to the hotel.

"Not like the Omo. We will sleep in trailers."

Trailers seemed strange, but it probably offered better protection against the elements than tents. I guess we'd find out tomorrow.

"We'll pick you up at 9:00," Nassos said, leaving us in the hotel lobby.

We had hamburgers and a couple of drinks and then called home before falling asleep. There are always conflicting emotions when away from home for an extended hunt. We missed the kids, but at the same time, we couldn't wait to get back in the field. At times, it made us feel guilty. Hearing they were doing fine helped us rest easy. We didn't get to call home often from Africa, but the kids were always on our minds.

Sleep came easy in the city, but the howls, shrieks and growls of the wild were replaced by the steady drum of tires and honking horns. A few hours removed from camp and we already missed it.

Nassos arrived a few minutes after 9:00 with Jason, who helped us load our heavy bags into the vehicle. Jason was a polite young man with a contagious smile. He may very well have been more excited about going hunting than we were.

"We will drive one hour to camp and hunt for kudu this afternoon."

"Is the population good here?" I asked.

"Very good. We have many kudu. We will get you a kudu here."

Our limited experience with hunting kudu kept us a little skeptical, but Nassos' confidence was addictive. According to Jason, who leaned up from the back seat, kudu were everywhere. He said we'd get one for sure. His conviction surpassed his father's.

The hour turned out to be a little longer, because we drove through a park, stopping a few times to view game. We soon discovered the animals in the park paled in comparison to the game at the hunting area in both number and quality.

"You should come hunt mountain nyala with us. It is one of the great trophies in all of Africa."

I don't know if he was prepared for my answer. I even shocked myself.

"How about next year?" I asked. Mary's eyes went quickly from surprise to enthusiastic agreement.

"Yes," she said. "That would be lovely."

"It is a very hard hunt," Nassos said. "The mountains are high, the weather is bad, and to find nyala is not easy."

"Sounds like fun."

Nassos seemed to ponder this for the next few miles. "I think we have an opening next year, but I must check the schedule at camp."

We'd have to consult our calendar as well, but I was committed. One of the great animals of Africa was too enticing to pass up.

"Will you be our hunter?" Mary asked.

"We will see."

The campsite consisted of three trailers overlooking the Awash River. Just beyond the embankment, the area was shady, painted with a verdant brush. It was cool in the shade, but the trailers were like giant-sized ovens. They soaked up the sunlight, baking the occupants. I made it a point to avoid the trailer until after the sun went down. Mary felt somewhat different, deciding the trailer could use a good cleaning.

"Dick, will you go get me some water?"

"From the river?"

"Yes."

"That water doesn't exactly look clean."

"Just do it, please."

I'd given the river too much credit. The water was far from clean. It was the color of mud and had a soft slurping bottom, but when I scooped a bowl full, it didn't look as bad. There were still little pieces of sediment, black foliage, and crud floating around in it, but at least I could see the bottom of the bowl. It would have to do. Mary took a towel and scrubbed down every inch of that trailer, paying particularly close attention to the bathroom.

"It's still not clean," she said as she emerged from the heat-box. "But I feel better about it."

We left camp at 4 p.m. and drove for an hour to the base of a mountain. We spent the next few hours climbing. We didn't turn back until nearly sunset, but the short afternoon had been highly productive.

The trees, though not tall, were thick with leaves and barely spaced far enough apart to allow the perfect amount of sunlight for the undergrowth to grow high and dense.

The going was tough. We stumbled, tripped, ducked and squirmed our way up that mountain, trying in vain to keep quiet. Over nearly every ridge, in every clearing, behind every wall of greenery and shadow, we saw game. Lesser kudu were everywhere. Many were females and the few bulls we saw were young, but the numbers were uplifting. In the course of a couple hours, we spotted more lesser kudu than we'd seen the entire trip. Their beauty, grace, and the eerie way they fade into the shadows, disappearing at just the right moment were elegant. We wanted more. As we staggered down the mountain in twilight, we knew, with certainty, the next few days would be unforgettable.

By the time we made it back to camp and finished dinner, we were exhausted. We went straight for the oven.

"At least it's not as bad as it was earlier," I said.

"No, it's not. And aren't you glad we have a clean bathroom to use," Mary said.

She knew if I'd been alone, I wouldn't have bothered to clean it. I was happy not to be alone that night as I brushed my teeth at the sink she'd scrubbed clean with river water. It could have been much worse.

Strange as it was, we did feel somewhat safer in the trailers than in tents or even thatched huts, but were left feeling as if something was missing. The sounds of the night were more muffled. To know only an elephant could disturb your quarters was almost too reassuring. I do enjoy the creature comforts, and as I age, roughing it becomes less and less alluring, but at the time, I remember longing for thatched huts.

"I really like Susan," Mary said as the pillow held her head in the darkness. "Jason's sure a good kid too."

"You can tell they love it out here. It was nice having them along today."

"I just wish we had more time."

"Well," I said. "We still have a couple more days and we'll be back next year."

"It always seems to go so fast."

"I know it does."

Time is the ultimate equalizer. Unable to escape its absolute grasp, we are, in the end, only in this world for a short visit. Though we humans come and go like the wind, Ethiopia would always be here. I'm thankful I was able to see it during the brief moment of my lifetime.

We spent the morning hiking in the hills, busting up kudu left and right. By lunchtime, we could describe the lesser kudu posterior in such detail it was nearly embarrassing. The ground conditions were poor for tracking and snap shots were out of the question – the kudu disappeared in a flash in the profuse undergrowth. Our danger alerting scent and our innate human inability to move through the forest in silence put us at a disadvantage.

As we ventured further from the river, we encountered less and less plant life. The Awash disappears somewhere in the sands of the Denakil Desert, but its waters support a vast array of life. The river's shores are vivacious with a large number of wild animals along its banks. Though sign of predators, like leopard, were always present, the lesser kudu we desired were plentiful. The mere hopes we'd see one or two of these striking antelope soon developed into a mission to find the oldest member of the clan.

For five hours, we hiked erratic terrain. Even Nassos, Alex and Jason, with his seemingly unending supply of youthful energy, were ready for a break. An open area where we could relax under the shade of a giant, lone tree was deemed perfect for lunch. It was there, in the bushes behind the tree, that Mary and Susan found themselves in a precarious position of which I did not envy them. It was in those bushes, after lunch, that they had an encounter with one of Africa's more deadly creatures. It all started with one of nature's most insistent calls.

"I think it's time for a potty break," Mary said.

"I'll go with you," Susan said.

Safety in numbers or something, I guess.

The rest of us thought they had a swell idea and positioned ourselves in strategic aiming points that were very close by, yet allowed each of us to conduct our business at perfect angles so as not to infringe upon the privacy of others or to have our own privacy infringed upon. In contrast, the women went on a trek. Only when they ventured deep enough into the flora that only the most experienced of trackers could locate them, could they determine it was safe enough to...well, you know.

We four men had scarcely zipped when the two women returned post-haste. Their eyes were wide and their britches held up with their fingers.

"That was quick."

"We almost sat on a black mamba."

The black mamba, though not really black, is one of the largest and most dangerous poisonous snakes in all of Africa. A victim of its bite must be treated quickly or succumb to the fatal venom. They can strike with lightning speed. Any movement they deem as threatening can result in a bite.

Nassos' and Alex's eyes widened and Jason asked, "Where?"

Mary and Susan were not impressed.

"Okay, okay," Nassos said. "What happened?"

They seemed a little reluctant to say. We gave them time.

"Well," Susan finally said. "I was just squatting down when I turned and no more than a foot behind me, I saw the snake lying still in the grass. I told Mary not to move any closer and we backed out real slow. The next thing I know, we're running back here as fast as we can."

"It's a good thing it didn't bite you," Nassos said.

"Why's that?" I asked.

"Because I'm not going to suck out the poison from back there."

The women, still shaken from their close encounter, didn't seem to find Nassos' humor as funny as the rest of us did.

"We should go now," Nassos said. "Alex knows a very good tracker who lives close. He may be able to help us find a kudu."

We began loading the truck.

"Wait a minute. I still have to go," Mary said.

With that, her and Susan found a nearby bush. After a cautious but thorough inspection, they disappeared behind it.

We picked up the tracker at a nearby village before heading for a new hunting destination. Not as steep as much of the area's terrain, this location seemed more choked with dense vegetation. The river was close. We shadowed our new tracker. His lithe silence and deft senses rubbed off on us. We became more aware, more predatory and even though we'd added a new body, we seemed to reduce our volume significantly. He read the trail like he was reading a book, feeling the story unfold – unfolding as a part of it. I observed him lift his nose to test the air on more than one occasion. The high number of kudu he led us to elevated his status in our eyes.

Many times his tensing muscles signaled it was time for silent steps. As he knelt at the edge of a small clearing, his posture was that of a leopard with a determined stare and an intense readiness to pounce. It was mesmerizing. Most bulls he put us on sported half curls and short horns, indicating their immaturity and we'd move on. The mature bulls, sometimes solitary and sometimes traveling with a vigilant female, found success in eluding our pursuits. The day, like so many before it, ended without the chance for a shot. Our perseverance for two remaining days was fueled by hope and a nameless native tracker who, through a deep connection to the land and air, had a knack for uncovering the haunts of our spiral-horned friends.

We dropped him home with a promise to return early the next morning. Like the regal kudu slipping silently into the shadows, he disappeared into his modest hovel without a word, a wave or a smile.

The morning arrived early – 3:00 a.m. always does. Alex and Jason were climbing into one of the vehicles when we emerged from our dark lair and they hurried to tell us goodbye. School awaited the young man.

"I'm sorry I cannot stay and finish the hunt with you," Jason said. "I tried. But my pleading fell on deaf ears. Good luck."

His captivation with the land surpassed even ours and his admiration for his parents was immeasurable. He was a credit to them.

They waved and the hum of the engine faded into the darkness. They were gone. Strange. They come and go, these people, weaving in and out of our lives like the seasons. Strange how their words and their faces sometimes fade, but their touch endures.

Our tracker was waiting in the dark when we pulled up. With a greeting similarly as absent as his farewell the night prior, he climbed in back. For five hours, we hiked and sneaked up to more lesser kudu than we could count. At one point, we stumbled upon an Abyssinian bushbuck while tracking yet another kudu. Bushbucks are the smallest of the spiral-horned antelope and, true to the nature of the tribe, they are both beautiful and highly reclusive. When a rare opportunity presents itself, it needs to be acted upon.

The bushbuck was alert, sensing danger was near, but as of yet, had not pinpointed the source. We all ducked. Nassos pulled me close and whispered.

"Dick, do you see him?"

I nodded.

"Shoot him now."

At that instant, the bushbuck stiffened, snapping his head in our direction. No time to think. No time to find a rest. I let one fly. Before I could reload, life had left the animal. So simple, yet so devastatingly complex.

Nassos covered the 75 yards to the bushbuck with hawk-like speed. By the time we caught up to him, his hand was out. I took it and he grabbed on with his other hand, shaking energetically.

"Congratulations, Dick. This is a very good Abyssinian bushbuck. This is very fortunate. Hunters come here for 21 days or longer and never get one. I am pleased. Kudu will be next."

When he finally released my hand, we knelt to admire the solid little antelope. We knew we had it on license. It was one of the animals we hoped to take, but with the time and effort exhausted in our continuous search for lesser kudu, we'd put many of the other species out of mind. Bagging the bushbuck had been fortuitous and though our optimism for kudu was diminishing, it made one last soar.

Nassos, ever mindful of fading days, asked the game scout if he would stay to field dress and skin the bushbuck while we continued on in pursuit of kudu. This allowed us two more hours of tough hunting before lunch. With time slipping away like a raindrop down a slicker, every second counted.

Upon our return two hours later, he had the bushbuck skinned and quartered. Our ability to get the truck close made the often arduous task of hauling skin and meat relatively painless. Following a picnic in the shade, in which the time-honored battle with ants and other insects was reenacted in grand fashion, a nap was had by all, save for Mary. She couldn't have slept had she wanted to between the snorts, wheezes, squeaks, and raspy discord of our snores. Instead, with a devotion I admire, she said her daily prayers.

I don't pretend to be so bold as to have the clairvoyance to see what my wife prays for, nor am I sure a high-horned kudu to culminate an already blessed hunt is something the Lord would concern Himself with. What I do know is that an hour after lunch on our second-to-last day, fortunes changed.

Sleek and graceful, surrounded by the shadows it so favors, encircled by a small halo of sunlight, the kudu we caught a glimpse of through a minute break in the shrubbery was like a magical vision. Almost as if he was purposefully placed in that very ray of sunshine. As romantic as the vision may have been, I wanted to shoot him.

The kudu we desired was right there, within 150 yards. So close, but not quite within our grasp. There was no shot. The line of sight we could see him through was interwoven with so many twigs, branches and leaves, the possibility of bullet deflection was too great. We had to make a move. The wind and silence of his stillness put us at a clear disadvantage. With nothing to lose, we began a stalk. It appeared as if the inches would be measured in hours when a remarkable thing happened.

The kudu began moving.

A few more steps and the wind carried our scent right to his nose, yet he walked right through the breeze as if he'd lost his sense of smell. If he kept his course, he would walk right back into the shadows and disappear from our lives forever. As we kneeled in voiceless astonishment, he veered just before he would've been gone. With soft deliberate steps, he made his way directly for us. There was still no shot. From our position, he would have to circle around and upwind of us. The tangle separating the kudu from Nassos and I permitted this marvelous beast to drop his hooves within mere yards of us without allowing a shot. Sweat hung from my brow, my leg bawled for movement. I wasn't sure I could hold on. When we could almost hear his breath, he again changed directions for no apparent reason. We lost him behind a thick, wide bush. If he reappeared on the other side, we'd have our opening. I shifted, resting my arms on my knee, rifle at the ready, and waited.

After a few stretched minutes, we realized he either stopped or chose

Nassos and Dick needed a ton of determination and a little bit of luck to finally get a lesser kudu.

a less fortunate course (less fortunate for us, perfect for him). We'd barely begun to stand when there he was, as if he'd been there all along. Maybe he had, cloaked by a color of gray; a perfect blend for the shadows.

"Shoot," Nassos whispered.

An unnecessary command, but reassuring to know I wasn't delusional. No mirage, no hallucination. A search which began weeks before had reached an apex. I would hit or I would miss. Missing was not an option at that range after the effort we put in, the effort Nassos and Alex expended. We'd earned it. Though hesitation when opportunity is measured in seconds can close the window, I delayed my squeeze. It had been a good day, a good moment I wanted to savor.

When the kudu fell and we were certain it would not rise, Nassos looked up with his knowing eyes. "That wasn't so hard now, was it?" he said.

"No," I said, laughing. "Piece of cake."

If you took away the weeks of laborious sweat, the countless days of disappointment, the misplaced hopelessness and the thousands of steps beyond what we thought we were capable of, I suppose that could have been true. But if we could do that, what would be the point?

Farewell: Mary

Last days in a hunting camp are difficult to describe. The weary urgency of making the day count, the sadness of leaving new friends and the anticipation of home, make for an emotionally exhausting day.

I should've spent this final day hunting for my lesser kudu, but it was not to be. My last day was stolen by illness. I felt a little sluggish upon departure from camp, but figured I was just tired. It would pass. Within minutes, I felt queasy, but it was the last day, so I tried to suck it up. I was kidding myself. When the terrible cramps, nausea, and cold sweats were joined by vomiting, I realized the hunt was over.

"Do you think we should go back to camp?" Susan asked.

"I don't think that's necessary," I said. "I think I just need to rest for a bit."

"How about this," Nassos said. "We will go on, and Susan will stay with you here. We will walk and leave the truck in case you need it."

When the men departed, Susan decided it was her job to make me more comfortable.

"It's too scrunched in the car. Let me make you a bed," she said.

I didn't have the strength to argue. All by herself, Susan took the back seat out of the truck and carried it under a shade tree to keep me from the sun. Her tiny frame was deceptively strong. With the men away, it gave us a chance for a little girl talk. Between my bouts of vomiting and dry heaves that is. I hated having her wait on me. I'm sure she would've rather been out with the guys, but I was glad she was there. She was kind, beautiful and intelligent. We'd already become very good friends even though I knew little about her.

"How did you and Nassos meet?" I asked.

A Greek professional hunter and the former Miss Colorado was more than enough to tickle anyone's curiosity.

"Years ago, I came to Ethiopia to do missionary work. When I met Nassos, I was immediately enthralled with him and all that surrounded the great white hunter mystique. We got to know each other and when he asked me to join him on safari, I jumped at the opportunity. I fell in love with him, with this place. We fell in love together and I never looked back."

You couldn't help but admire her courage. It was like something out of a storybook romance.

"Do you have any other children, or just Jason?"

"No we have another boy, Niki."

"And where's he?"

"London. He's at a Catholic rehabilitation center for cerebral palsy."

"How's he doing?"

"Very well. He is the sweetest kid. He brings so much joy into our lives."

"I would like to meet him," I said.

"I'd like that too."

A few minutes later, my body succumbed to the sickness and I fell asleep. Over an hour passed before I awoke. I saw Susan talking to the tracker who had left with Dick and Nassos. She came right over when she saw I was awake.

"How are you feeling?" She handed me a bottle of water.

"Much better. Thank you. Where are the guys?"

"Still hunting. We're supposed to take the truck and pick them up down the road a few miles. Do you feel up to it?"

"Yes, I think I'll be fine. My stomach feels much better." I didn't wish to spend the whole last hunting day asleep.

The day had heated up considerably. I couldn't imagine what the trailer was going to be like. We found Dick and Nassos right where the tracker said they'd be. They were waiting in the shade. It was too hot to continue hunting, so we found a cool shady spot by the river to have lunch and rest for a couple hours.

Susan, apparently undeterred by our earlier encounter, went to search out a bit of privacy behind a nearby bush. Barely able to stifle a scream, she was back in a flash. This time it was a cobra and she was lucky she didn't try to sit on it like the black mamba. After that, we held it as long as we could, only choosing a bush after thorough investigation.

During the final few hours of our last day, Dick's crosshairs found their mark on a dik-dik. We also ironed out an agreement for our return in November of the following year. Mountain nyala would be our main focus, but other game, such as hippopotamus, would also be on the list.

On our way back to the Awash, we stopped in a village where Nassos wanted to visit with an old woman. She was the mother of one of his best childhood friends who had recently been killed in a car accident while on safari. The old woman smiled politely and touched his hand before he left. She was glad he stopped. It was a good visit. All our spirits were uplifted.

Two days of shopping in Addis was an adventure in itself. What we would've paid without Susan's negotiating skills is frightening and without her at our sides, we never would've strolled into a small, dark, market that had the strange pungent aroma of spices and sewage. The beautiful baskets we found there made the gagging smell endurable. We were glad we ventured into the market – even if the fleas wouldn't.

Goodbyes are always difficult. The knowledge you may or may not see a stranger, who has taken a piece of you and molded it with a piece of themselves until it formed a friendship as solid as iron, can hit you hard, again. We had plans to return in a year, but it appeared as if Susan wouldn't be hunting with us and much can happen during the course of a year – especially in Africa, where instability is redefined with regularity.

"We had a wonderful time," I said as they dropped us off at the airport. "Thank you."

"No, thank you," Nassos said. "It's not every safari we get to enjoy ourselves so much. The Colonel here will assist you with customs." He introduced us to a man who suddenly appeared from across the street.

A few teary-eyed hugs (especially from Susan and I) and we followed the Colonel into the airport. We turned before the crowd engulfed us to see Nassos and Susan wave one last time.

Thank God for the Colonel. He shuffled us painlessly through customs, whisking us to our departing gate without delay. It was one of the all-time easiest departures from a foreign city. It certainly could've been excruciating if not for the Colonel. We tried to tip him, but he declined. He asked instead for us to send the money to his son attending college in the United States. We agreed and he gave us the address. Then this refreshingly trusting man disappeared into the line of bustling travelers.

During an uneventful flight back to the states with Dick asleep beside me, I said my prayers, asking of God more than I had the right and thanking Him for giving so much more than I deserved.

Part Six:

The Quest for Mountain Nyala Begins

1990: November 5 - December 4

<u>**A Learning Experience:**</u> Mary

By November of 1990, of our nine children only Joseph remained at home, entering his junior year of high school. We'd taken some of the kids fishing with us to Alaska and Mexico, but had never taken them on an international hunt. Joe would be the first. He and his brother, David, hunted rabbits and other small game with bows and arrows when they were young, but Joe hadn't shown a major interest in hunting for many years. Teenagers often find girls and friends more interesting than upland birds and deer, definitely more than their parents. We weren't sure how he'd react when we approached him with the idea. The opportunity to miss a month of school had him counting the days until we left. A discussion with his teachers and school officials confirmed they thought it would be a great opportunity for Joe to better understand another part of the world and another culture. They requested he take lots of photos and give a full report to the school upon his return. Dick and I thought it was a good idea, but Joe, typical teenager he was, thought of it as homework and agreed grudgingly. There was the possibility his teachers were glad to have him out of their hair for a month. Come to think of it, they did show more excitement than might have been expected. Nevertheless, Joe was going to Ethiopia with us.

Although we'd been to Ethiopia the previous year, we'd be traveling to a new area, hunting a species we didn't even know existed before our friend, Nassos Roussos, told us about them. So, in essence, this trip would be as much a new experience for us as it was for our son. We hoped the journey would reinvigorate a passion for the outdoors he embraced as a youngster. My first experience with Africa changed me forever. If it touched our youngest son the same way, it would truly be something.

Our hometown of Sidney, Nebraska, is nearly three hours by car to Denver and the nearest major airport. Halfway there we realized we'd forgotten to visit the doctor that morning for the last of a long list of shots we needed for travel into remote Ethiopia. It was a good thing our flight didn't leave until the next morning because the return drive to Sidney set us back a few hours. What a way to start a trip. We hoped it wasn't an omen. When our flight to Rome was delayed until the next evening, we feared it just might be.

Rome, though fascinating and moving as it is, was unable to distract us from the string of misfortune wrapped in red tape the airlines continued to gift out. Our extended wait in a short line at customs put us in a rush to reach the church in time for Mass. We were late, but at least we made it. Standing in the Vatican, I was overcome with reverence and cried.

One full day is not nearly enough to absorb even a little of Rome's rich history, but that was all we had and a visit to the catacombs at St. Sebastian's would be a powerful history lesson for not only Joe, but us as well.

The massive burial site of some 500,000 people was disheartening. The fact that 25 percent were babies and small children was tragic. Frescos depicting Jonah and the whale, the Last Supper, and the dove with the olive branch adorned tombs lining the sides of the excavation. They were the remains of Christians and others Roman law didn't allow to be buried in the city. We left there with a greater respect for the freedoms we are blessed with in our own country and own time. Often, we are guilty of taking these things for granted, sometimes failing to realize the greatest threat to our unequaled liberties is the failure to grasp just how precious they are. We are the only ones who can destroy the liberty our forefathers entrusted to us.

We were glad we made the visit to the humbling catacombs, brief though it was, and were gratified to expose our son to a world and history reaching far beyond the rolling plains of Nebraska.

The enlightening day ended with a red-eye flight to Addis Abba, but not without more delays and complications which began when we forgot our shots back in Sidney. Checking the rifles was almost more hassle than it was worth. A clueless, but opinionated, official made a show of the fact his uniform gave him the right to bully us. He inspected our documents closely. When he grabbed one of the guns, peered down the end of the barrel, then scratched at the stock with his fingernail, we understood we were dealing with a fool whose self-importance could very well cause us to miss our flight. The last thing you want to do to a fool who has the ability to complicate your trip is to point out to him he is a fool. We took his verbal abuse as cordially as we could, jumping through every hoop asked of us.

Luckily, the scene he created brought forth a pleasant, young blonde woman who apparently outranked the fool who thought the best way to inspect a gun was to close one eye and look down the barrel without checking to see if it was loaded. Upon her arrival, his pompous bantering ceased and he retreated to the corner. The young woman took one quick look at our documents before sending us on our way.

The man in uniform's angry scowl at our departure should've alerted us to the further hurdles we'd have to clear. We rushed to the gate only to find our flight delayed until 1:30 a.m., which mockingly changed to 3:00 a.m. before our eyes. We'd no sooner found a seat in the lounge when a young man tapped Dick on the shoulder, requesting his presence at the loading dock, where they were once again rummaging through our luggage. He was gone so long, I began wondering if he'd been arrested or something.

He finally returned a few moments before we boarded.

"What happened?" I asked.

"Oh some yahoo decided to check the luggage again. When they found the ammo box, they were certain they'd discovered incriminating contraband of a serious criminal. I finally got it worked out."

"What did they say?" Joe asked.

"I'm not sure. They couldn't speak English. Finally, an old guy showed up who knew English, asking me to sign a declaration for the ammunition, then he shook my hand and sent me on my way. It wasn't that big of deal. I think some of them just didn't like me."

Nassos and the Colonel met us at the airport in Addis Ababa. After checking into the hotel, we all went to lunch. Susan's appearance was a pleasant surprise. We spent much of the day remembering our last hunt. They hadn't changed much. Susan was as beautiful as ever. Nassos might've had a little more white in his beard, but his quick wit and dry sense of humor were, if anything, more prevalent. A year earlier they were strangers. Today we were in the company of old friends.

The next morning, we loaded into the vehicles and just over seven hours later, arrived at the nyala base camp nestled neatly at 12,000 feet. What began as a lovely, clear, 85° day became cold and dreary as our long, slow climb up the mountains progressed. By the time we reached camp, the temperature hovered around freezing. The warm fire became the focal point. The untouched beauty of the region was awe-inspiring. If not for the cold, I may've spent more time in quiet admiration. Instead, I bundled up and shivered closer to the fire, mesmerized by its glowing warmth. How Joseph could be comfortable in just shorts and a t-shirt was beyond me. Nassos just thought he was crazy.

"Both guns were four inches low," Dick said after checking them. "We had them zeroed at two inches high."

"You're kidding."

"No. It just goes to show you how important it is to sight your gun in after traveling. Could you believe the mess we'd be in now if we hadn't discovered this until later?" Dick shook his head.

"Well, I'm glad you checked them. I'm too cold to leave the fire."

"The altitude's a killer. My heart is beating faster, I'm having trouble breathing and the thin air is giving me a massive headache. According to Nassos, we'll be climbing higher to hunt the mountain nyala. Over 13,500 feet. This is going to be one tough hunt."

"I just hope it warms up. How are we supposed to stay warm in those canvas tents?"

"We've got good sleeping bags and Nassos said he had some blankets placed on our cots."

I wish I could say I didn't freeze that night. It was one of the most miserably cold, sleepless nights I've ever experienced. Inside our sleeping bags, we were under two heavy blankets and still froze. It was a damp cold that made us feel like we were surrounded by those cool gel packs. I bundled up in my long underwear, jogging outfit and two pairs of socks, but still froze. I dozed off a few times, but couldn't get warm enough long enough to sleep more than a few minutes at a time. Dick had it worse than I did. Along with having to endure the cold wet night, his heart was beating like uneven war drums and his lungs felt like shriveled prunes.

Only after numerous attempts to wake him did Joe finally join us for breakfast.

"Morning," he said.

"Good morning. How did you sleep?"

"Fine, why?"

"Your father and I had a rough night. Weren't you cold?"

"No, I was fine."

At least he was wearing pants and a long-sleeve shirt. The rest of us had on triple layers and heavy winter coats. The entire camp took to Joe right from the start. He was young and full of energy, if not a little cocky. His long, blond, rock-star hair was something many of them had never

Base camp for mountain nyala was at 12,000 feet.

encountered. He made friends easily with the entire staff. Despite the unfathomable cultural differences, there seemed to be a connection between him and some of the others. It would be safe to say he was a real hit in camp.

"Joe, you will go with Kidane to higher ground today," Nassos said as he joined us after breakfast. "Dick, you and Mary will hunt with me around this elevation."

We would've liked to hunt with Joe, but Nassos said Kidane was a very good nyala hunter. They should have some good luck if the fog lifts.

I hadn't ridden a horse in ages. I don't think Dick had ever ridden a mule, but that was the situation we found ourselves in as we ambled up the mountain. Although I found it more agreeable than walking that first morning, my feelings would become mixed on the subject as the hunt progressed. My rear-end would eventually scream the loudest, but for the time being I preferred the horse to the tiring thin-air hike that so easily wore me out. During the ride, a young nyala bull crashed off ahead of us, but the challenge of hunting a wily old bull is much of the allure. We merely smiled as the youngster dashed away, more educated than before.

The mountain nyala is more closely related to the greater kudu than the southern nyala, but like all spiral horned antelope of Africa, they lead secretive lives. They stick to thick cover during daylight hours, but in the hazy light of twilight and dawn slip through the heather, browsing on what vegetation is available. The solitary life of old bulls we were after made finding them in the high, dense heather the equivalent of locating a grain of wheat in a bushel of corn. The hunting method of choice is similar to hunting mountainous species the world over – glass, glass, glass. The thick morning fog made our binoculars worthless for the time being.

We worked our way up to an outcropping of rocks at the top of a mountain to wait out the fog, clinging to the mountain like cold sweat. Visibility was measured in feet fewer than ten. It wasn't long before keeping warm took precedence over hunting an animal that had every advantage in the dreary haze. I hunkered down behind a boulder, pulled on my stocking cap, and cinched my hood over my head tight. I could just barely see. With the bulky teal coat I wore, I must've looked like a cartoon character. I didn't care. It was cold.

Low clouds held tight to the mountain, showing no sign of letting go. We remounted and climbed to higher ground where we could eat lunch while waiting for the fog to lift. The spotting scopes we hauled were absolutely useless in such an environment. If the mist didn't dissipate soon, I wouldn't have been opposed to returning to camp where a toasty fire could thaw me out.

When lunch ended, the fog retreated. It was replaced by a threatening dark cloud that moved with menacing speed and purpose. Umbrellas began popping up among the trackers and porters. We were handed one seconds before a rain pelted us and soaked all our gear. We found a relatively dry spot to hunker. I sat down, pulling my knees to my chest. I cared little about nyala or anything other than a dry, warm bed.

The rain washed away the fog, opening up hills and mountains covered with heather and rocks. The valleys and mountainsides were green and lively in every direction. Small, jagged outcroppings jutted into peaks. A low cloud moved in, hanging a few meters above our heads. At times, the mountain seemed to fight to keep the fog at bay, at other times, it appeared to will it down. It was as if the mountain was struggling with two separate personalities. The more welcoming side was winning, but how long it could hold out was anyone's guess.

The window of opportunity prodded us to lookout points where we could glass. Within moments, nyala were spotted on opposite hillsides by Nassos and Hussein. Both were young males. Thorough glassing in all directions revealed four more, two females with a young bull and a single female two ridges away. The rain had them moving, but the fog could roll back in at any moment.

"I think we will go take a closer look at that female," Nassos pointed across the vast, green landscape. "There may be a bull bedded down nearby."

Mary bundled up, but still found keeping warm while shrouded in fog and rain a losing battle.

Hussein prepared the horses. We hunted with another Hussein during our previous trip, but this short, thin man was native to this area. Most days he wore olive greens and a shiny silver watch on his left wrist, given to him by a previous hunter. He had a distinct light and lively laugh. We rarely saw him without a smile. His English was almost non-existent, but his hard work, exceptional hunting skills and exuberant sense of humor substituted for conventional communication in grand fashion.

We couldn't see the cow with our naked eyes. She was just a small dot on the mountainside with our binoculars. It seemed so far. The altitude was high, but not excessively steep. If not for the lack of oxygen, the trekking would've been more pleasant. Thin air strained our unaccustomed lungs into tight, little balloons.

Moments after we mounted up to head off, my legs and back stiffened. I dismounted to walk my steed. The air sucked at my lungs like a vacuum. Before long, I was back on the horse, opting for a pain in the ass over a caving chest cavity. I found myself on a tedious routine, not nearly as tough as I thought I was. On again, off again. Ride, walk. After a while, my horse became impatient. He wouldn't stop when I wanted him to. He'd nip at my jacket and take a step forward whenever I tried to get on or off. Irritability summed up our woman/horse relationship quite well before the day ended – the first day.

The distance to the nyala had been closed. If she were still where we'd last seen her, she would be just over the next ridge. We left the horses and Dick's mule with one of the trackers before proceeding up the hill in a back-straining crouch that became a crawl as we reached the apex. She was gone. If she'd held the attention of an amorous bull, he disappeared with her.

We hunted back to camp. Between my intermittent forays in and out of the saddle, I took in the beauty around us. When my horse wasn't acting up and as long as my rear could stand it, I especially enjoyed the higher vantage point upon his back. The mist closed in around us. It didn't take long for the mountain tops to be swallowed up. One by one, peaks disappeared and fog billowed into the shallow valleys. Our elevation was high. To look out at the topography, you wouldn't realize it. It was more reminiscent of the rolling foothills of eastern Colorado, only much greener and near 13,000 feet as opposed to 6,000 or 7,000. At the same time, the terrain was mountainous and we felt it. The inclines, though not always abrupt and sheer, were the type that went up forever. They burned our legs, tested our stamina.

In many areas, we found ourselves blocked on one side by steep walls, becoming too treacherous to continue riding horses. Heather covered the hillsides; in some areas it was higher than our horse's heads. The quest, the honest and intimate relationship with nature pushed us on.

Three duikers stared inquisitively as we passed by. Hares were darting every which way. Ravens as big as vultures were always present. I began to wonder if they were following us. I felt like I was one of those cowboys riding in the old westerns, hanging on by a thread with vultures circling overhead. Only our vultures were huge, black undertakers perched on rocks, slowly turning their heads as we sauntered along, ogling us with their empty black stares.

The fog eventually overtook us as we dragged ourselves into camp without becoming scraps for scavengers. Camp, a series of canvas tents, became our sanctuaries when rain pelted the roof and wind whipped the flaps. The focal point, as in most hunting camps, was the fire. Its warmth was always comfortable after long, cold, wet days. If it wasn't raining too much or the wind wasn't howling, we were drawn to the blaze, mesmerized by its flickering flames.

Joe found us beside the fire when he finally strolled into camp.

"So? How did you do?" I asked.

"We walked a lot."

"Did you see any nyala?"

"One, but it was way off in the distance. We went up to the top. Over 13,000 feet."

"You must be tired."

"I'm okay. It was easier for me to walk than ride the horse. We walked for six hours straight, the wind started blowing and it was pretty cold."

"Pretty cold? I was freezing," I said.

"Did you guys do any good?"

"No," Dick said. "We saw a few when the fog cleared, but that was it. Maybe tomorrow. I guess we'll be going where you went today and you won't be going so high tomorrow."

The fire couldn't hold off chilly night air for long. We bundled up and headed straight for bed right after dinner. It was a cold, restless night. I wasn't used to sleeping in a stocking cap.

"It's a little chilly out this morning," Dick said, slipping back into the tent after his quick morning visit to the bushes outside. Men have it so easy.

"That's the understatement of the year. It's freezing."

My husband smiled and blew warm air onto his fingers.

I wrapped myself up in four layers, mobility be damned. Before I knew it, I was back in the saddle again – literally. The fog was thick again. It was like trying to navigate through whipped cream. Frost clung to the heather in the damp, frosty air. I felt like the heather, surrounded by an icy blanket I couldn't escape. After nearly three hours up and down the mountains on that cheeky beast of a horse, I couldn't take it anymore. My rear end and back felt like Roger Maris had been using them for batting practice. I remembered riding horses when I was young as a lot of fun. I guess time and lethargy chew you up and spit you out. Nassos promised I would get used to the saddle, but I thought he was just saying that to keep my spirits up. I was beginning to think this mountain nyala hunting was more trouble than it was worth. After all, I am not a masochist.

I had to remind myself we were only a couple days into the hunt. I had similar misgivings on other trips that turned out to be some of the greatest adventures of my life. I'd stick it out for a few more days before passing judgment. I just wished the weather would clear a bit.

The fog broke. Within a few minutes of stopping to glass the hillsides, we spotted a mountain nyala.

"That is a good nyala," Nassos said. "We will glass him for a while. See what he does."

It didn't take long for him to bed down.

"We're going to have to climb to the other side of the mountain, get downwind and come up over the top of him."

"Will he stay that long?"

"Yes, he should stay. Let's go get your nyala."

Two hours and a barrage of aching muscles later, we crested the mountain, finding ourselves staring down into an empty canyon. I started glassing – maybe we didn't see it – maybe it was behind some heather. Nassos knew right away.

"This is the wrong canyon. We came one canyon too far." Nassos turned away. "Let's go."

We hiked back down to where we'd tethered the horses.

Backtracking slowly, I paid attention only to the next foot of ground ahead of me. I was in a daze until one of the spotters stopped and pointed.

"There he is." Nassos said. "There, in the clearing. Come Mary, grab your gun."

The nyala had seen us as we crossed over the ridge. He was at that brief stage when his decision to bolt for safety was imminent. He stared at us, rigid and tense, recognition transforming to alarm. Seconds were a luxury we didn't have. By the time I shouldered the rifle and found him through the scope, he was on the move. He glided over the ridge in effortless bounds, vanishing into another canyon. Dick and Nassos ran after him. I just didn't have the energy to run. They saw him slink into a patch of heather. They waited a few moments, Dick's rifle ready, but he didn't reappear.

"We will sneak down around that boulder to see if we can find him," Nassos said, wiping his forehead with his palm.

They worked their way down. When they peered around the rock, the bull had moved. He was looking back up the canyon, checking his back trail for pursuers. Despite the cold temperatures, Dick's brow was thick with sweat. Steam emanated off his head from the rush up the mountain. His breaths were hard and short. His lungs struggled to find oxygen, his glasses fogging over from the heat rising off his body. There was still time. The nyala's attention was focused on the canyon's rim and they were nearly level with him. Dick rubbed his glasses. It left streaks of condensation that blurred his vision. At least he could see. Good enough to shoot the spiral horned antelope 150 yards away? Just barely.

He took his time, trying to pull his focus from the droplets on his glasses and project it to the mountain nyala. His finger edged to the trigger. He touched it lightly. Then the nyala briefly stiffened and was gone the next instant. Nassos and Dick stood to find the nyala's source of panic. At the top of the hill, a water-bearer stood tall – he was smiling and waving at them, oblivious to his blunder.

By the time Dick and Nassos made it back up the mountain, they'd cooled off some and held their tongues. Nassos put his hands on his hips, studying a black cloud picking up power as it crept darkly toward us.

"Rain's coming," he said. "Three hours by horse back to camp. We are going to get wet."

We mounted up to head down the mountain, but the massive cloud rolled in like a freight train and swallowed the sun. Day's brightness curled into shadows in a matter of seconds. A low distant rumble was the only warning to a deluge that all but stole away visibility. We had no way of knowing if we were walking close to the edge of a cliff or deep ravine. I could barely see the ground under the horse's feet, but we pressed on. My horse stumbled several times. I heard the other horses slipping as well. I could just make out the rear end of the horse ahead of me. As long as I didn't hear any loud crashes or shouts, I felt some comfort. These guys know what they're doing, I told myself. They live here – have to deal with this all the time. But in the end, I was kidding myself.

We had to be lost. How could anyone know where they were going in such blindness? I was fearful my horse might lead me over the rim of a canyon, prayed that he wouldn't. I was drenched and cold. Nobody said a word. How could they all be so calm? We'd never make it back to camp. I wouldn't make it another hour. Fear and cold rain flowed through my veins. It was all I could do to keep them from consuming me. I remember thinking to myself that if we made it back to camp, I would just stay there the rest of the trip.

It wasn't beyond me to exaggerate and lie to myself in distressing situations.

Just when despair took over, my beloved horse stepped onto the road. The road. It sounds so trite, but at that moment it was as soothing a sight as I had seen. It wouldn't be much longer.

All doubts of making it back to camp washed away with the rain. The knowledge we weren't lost and thoughts of dry clothes supplied me with all the energy I needed for the last few miles. I had made it. We'd never been in any real danger and Nassos and the others knew right where they were going, but I didn't know that. Sprinklings of panic had begun to form in my stomach. With sheer grit and trust in our guides, I was able to suppress it. I arrived in camp exhausted, wretched and sodden, but relieved and maybe just a little wiser.

I was initially worried that Joe wasn't back yet, but he arrived shortly after us and those inescapable motherly fears were alleviated. Though he was wet like the rest of us, he looked no worse for wear. He and Hussein were laughing. I thought maybe they found their nyala, but they had merely demolished the walls of communication. They found humor and friendship didn't rely on words. The two of them made quite a pair. Joe was the tall, American teenager with long, blond hair, a lip full of tobacco and a look of wonder in his eyes. I've met few teenagers who do not know everything. Confronted with a situation far from anything he'd ever encountered, I believe Joe began to understand how little we all ever really know a bit sooner than he might have.

Hussein, on the other hand, was a thin, short native who'd spent his entire life in Ethiopia. His cheerful personality allowed little room for sorrow or anger. His eyes missed nothing. They revealed a man of understanding who found pleasure in other people's enjoyment. He and Joe, though strikingly dissimilar, were the genuine article. What you see is what you get. They felt no need to be something they weren't. I think they saw this in each other. A common link distinguishing them as pals almost instantly and without effort. I drifted off to sleep that night knowing with certainty that bringing our youngest son along to Ethiopia was the right decision.

Call of the Wild: Joe

Though I didn't realize it then, Ethiopia was a revelation, an enchanting land of wonder and possibilities. If I'd known the incredible gift I'd been given, I would've taken a closer look around – removed the blaring headphones from my ears and lost the batteries to my Gameboy. But what did I know? I was a brash kid, more excited about missing a month of school than becoming a world traveler because my parents' generosity knows few bounds.

I never hunted much before then, not since my brother David and I were on the outside of adolescence looking in. I guess after my sense of wonder focused all its energy on the opposite sex, I let that part of my life fade. I didn't know it then, but Ethiopia re-ignited a spark that had been nearly snuffed out; left at Lake McConaughy with two hand-me-down recurve bows and the memory of two young brothers chasing cottontails without a care in the world. We knew true freedom then, doing only what came natural. There were moments on those rolling plains that were perfect, moments when a clear understanding of what it means to be brothers touched our souls and became a part of us forever. Sure, there were times when our ignorance lost sight of that understanding, but bonds molded by blood are not easily severed. There would be days in the future when two brothers, no longer young, would stalk game in silence and for fleeting flashes, know what it means to be free, what it means to be brothers.

Ethiopia had a hand in this. I arrived in Africa a young punk whose view of the world was narrow at best. I like to believe I left a little wiser with the help of a wild untouched land, a non-English speaking native named Hussein, and a small Greek who taught me how to shoot. Nassos learned the hard way I wasn't as skilled as I thought I was.

Mom and Dad tried to get me to the target range with them to teach me how to shoot properly. The few times I went, I usually brought a buddy, caring less about learning proper technique than trying to impress my friends. All their instructions and attempts to show me the way, "went in one ear and right out the other," as Mom often said. I hit the targets a few times at 100 yards in optimal conditions, naïvely believing I was a good shot. The day Nassos led me to a nice mountain nyala was the first, but far from last, time hunting taught me humbling lessons.

"Have you ever shot a gun before?" Nassos asked.

My appearance apparently wasn't that of a great white hunter.

"Yeah, I've shot targets with my mom and dad."

He didn't ask if I was any good, so I let him think I was, even though deep down I was beginning to feel I'd spent an inadequate amount of time practicing. From what I could gather during the first few days of hunting, my target wasn't likely to be standing still 100 yards away under good conditions. Quite the contrary. Conditions were harsh. Wind, rain and fog were constant and few animals stand still in the open at 100 yards. Mountain nyala were often on opposite hillsides at 300 yards or more, half covered with vegetation and rarely motionless. But, like I said, those thoughts were buried. On the surface, I was still the know-it-all teenager. At that age, believing you know more than an adult often trumps all other cards.

Later that day, we were glassing from the side of a steep incline. Using rocks and heather to break our outline, we stayed a few yards from the top. I wasn't paying much attention and, to be totally honest, was a little bored. We hadn't seen a nyala all day, except for a few females four or five ridges away. I figured by the time we saw one, it would be so far away we wouldn't have time to reach it before dark anyway, so I wasn't as into it as I should've been. I scanned the mountains for a while, daydreaming.

"Joe. Get over here. Hurry."

Nassos was a few yards below. I grabbed my rifle, questioning him with a look. He shook his head up and down, a little agitated.

When I positioned myself next to him, he said, "Do you see the nyala there on the next ridge?"

I didn't see it.

"Level with us, straight across."

I finally found it.

"The one below that big rock?"

"Yes, get him in your scope. He's about 300 yards. Do you have him?"

"I can't find him," I said.

"Find him over your scope and then find him through it. Can you see him?"

"Not yet."

This was nothing like shooting targets back in Nebraska.

"He's right there. Look at the tree and come down." He looked at me with wide, irritated eyes.

"Okay, I found him."

"Good. Shoot him on the shoulder."

I missed so badly Nassos wondered if I really did see him. The nyala was suddenly alert, but in his confusion as to where the shot came from, he froze.

"You missed. Shoot again."

Taut seconds ticked by. I tried to find him in my scope again with similar troubles. Eventually I found him. Neophyte that I was, even I could tell he wasn't sticking around much longer. Before I could get the crosshairs on his shoulder, he started to move. After two steps he hesitated.

"Shoot. Shoot."

It was now or never. I fired.

"You hit him."

I don't know who was more surprised: me, Nassos or the bull.

"You better shoot again."

By the time I reloaded and found him again, it was too late. He was gone. And he wasn't hit well.

"In the guts, I think," Nassos said.

We searched until dark without luck. A heavy dose of rain and sleet didn't simplify our task. Downtrodden, we proceeded to camp. I'd been knocked down more than a few notches. During our return hike, I caught up with Nassos who had a surprisingly long and fast stride for his size. I didn't know where to start. He waited patiently for me to begin.

"Obviously, I don't shoot as well as I thought. You think maybe you could...uh...teach me to shoot better?" I'd left my pride on the track of a wounded nyala.

I wasn't hungry and didn't feel like hanging out at the fire, but Mom and Dad were already there, sipping on drinks. They were smiling when we joined them, but that changed at the sight of our somber expressions. I felt sick to my stomach, wanting only to retreat to my tent. Mom and Dad wanted to visit for a while.

"Kidane and the men will go find him tomorrow," Nassos said.

I didn't share his confidence. A half-hearted smile was all I could conjure.

"We will find him," Nassos said, placing his hand on my shoulder.

I tried to force a smile.

The words I left unsaid jumbled into a knot, churning in my stomach. I wanted to go to my tent, but took a seat beside my father instead.

"How'd you guys do?"

Maybe their day had been better than mine and maybe, if I did my best to listen, a gut-shot mountain nyala suffering in the dark might not consume my thoughts. A little respite would've been nice.

"We spent the day riding and walking," Mom said.

"I couldn't tell you which hurts worse," Dad said. "My butt and back from riding or my feet and legs from hiking up and down these mountains. We went back to the top. I think I'm going to pay for it the entire hunt. I hurt all over."

"I think the riding was much worse," Mom said. "My backside's still numb. This high altitude takes everything out of us so quickly. If it weren't for the horses, I would've collapsed a long time ago. Then when the fog and rain and darkness set in, I thought we wouldn't be able to find our way back. I thought we were lost. It seemed like we stepped over more rocks and through more streams than we had before. I always feel better after we hit the road. Anyway, we didn't see any nyala."

I only ate a few quiet bites at dinner.

"You know, it happens to everybody," Mom said.

"Yeah, I know." I excused myself and went to bed.

I didn't sleep much. Heavy rains and strong winds pelted and ripped at the tent. The canvas whipped violently throughout the night. Though we didn't get flooded out or blown away, it did little to aid sleep. The nyala's blood and tracks would be washed away. When morning's bustle stirred me, I felt weak and ill. My legs were unsteady. I felt lightheaded and nauseous. A few minutes out of bed proved to be more than I could handle, so I laid back down.

"Are you going hunting today?" Mom asked from outside the tent.

"I don't feel well."

"Can I get you anything?"

"No, I'll be okay."

"Do you want me to stay with you?"

"No, Mom. You go ahead; I'll be fine."

It was a nice gesture and I knew she meant it, but I wasn't that sick. For her to stay in camp would only serve to waste a day of hunting for two of us.

"Are you sure?"

"Yes, I'm sure. Have fun."

"Okay. Kidane and some of the others are going out to look for your nyala. I sure hope they find it."

So did I. I drifted in and out of sleep until about midday. I had some strange dreams. Dreams of mountain nyala with long, sharp teeth eating each other and chasing me down with mouths full of foam and fire in their eyes. Those images could've given Rip Van Winkle insomnia.

When I emerged from the tent, I was greeted with a clear, sunlit sky and a slight breeze. A low, dark cloud hugged the mountaintops in the distance. The weather wouldn't last. I ducked back into the relative comfort of the roomy tent. Resting my head on the pillow, I stared at the ceiling. I drifted down to thoughts deep within myself, thoughts left unsaid. I was by no means a deep teenager, but neither was I as shallow as I pretended to be. Quiet times often force us to confront ourselves. I had unasked questions with unspoken answers. I wondered why anyone would want to hunt if it made them feel the way I did. I wondered why my parents put themselves through physical challenges that pushed my youth to the edge just for hunting. I never thought about these things when David and I were flinging arrows at cottontails. We were just following the primal instincts of boys. Did I still have that? Did I care?

I had no answers, but was determined to find them. I didn't know if I could find the answers in the mountains of Ethiopia or not. I was sure I wouldn't find them lying on a cot in a tent. I didn't know if my thoughts were even worth the trouble. I was just a kid after all. But it was that kid in me that gave me the courage to try.

I don't know how long I laid there staring at bare canvas, but when I left the tent, the sky was still clear, the black cloud had inched closer and the temperature had fallen. Mom, Dad, Nassos and Hussein were by the fire. Hussein and Nassos seemed to be in a playful argument.

"No, no, no." Hussein said. I couldn't understand the rest, but he was pointing at himself triumphantly.

I took a seat by my mother.

"Are you feeling better?"

"Much thanks. You guys are back early."

"It was so rainy and cold, we decided to come in early and have a shower. We haven't had one for a few days. I feel so skuzzy."

"What's going on?" I pointed at Nassos and Hussein, who began laughing.

"Oh they're arguing over who won the race."

"What race?"

"When we hit the road, they decided to race back to camp, galloping off on their horses. One of the boys leading the horses tried to hand me the reins and give me a brush from the heather, gesturing I should race too. I had to laugh at that. I told him the horse would take over and I'd probably end up in Addis. I don't know if he understood me, but he didn't press it any further."

Nassos strolled over, and before he walked by, he leaned down and said, "I won."

"No, no, no," Hussein shouted, pounding his chest with his fist, a stern but fake expression on his face.

Joe decided he'd better hone his shooting skills before trying for another animal.

"Looks like rain again," Mom said. She made no attempt to hide her disgust. "I better try and have a shower before it starts."

Nassos returned holding my rifle and a box of shells. "Come, Joe. I will teach you now."

I knew if I truly wanted to discover if hunting was for me, I'd have to learn to shoot properly. I listened closely to all Nassos' instructions, even feeling a little excited to learn something new. My instructor was patient with a genuine desire to show me what I was doing wrong and teach me as much as he could in the short time we had.

"You will still miss," he said when we were done. "And every hunting situation will be different. You will be learning as the trip continues, but there are a few things to always remember and apply to every shot. Always be certain of your target, remain calm and remember to squeeze easy like I showed you."

About that same time Kidane returned with some of the trackers. Their solemn expressions were all the evidence I needed. Their search for my nyala had been fruitless. I turned to head for the tent, but Nassos stopped me.

"I will find your nyala, Joe. I promise." His penetrating stare was a laser of sincerity.

I appreciated his effort, but a gut-shot animal can travel great distances before dying. With its trail washed away in the rains, I was painfully aware they'd never find it. After that, I tried to put it behind me, but Nassos, true to his word sent trackers out to search the heather everyday for the remainder of our trip. Men, whose jobs included other duties, spent countless hours in an attempt to rectify my mistake. As a result, the entire camp staff had heavier workloads. I should've been out there looking for it, but Nassos would have none of it. He said I hadn't come halfway around the world not to hunt. They would exhaust all efforts to locate the bull. I should try not to worry about it.

I attempted to push it from my thoughts and would be lying if I said I totally failed. It was the silent nights, alone in my tent, that were hardest. I saw the mountain nyala hunch over and gallop over the crest of a hill. I could picture it lying under heather in a dry spot, panting, losing life with each breath, slowly dying. But this was Africa, harsh and cruel, where one creature's misfortune is another's reward. I could only hope a leopard or other predator found life in a young man's painful lesson.

The morning was a different story all together. Stretching muscles, dew dripping off plants, the scent of sweet, purple clovers and a bustling camp all signaled the promise of a new day. Later, methodically glassing for a bushbuck in a deep tree-covered valley, I watched a nyala feed into a clearing before disappearing around a bend. A soothing peace came over me. How had I missed the beauty of these antelope – sleek coats, graceful stride, powerful physique? How had I failed to notice the beauty in which the nyala lived?

A stubborn mist blurred the line where earth met sky. I never knew so many shades of green existed. It was there, watching the shadows for movement, losing sight of the treetops in the haze, I began to understand how fortunate I was. Not from anything I'd done, but just because I was born to the most generous people I would ever know. Dad believed in hard work, demanding nothing less of his children. If we were to find financial success, it would be on our own. My parent's generosity came from a much deeper love. They tried to give us a piece of themselves, a look at the world the way they saw it, a perspective unencumbered by mist.

Few people see things so clearly. The world is an opaque prism; too often, it is our own self that is most difficult to recognize. They know who they are and exactly who they aspire to be. They revealed a part of themselves I had never seen and led me to a part of myself I had never known. That kind of generosity cannot be repaid.

I saw my mother and father in a different light around the fire that evening and listened with interest to their stories. Something told me to relish the moment. Such times are too often rare and fleeting.

Dad was always direct and to the point. His answers to queries were often condensed to a few words. This conciseness belies a high intellect and large vocabulary. Success of the kind he has attained is never acquired by dumb luck.

"How are you doing?" is most often followed by "fine." "What are you doing?" by "I'm working." "What did you think of that book?" "It was okay." or "It wasn't bad." or in some cases he just stuck his hand out palm down, tilting it back and forth. So when I asked what he did that day, I was not surprised by his answer.

"We hunted nyala."

"Did you see any?"

"Not today. That's why they call it hunting."

"Did you have fun?"

"It's always fun."

"Did you go up high again?"

"Yeah, about 13,000-feet, but we couldn't see through the fog and rain."

Mom was always more detailed than Dad.

"We sat up in that cold, wet, rainy fog from 7:30 until 11:30 before we were so cold and wet Nassos started a fire to warm us up," she said. "We couldn't see far anyway. If it was up to me, we would've started the fire at 7:30. After lunch, it started to clear, but the clouds were just teasing us, because right after I pulled all my raingear off, folded it up and put it away, the clouds came barreling back in and it started to rain again. I hope we get our nyalas soon so we can move down to the hippo camp where it's warmer."

She scooted her chair closer to the fire and pulled on her hair in a hopeless effort to keep it from going flat.

"It sure is beautiful though. I can't believe how many flowers can stay so pretty in the cold weather. At first glance, all you see is heather, but there's a wide array of plant life – even on top of the mountain where trees don't grow. Today I saw snap dragons, clovers, flowering cactus and three different kinds of moss. I also saw some pretty yellow flowers, which bloom flat to the ground in the game trails, some flowers that look like our strawflowers, rose moss and alyssum. It sure is beautiful, isn't it?"

I nodded. I tend to take after my father, but I enjoyed my mother's energy, so I gave her another nudge.

"You see any animals?"

"We caught a glimpse of a leopard in broad daylight, which was exciting. We also heard a gunshot around that same time and thought you'd shot your bushbuck. It turned out the shot came from a nearby village. Nassos said they were mourning a death. Other than that we saw two klipspringers on top of the mountain and two nyala – a cow and a young bull. We saw the female first. She looked like she was alone, but

Nassos thought there might be a bull lying nearby. We snuck into position and then one of the trackers gave out a call with his mouth that sounded like a distressed hare. Sure enough a young bull stood up. We didn't see much after that – except for fog and rain."

"You know the rain is like a bad stomach," Nassos said. "You get the diarrhea until you get rid of the bug. It's cloudy, windy and rainy until the front clears."

A pungent aroma emanated from the rain after that – or, at least, I thought it did.

The front must've stalled directly above us the following morning. Keeping dry would be futile. It would be for Mom and Dad anyway. They climbed into the heavy stuff while Hussein and I worked our way to a lower elevation in search of Menelik's bushbuck.

I didn't know it, but a few of my unasked queries were about to answer themselves.

At one point during our descent, I slipped on a moss covered rock, catching myself with the aid of my behind.

"Shit."

Hussein gave me a questioning look without concealing his smile. He extended his hand to help me up. When he noticed mud had transferred from my hand to his, he held it up and said, "Sheet."

We both laughed as he wiped it on his pants. Hussein's pronunciation of my English expletive was, from that point on, our favorite common word. For Hussein in particular.

If he lost a track, "Sheet." When the fog set in, "Sheet. Sheet." When we blew a stalk on an animal, "Sheet. Sheet. Sheet." His new-found vulgarity was often accompanied by a lowered head and a stomping foot, but he almost always ended it by looking up at me, smiling. His frustration was genuine enough, but he realized, better than anyone I've ever known, that life without laughter would be a boring life indeed.

When we jumped a female bushbuck, we both ducked as we watched her crash into the bush.

"Sheet."

I decided to throw him a loop.

"Son of a bitch."

Hussein looked over wide-eyed at first, then with a more quizzical stare. He appeared to be in great concentration for a few moments, then shook his head up and down.

"Sunabeech," he said, smiling.

I couldn't hold it in and began laughing. Hussein stood up with a big smile and a more pronounced nod. "Sunabeech," he said, slapping my shoulder. "Sunabeech."

He was quite pleased with the new addition to his vocabulary. If he didn't understand what it meant, I'm sure someone would eventually let him know. By his use of *sunabeech* over the next few days, I'd guess he was fully aware of its connotation.

The rain hadn't bothered us for over an hour, but the air was like a damp cloth. Tree limbs drooped with the weight of the season. We led a few mules with assorted gear, but none of us elected to ride. There were six of us. Hussein and I; two young Muslims, whose names I couldn't pronounce; a heavyset native, Boletto; and a tall, mysterious looking fellow whose manner was cool, calculated and fluid, that of a warrior. He wore a lavender sash over his left shoulder and kept mostly to himself. He seemed to have a grievance with one of the Muslim boys, but he worked hard and was one of the best trackers in the group. The way he stood tall with his head high, his deep-set, predator eyes and unyielding features gave him the appearance of being unapproachable. I admired his tracking abilities from a respectful distance, doing most of my communicating (or lack thereof) with Hussein and to a lesser extent Boletto. The six of us made an eclectic, if not strange, group of hunters. Other than the apparent rift between the young warrior and the Muslim, everyone worked together well and the hunt progressed smoothly.

We'd just walked through a clearing, into the dark shadows and thick undergrowth of the forest when Hussein suddenly dropped to one knee. I followed, scanning the brush ahead of us. We were frozen for a long moment, Hussein's gaze focused and intense; my own vainly scanning for confirmation of game. Then, without taking his eyes from the target, Hussein pointed through a miniscule hole in the vegetation, a line of sight squeezed hard by patchy edges. The lane my bullet had to travel would need to miss crisscrossing twigs by inches to penetrate the left shoulder of the bushbuck. His horns were aged with spiral length, his ears flickering this way and that way to pinpoint the source of danger it sensed nearby.

I was suddenly alone, but part of something bigger than myself. I was connected with intimacy to the earth beneath my feet, the breeze caressing my cheeks, the thin tree trunk providing balance, and the small-bodied bushbuck giving spark to a primal fire burning within me. Without conscious thought, without the human need to question why, I sent a bullet into the bushbuck's heart, instantly ending its life.

Hussein was on his feet, running, the others on his heels whooping and hollering in excitement. Boletto shook my hand as he went by. Standing back in the shadows, unwilling to dash off in a show of emotion, the young man with the lavender robe over his left shoulder looked into my eyes and gave a slow nod. I returned a half smile and nodded back before marching off to inspect my first big-game animal.

I was greeted by smiles, handshakes, thumbs up and one exhaled

Joe and the crew with his bushbuck.

"Sunabeech". I didn't completely understand, but in that moment I realized I was a hunter. I knew I would continue down that path. The emotions were overwhelming – some joyous and exhilarating, others sorrowful and draining. I'd never known anything like it. But it was more than those feelings. It was the pride I felt in shooting perfectly and calmly, squeezing just as Nassos had instructed. It was the camaraderie of men, hunters. I could barely communicate with them, but knew with absolute certainty that, despite all our differences, we understood each other. The link we shared was a bond that had been part of us before our births as surely as the sand was part of the earth. It was a brutally honest relationship with life and the most intimate understanding of my parents I would ever know.

Part of the safari experience is having the luxury to hunt as hard as you can without the added chores of cooking, cleaning, field-dressing, skinning, packing, building fires and setting up camp. You are free to hunt more and work less; it's all part of the cost. Many safaris are encumbered with hardships, especially those when the industry wasn't so popular and the operators were not constantly improving their outfits. As competition grew fiercer, few traveling sportsmen have been required to spend much time with the inevitable work that accompanies all hunts – not unless they wanted to.

I've always enjoyed hard work. I find pleasure in working with my hands. Though I knew little of game cleaning and skinning, I dove right in and got my hands bloody. Hussein tried to stop me at first, but shrugged his shoulders at my resolve. The others looked at me as if I were crazy. I had the feeling they hadn't seen such behavior from western hunters often. But that's what I wanted. One of the other great things about a safari is that those footing the bill are usually accommodated. I dug in with both hands, receiving numerous guffaws when I pretended to take a bite out of the raw heart. Hussein thought it so funny he just had to have a picture.

Upon our return to camp, Nassos was the first to congratulate me.

"I hear you shot very well. A steady, one-shot kill according to Hussein. Good job."

"Thanks."

"We finally have some fresh meat for camp. We were all getting tired of chicken."

I was on top of the world. Everyone was excited about the trophy I'd taken and the meat from the bushbuck was tender and succulent. After I recounted the story for the last time that evening, I said goodnight to my parents. The admiration in their eyes was comforting. My respect for them grew that day. Their pride supplied me with a cache of confidence that would last me throughout the remainder of the hunt.

I slept well, dreaming of another time. A time when two brothers chased cottontails with recurve bows and a life free of limitations. A time when these two brothers knew, without question, the world was a bottomless bowl of possibility.

Bandits: Dick

"It was cold again last night," Mary said. "Like fog was wrapping around the back of my neck. I felt wet all night."

"I wonder why they didn't wake us up this morning," I said. "It's already seven."

"Probably because the weather is so bad. We'll be lucky if it clears up enough for us to take a nyala. Nassos even seems to be getting nervous about it. I guess I can't blame him, but he doesn't control the weather. We could be hippo hunting at Langano."

"I really want to get a mountain nyala though. I'm convinced it's the toughest hunt in all of Africa."

At the time, considering my somewhat limited exposure to "all" of Africa, that was a bold statement. Fourteen years and more than 25 safaris later, a sound argument can be made to defend that statement. I would rank bongo and Lord Derby eland in the same class, but in only a week of mountain nyala hunting, I knew there couldn't be too many hunts anywhere in Africa that could push you to such physical and mental limits day in and day out. I was frustrated, but I wasn't willing to give up. Like Nassos, I do not control the weather.

"I'm sorry," Nassos said at breakfast. "It's just raining too hard to hunt. I am really sorry."

"Hey, the rain isn't your fault. We know that."

Nassos smiled, but it wasn't genuine. "When the weather breaks, we will go shoot a nyala."

While cleaning up after lunch, Nassos sat down between Joe and Mary exacerbated. "If the rain does not abate by 2:00, we will have to forget about hunting today. It's too far up the mountain. I am sorry." He started to the kitchen tent, then turned back. "Be ready, just in case."

He looked up, letting the cold rain spatter his face, shrugged his shoulders then disappeared.

Mary, Joe and I stayed in the dining tent. Nassos had set up a Hibachi with hot coals for our comfort. At 1:30, Joe poked his head out.

"It's hardly raining," he said.

"Yeah, sure." We weren't as gullible as he thought.

"No, seriously. Here comes Nassos. I better go get my stuff."

When he took off for his tent, Mary and I looked at each other. Maybe the weather was clearing.

Nassos slipped into the tent and put his hands on his hips. "Ready?"

We rushed to our tent, threw on our jackets, grabbed our rifles and hurried to the horses. We all went together, but it turned out to be more of a family horseback ride (mule-back in my case - I think it was the only beast indifferent enough to put up with me). We glassed a few times and saw nyala so far away attempting to reach them before dark would be foolhardy. So we headed back to camp without a nyala once again. Frustration was beginning to rear its ugly head. My attempts to suppress it were beginning to fail. A new ingredient was added to the brewing dissatisfaction; an ingredient that, left unchecked, could permeate through your veins and consume you. A tiny grain of obsession had been added to the cauldron. Caution must be taken not to allow it to boil over.

A strange thing happened that night. Around midnight, Mary awoke from a stirring sleep.

"It's so hot," she said.

I rolled over and mumbled, "Good, maybe we'll get a shot at a nyala tomorrow."

I should've kept my mouth shut.

A rooster crowed at 4:30 a.m. waking us up half an hour early.

"Where the hell did that rooster come from?"

"How am I supposed to know," Mary said. "Someone must've brought it into camp yesterday."

"Hey, listen."

"To what."

"Just listen. What do you hear?"

"I don't hear anything."

"Exactly. It's not raining."

Outside the air was cool, but not cold, with a slight breeze. What little fog there was appeared to be lifting. Camp was alive with optimism. Breakfast was hurried as anticipation burst from the dining tent. Nassos showed up as we were finishing, apologizing for the crowing early in the morning.

"I was having a good dream too," he said. Then, more to himself than to us, he said quietly, "I must find that rooster."

We never heard the rooster again and don't know what happened to it, but Nassos seemed to enjoy the breaded chicken that night with a bit more satisfaction than usual.

"I will take Mary and Joe today," Nassos said. "You and Kidane will go to the high mountains; a very good spot for nyala. Is this okay?"

"Whatever you think is best."

"I think it would be best if you would shoot a nyala today. Do not let Joe show you up with his bushbuck. He's walking around in the cold with no shirt on, hair waving in the wind."

Nassos imitated Joe's walk and waved his hands behind his ears to demonstrate Joe's long hair. "He will leave here with a big head, thinking he is the greatest hunter around. I do not think you should let him do that." Nassos smiled.

I laughed. "I'll do the best I can."

"You go get your nyala Dick."

It was a beautiful day. The best we'd had. You could see for miles. Every now and then the light clouds high in the sky would part, revealing a brilliant blue picture we'd almost forgotten existed. When the sun shined through, it was as if heat rose from the earth. Spotting scopes were unpacked and distant mountainsides scanned. Females and young bulls, apparently awakened by the new day, appeared on every hill, feeding leisurely. Had it not been for the heather, I wouldn't have recognized the mountain.

"Nyala." Kidane held his hands apart from each other to emphasize it was a good bull as he offered up his spotting scope for me to have a look.

He had the scope lined up perfectly. When I peered through, I saw a grand bull. He carried himself differently than the females or the young bulls. He was royalty and knew it. Each step was confident, bordering on arrogance. When he slipped behind a boulder, Kidane snatched up the spotting scope.

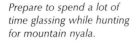

Prepare to spend a lot of time glassing while hunting for mountain nyala.

"Come, come," he said.

I followed him down the slope. Halfway down, we stopped and used our binoculars to relocate the bull. He had laid down in a large opening, making a stalk difficult. Once we started up the slope he was on, it was a slow going affair. We inched along, belly crawling from one patch of heather to the next, using slight undulations and rocks of all sizes to conceal our advance. We worked our way up the mountain until we were level with him. A slight fold on the hill was the only thing separating us from our quarry. If we could reach the fold without detection, we could use it to move within shooting range, slip up over its edge and pop him. It was a good plan, but it wouldn't be easy.

Two hours later, we'd closed the distance to 100 yards. He was still bedded down, oblivious to our presence. A shot at a bedded animal is risky, especially when the vegetation directly surrounding it conceals much of its body. In hindsight, I maybe should've taken the shot. I had a good, comfortable rest and was well within the range of my shooting capabilities, but we made a different decision. If we could just get him to stand up, I'd have a much higher percentage shot.

"Ready?"

Before we made a move, I felt a tickle of air behind my ear, a tiny gust, swiftly and silently sweeping our scent across the hillside directly into the nostrils of the nyala. The bull recognized the odor immediately – the scent of man, the scent of danger. He didn't stand and freeze to test the air for assurance. He didn't need confirmation. There was lightning in his feet, instant reaction. Second-guessing in Africa is too often fatal. This old bull had learned that long ago. He never glanced our way. He sprung to his feet. I fired, but he was ten yards down the mountain by the time my bullet embedded itself harmlessly in a bed he no longer occupied. I could've flung another shot out there, but it would have been in desperation.

Tension slipped from my shoulders and my chin dropped to my chest. All the miles walked and ridden, all the dreary days of fog and rain, every missed stalk; frustration came crashing down on me. That had been the moment of truth and I knew it. What we were here for – the long, hard days, the freezing nights, the overworked muscles from walking and riding. We endured those tribulations with gratitude. It had all come down to one instant. I blew it.

At such times, self-pity and despair can most easily have their way with the hunter. To come so close only to fail because of your own mistake is enough to make you concede. I, myself, have taken such situations with a grain of salt, saying "oh well, I had my chance." Other times, I berate myself with "should haves," "only ifs" and just plain feeling sorry for myself. But this time, my reaction sprung forth from deep within. Its name was resolve. It was then that my obsession with mountain nyala hardened. If I wasn't successful this time around, I'd be back. A few more days were all we had left in nyala camp. If the past week was indicative of the future, our chances were slim indeed.

I wouldn't have minded staying, but we'd paid to hunt hippos and other game and it wouldn't be fair to Mary and Joe. I missed my opportunity. Another chance would be great, but if it didn't present itself there was nothing I could do about it. All throughout our lives, in all our endeavors, we are restrained by time, and days were quickly dwindling. A fact of life, plain and simple. I would have to check Nassos' future availability, but a well-known, highly respected outfitter like him is most often booked up years in advance.

Under the recent developments, optimism was unable to gain a foothold. Thick fog rolling in only added to the gloom. With visibility nearing zero, the day's hunt ended two hours before it should have. Each clack of the mule's hoof on rock signaled another second we couldn't get back. There was so much I'd never done, so many mountains I hadn't climbed, so many places I'd never see, so many hunts I'd never experience. Life is too short. Nyala do not care about such human ponderings, so I to pushed those thoughts from my head. Focusing instead on the last days of the hunt.

Camp slowly began to take shape through the mist. First a blurred dark object, then an outline of a tent, then another, until we were surrounded by the familiar. What would a hunt be without the return to camp? The day's hunt over, replaced with a new anticipation, an eagerness to drift to the fire, to gather and reconnect with friends and loved ones in an open moment of storytelling and conversation unmatched in any other setting.

That evening's campfire wouldn't be disappointing. Mary and Joe hadn't yet returned, so I used the time to take my first shower in several days. It was refreshing to wash away the old stinky layer of grime and sweat and shave the stubble off my face. By the time I returned to the fire, Mary, Joe and Nassos had pulled up chairs and the high-spirited laughs suggested their day had been better than mine.

"Hey, Dad. How'd you do?"

"I had a chance, but missed. Did you guys get anything?"

"Joe shot a klipspringer," Mary said. "It was a difficult shot and he hit it perfectly. It's looking like he is the only one who's going to shoot anything this trip."

"No, no," Nassos said. "We will get more animals at the hippo camp. It will not be as hard as nyala."

I kept my thoughts to myself. Not wanting Nassos to think I was becoming too discouraged. It was probably apparent.

"So, what happened?" I asked.

"We were on our way back to camp after the fog set in," Mary said. "As we made our way down the mountain, the mist began to dissipate and for a few minutes lifted all together. The sky was even blue in patches. That's when Nassos and Hussein decided to stop. They thought it was a good spot for klipspringer. We sat behind a boulder surrounded by heather and Hussein began to make a kind of high-pitched whistling sound. Within a few moments a klipspringer bounced down the mountain, hopped on a rock and stared at us. As soon as Nassos said to, Joe fired, hitting it perfectly. The klipspringer dropped in his tracks. They sure are amazing little antelope, the way they jump around on the rocks effortlessly."

Joe sat listening to his mother's version of the hunt with an attentive smile. It's hard to read your teenage children at times, not knowing what's going through their minds, but the smile on his face and the glow in his eyes was the look all parents wish for their kids.

I hadn't seen any klipspringer yet, but that wasn't completely odd considering we were concentrating our efforts on nyala. The klipspringer's size and color allows them to blend in easily. They can move about behind heather and other vegetation without detection. The name klipspringer means "rock jumper". They live up to that name in grand fashion. Sheer rock faces are but a small hurdle for these hardy creatures, preferring the feel of rocks below their hooves to the softer soil in flat country. Klipspringers have a few distinguishing characteristics which make them a unique and desirable game species. Besides their adaptation to rocky outcrops, their meat is tasty. Klipspringer are fond of bouncing around on their blunt-tipped hooves and have a unique coat of stiff, hollow hair – a feature that, at one time, found them widely hunted because this hair was in great demand. It's a highly sought after trophy for safari hunters. The fact that Joe was able to attain one was fortunate. It would've been nice if he would've shared his luck.

The following day was filled with more frustration. Controlling my emotions was becoming a challenge. Long hard days were taking their toll. We started out together, Mary, Nassos, Hussein, Kidane and I. Joe stayed in camp to work on the presentation he had to give upon his return to school.

"You're going to get bored here in camp all day," I told him.

"I'll be fine," he said. "There's nothing left for me to hunt here anyway. If I get done early, maybe I'll go with some of the guys to look for the nyala."

They'd been looking everyday without luck.

Eventually we split up. Kidane and I began a long arduous day of riding, climbing and glassing, followed by more riding, climbing and glassing. I was dead on my feet while we hiked and dead on my ass when we rode. We spent maybe ten percent of the day glassing and the rest on the move. The most maddening aspect of the day was all the mountain nyala we encountered. Thirty of them, all cows. It was a trying day. High anticipation each time we saw a nyala, followed by a valley of disappointment each time it became apparent there was no bull in the vicinity. We rode this emotional roller coaster all day until I began to question the existence of mountain nyala bulls and, shamefully, the ability of the guides who were putting their best efforts forward for our sake.

Upon our return to camp that evening, I found Nassos adding wood to the fire.

"Did you guys see anything?"

"Just a few females and a baby klipspringer," he said. "You?"

"Thirty females. There are no males in the area," I said, only half-joking.

"We still have many days left. Our luck will turn."

I made a decision right then and there, diverging from the obsession for nyala that had its hooks in me.

"No, we have little more than a week left on our three-week safari. Mary and I might come back someday, but we brought Joe so he could experience Ethiopia. He just spent an entire day at camp because there is nothing left here for him to hunt. It wouldn't be fair to him to stay any longer because there aren't any nyala on this mountain. It's time to move on."

"I am sorry Dick, but I would really like you to get a nyala."

"Forget it. If we stay any longer, we won't have much time at the hippo camp."

"We do not need as much time there," Nassos said.

I wasn't really listening. I'd allowed all the built up frustration to speak for me. I'd left my common courtesy somewhere up in the shroud of fog. I was nearly to our tent before I turned around and approached Nassos again.

"Look," I said. "I'm sorry. I'm just tired and a little discouraged. I didn't mean in any way to imply this hasn't been a good hunt. I know you can't control the weather or the animals. However, I think it's important to move to the hippo camp soon."

"It is okay Dick, I understand. Let me apologize to you. I truly want you to get your nyala. If it was anyone else, we would be packing up right now and leaving for the other camp first thing in the morning. I understand you are frustrated, but I think we should give it one more day. If nothing," Nassos lifted his palms and shrugged his shoulders. "We move on."

"Okay," I said. "We'll hunt nyala tomorrow and leave for hippo camp on Sunday."

"Very good. We will see you for dinner."

We ate steaks from Joe's klipspringer. It was our best meal of the trip. The meat was tender and mild, served with a bean sauce. We also had macaroni and rice soup, fried potatoes, beets, carrots, and purple cabbage to complement the klipspringer. We devoured it. During a much needed break in the feast, we finally had an opportunity to talk.

"Nassos told me you saw a baby klipspringer today," I said to Mary.

"Oh it was so cute. The trackers spotted it hiding in the bushes just a few yards from where we were. Nassos was able to catch it so I could have a closer look. It started crying and shaking, so we took a quick picture and let it go when a male and a female showed up in response to its screams. It would've been a good opportunity to take a nice male. I really didn't want to shoot one under those circumstances. It was such a cute little thing, but it was frightened. We felt sorry for it, so we released it and it hopped off back to its family in the heather. That was our excitement for the day. Did you tell Joe tomorrow was our last day?"

"Yeah, I know," Joe said. "Nassos said we'd be hunting hippo from some kind of canoe or something."

"That sounds a little scary to me. But I guess we'll see."

There was a lull in the conversation for a few minutes as we all leaned back, suffering the consequences of overeating. It was Nassos

This young klipspringer sprung back to the safety of the rocks after Mary let it go.

who finally broke the silence.

"I think you should come with me to the high mountains tomorrow, Dick. We will go far and stay out very late, give it one last good effort before we leave. I think it's important for you to get a good nyala. You are my friend and the mountain nyala is one of the great trophies of Africa. You deserve to get one. Then we will try early Sunday morning before we leave for Lake Langano and the hippos. Is this okay?"

"That'll be fine," I said.

I felt bad for venting my frustrations earlier, but he seemed to understand. It appeared to be forgotten already.

The next morning we left camp not as frustrated guide and client, but as hunting buddies. Granted, Nassos and his crew did a great deal of the work that accompanies any hunt, but that's part of what we pay for. If he came to Nebraska to hunt, I'd take care of everything, including having the area scouted out. Good outfitters and professional hunters are worth their weight in diamonds. Nassos was one of the best. He was still working hard for my benefit and I was still paying him, but we considered each other more than just friends. We were two hunting pals on a quest. The air was filled with camaraderie, but at the same time embedded with the urgency of a final opportunity. We left camp with smiles and determination. I knew our chances were slim, but wasn't going to let disappointment overtake the pleasure of the things that truly make a hunt great.

I considered it as good a time as any to prod him about a future hunt.

"Mary and I were thinking we'd like to come back and give this mountain nyala another shot. Think you can put up with us for another hunt?"

Nassos laughed. "I was examining the schedule last night. I would very much like for you to come back, whether we get one today or not. Our next open date is not until 1992."

"Hold the date. Once we get back to the States, we'll iron out the details."

"It would be my pleasure," Nassos said, smiling gently. "It is cool today."

"Cool? It's freezing. My hands and feet are numb and the damn fog is as thick as butter again. I'd be cussing at my mule again if it weren't for the fact that he's keeping my ass warm."

"Just one more reason to like the mule. I believe that is one of the best things any client has ever said about our beloved mule. Next time someone complains, I will have to remind them of his redeeming feature – a built-in backside heater."

"Don't forget his stench. If you're real cold, you can just take a big whiff and it will melt your nostrils." The mule jerked his head back in apparent annoyance. "Whoa," I said. "I was just joking."

A few moments later, Nassos lifted his hands in disgust. "This fog is no good. We will go up to a good spotting place and start a fire to warm up while we wait for the fog to lift."

"So, in other words, we'll sit by the fire all day long."

"You must think positive Dick. Look at how far positive thinking has led us."

"I'm positive I am sick of fog, rain and cold. That's about all the positiveness I have left."

We warmed up by the fire for over an hour before the fog finally lifted. After that, we glassed several canyons with the luck of a two-legged frog swimming in bass-infested waters. As the day wore on, what little optimism remained vanished with the passing minutes. The resulting resignation was palpable. Even the mule's head seemed to droop a tad lower on our long trek back to camp. With an hour of daylight remaining, it would've been foolish not to pause and scan the mountains at regular intervals. We did, though we had seen no nyala in the area since the hunt began.

Of us all, Nassos retained some diligence. He would stop, dismount, find a comfortable spot and glass with quiet intensity just as he had done since the first day. I lacked his patience. I hadn't always lacked that patience. In fact, it was that same fortitude that kept Mary, my brother,

Sometimes the fog would lift allowing us to see for miles, but it was still cold.

Jim and I and on track during the formative years of Cabela's, the years in which we chose growth over salary and held other jobs to pay the bills. I knew patience well then. But that was a different kind of patience. I believed with certainty the long nights and endless weekends ignoring leisure, among other things, would eventually pay off. I didn't have that same confidence on the last day of a mountain nyala hunt in which less than a handful of bulls had been seen in nearly two weeks. The next mountain nyala I would see would probably be in 1992.

I was so unprepared when Nassos sprung to his feet and yelled at me to grab my rifle that I fumbled with it for several seconds before falling in beside him. He pointed out a fine bull two canyons away. Nassos marched off at a pace more than a little difficult to keep up with. At times, we ran, the heather slapping me, the rocks and weeds twisting and gripping at my ankles. I stumbled enough that a brisk walk turned out to be a better speed. You know, slow and steady wins the race and all. I had no problem playing the role of tortoise.

There was a dogged determination in Nassos' step as if he were racing to beat a storm. We traversed two canyons, maneuvered around heather taller than us and scaled small rock faces. I slipped once and twisted my bad knee. The day was fading around the edges and the nyala had been on the move when we first spotted him, so resting to lick my wounds was not in the cards. I limped the rest of the way up the last hill. When I peered over, huffing and puffing, barely able to lift my rifle, too fatigued to care, the nyala started running. The gun shot up to my shoulder, apparently by its own will. I jacked a shell into the chamber, focusing on the moving target instantly.

This was it, I'd been given another chance, one final opportunity at what some consider the greatest trophy animal in all of Africa. My finger tickled the edge of the trigger, but the heaving of my chest as it struggled for oxygen and the shaking of my tired arms protested. The rifle slumped from my shoulder as I watched the antelope disappear over the crest of the hill. I couldn't take a steady shot even if he stopped.

Neither of us said anything for some time. We just stared at the spot the deep-spiraled bull had once stood. When it was time, we climbed down the mountain to camp more satisfied than we deserved to be.

Mary and Joe were at camp by the time we rolled in well after dark. Mary had seen a fleeting glance of a bull, but that was it.

"A shepherd led us on a wild goose chase," she said. "We met him out in the middle of nowhere and when Kidane told him we were looking for bushbuck, he said he knew where they were. He sent us down through the forest, back up through the forest and over to the other side of the mountain. We finally told him we'd had enough and we were going to rest. He ran off, and within minutes returned with an entourage. Half the villagers and all their cattle and sheep came around the mountain to stare at us. The sudden influx of bodies and ensuing commotion made hunting a moot point in that area, so we left after Kidane explained they shouldn't follow us. It was back near camp that we saw the nyala, but he wasn't sticking around for us to climb up the hill and shoot at him. I guess I'm not supposed to get one on this trip," she said.

"Nassos said he has an opening in January of 1992. What do you think?"

"I think we'll plan to bring more appropriate clothing," she said.

We sat around the fire, laughed, drank a beer, told jokes and relished the moment. I've always had a soft spot in my heart for campfires. There are few settings as revealing. A person's character can present itself more easily in the shadowy glow of a nighttime gathering. Something about the romance of it all makes us feel secure, allowing us to open up in ways we normally wouldn't. Senses of humor, or lack thereof, are quickly brought to surface, sensibilities and temperaments are close behind. Ultimately, if you can't find common ground before a campfire, then there isn't much hope out in the field or on the water.

Our fire in Ethiopia was surrounded by laughter. Nassos made sure of that. His quick wit and joke-telling abilities made each evening a pleasure. Professional hunters are a colorful lot. Most can spin a yarn with the best of them and if the company is relaxed and familiar around the campfire after a long hard fruitless day then, no matter the hunting conditions, your trip will be unforgettable. The best of the best can pull this off. Nassos made us feel more at home than we could have wished for.

It was after dinner, around the campfire, that we saw a side of Nassos we hadn't seen before. I'm sure he wished we hadn't, but circumstances dictated the moment.

"That's strange," I said walking to the tent with Mary. "I thought I closed the tent all the way."

It was halfway open.

"Maybe you forgot."

"No, I'm sure I closed it all the way."

We approached the tent warily, pulled back the flap and peered in. The contents were a mess. We'd been robbed.

The train case and our two aluminum bullet cases were gone, as well as all of Mary's jewelry, my billfold and all our travelers checks. Mary's make-up, all her cosmetics and medicines were gone. Our money, traveler's checks and Mary's jewelry were locked with all our .375 ammunition in the aluminum boxes. A quick dose of panic was quickly replaced with resignation. They didn't take anything that wasn't replaceable. Mary's jewelry was mostly of the costume variety, but there were a few genuine items included. It could've been worse. They could've taken all our clothes, our boots, and our guns. That would have been a tragedy.

"That is not the point." Nassos said when we approached him at the fire with our predicament. "This is unacceptable. Show me the tent." On our way he turned back and yelled to Kidane. "Round everybody up and bring them to the fire." He paused a moment. "Don't tell them why."

"Everybody?"

"Yes, everybody. Now."

He looked in our tent with disgust. "Take a closer look to see if anything else was stolen," he said, shaking his head. "Over ten years in the safari business, nothing like this has ever happened." He looked at us somberly. "We may not ever find your stuff – especially the money, but we will find these criminals. I will give you money to get home. I am so sorry."

He kicked at a basket outside the tent before stomping away with his hands on his hips.

We stayed away from the interrogations. There was a lot of yelling – mainly from Kidane and Boletto, but in the end Nassos came to us with his head held down in defeat.

"No one has confessed," he said. "And nobody will give anything up. Unfortunately, because of this, they all will suffer. Nobody is talking, but the way things are done here, the police will arrest them all and throw them in jail until one of them tells what they know. I'm sorry this has happened to you."

"It's okay, Nassos. It's not your fault."

It was more of an inconvenience than anything else, but Nassos seemed to have been affected deeply by the incident. He was an honest man and expected the same from everyone else. He'd been near rage earlier, but that overwhelming anger had abated. He was now somewhat despondent.

"I've sent everyone to their quarters, under close supervision by my most trusted men. We will have to take them to the nearest town in the morning. We will not be able to hunt nyala tomorrow. When we get back, we will go to the hippo camp." He turned to leave, but stopped short. "Did they take all of your ammunition?"

"We had most of our 7mm rounds out of the ammo boxes since that's what we've been hunting with, but all the .375 ammo is gone."

"I do not know if we can hunt hippos with 7mm. We really need a heavy caliber with solids. Hippo hunting can be very dangerous. They have thick skulls. Soft points may not penetrate. We mostly shoot them in the head while they are in the water. Often big bulls do not come out to feed until after dark so hunting them on land is not normally a viable option. I'm sorry. I do not know if we will be able to hunt hippo."

"I have a box of 140-grain 7mm solids."

"That is a small bullet for hippo, but under the circumstances it might just work. We will try and see."

Sleep was cold and fitful our final night in nyala camp. It was a rotten way to end a hunt, but we pushed ourselves beyond all conception of what we thought we could and walked away more educated in many ways. Two years seemed like an awfully long time to meet the mountain nyala again, but like most things it would be here before we knew it. Many hunters come multiple times for the nyala found only in Ethiopia's mountains and leave without having fired a shot. I knew I was making a rather bold commitment to myself, but whatever it takes crossed my mind more than once. We'd be back. I'd meet the spiral horned antelope on those mountains again.

The next day, as we pulled away from camp, I stared up at the mist-covered mountains and thought of a majestic mountain nyala standing tall above the heather, surveying his mountain with wise and wary eyes. In two years, he'd be older, wiser, warier – and bigger.

Among the Hippos: Joe

"What kind of boats?"
During the drive to hippo camp, I tried to envision hunting from the water. Nassos tried to explain.
"Don't worry Joe. They will float – most of the time."
"Do you shoot from the boat?"
"Sometimes, if it is necessary."
"When would it be necessary?"
"If the hippo was eating the boat," Nassos said smiling.
I wasn't going to get a straight answer.
When we finally arrived, Boletto was already there. With the help of a local crew he'd hired, the last tent was going up. Camp was situated along the shore. The mosquitoes and flies were thick. They gave new meaning to the word fog. We would've given just about anything for the mist in the mountains as opposed to this intense cloud of biting insects that replaced it.
After we slapped, whapped and dodged our way through the haze of insects, camp was quite scenic. After settling in, we strolled down to the beach just in time to see the sun set. We'd hoped to see some hippos, but were content to watch the sun dropping past a line of hills, sparkling golden off the lake. The water was smooth, lapping rhythmically against the shore. We stood listening, enjoying the day as it faded around the edges.
Except for the bugs, we couldn't have asked for a better setting. The view was awesome, we were close to the hunting grounds, the tents were comfortable and roomy and the grass was green. Hippos are voracious grazers, and like all other grazing animals prefer the taste of lush, green fields.
I slept well that night, unaware of anything outside my tent, but the next morning, Mom was a little rattled.
"Did you hear the hippos in camp last night?" she said.
"I didn't hear anything."
"I was sleeping well too, until about 1:00. At first, I thought there was a cow feeding outside our tent. I could hear it chewing and breathing. I woke your father. He just got up and went to the bathroom. When he came back, I asked if he saw it. I told him it was right outside our tent, but he fell asleep as soon as his head hit the pillow. Then I heard a grunt and knew it wasn't a cow. It was a hippo. They're the most dangerous animal in all of Africa you know. They kill more people than any other animal."
The look on her face reflected the skepticism on mine. I thought she was overreacting, but I let her continue.

"I'm serious. I was scared after I figured out what it was. I stayed awake all night listening to see where the hippo was and what it was going to do. He was right by the tent. I tried to wake up your dad again, but he just rolled over and started snoring. I was petrified one would come right through the tent."

Dad just smiled. Nassos had joined us and was standing beside Dad with a similar smirk on his face.

"She is right," he said. "Hippos are very dangerous, especially if you get between them and the water when they are on dry land. You should be careful at night and shouldn't leave the tent unless you have to. They can be very territorial. Old ones will defend their space fiercely."

Then he smiled again.

"It will be okay," he said before marching off to prepare the Zodiac, a type of inflatable raft with an old outboard motor and room for four passengers.

It didn't look seaworthy. Heck, it didn't look bathtub-worthy. It looked like it would sink with much weight and that a strong wave could flip it. It would be nothing for a hippo to tip us over and thrash us around like a dog playing with a soft rope.

The lake was big enough that traveling by boat to find a hippo made the most sense. However, we usually employed two methods. One was to spot from the boat. The other was to move around the shore, hoping to catch one on dry land or close enough in for a shot. The problem is hippos most often only leave the water to feed at night. Shooting them while they're in the water is one of the few successful ways to hunt hippo. Although hippos can be dangerous and aggressive animals, hunting them is usually not a harrowing affair. It's mostly a matter of finding a good bull with enough of its head out of the water, then making a precision shot into the brain. The tiny target offers the most difficult aspect of the hunt. If you drill him precisely, death is instant, but if you're off by mere inches, you have an angry hippo with a mean headache. A complete miss is much better than a shot into the hippo's nose or jaw. In most cases, after finding a good bull, you take the shot. If your aim is true, you wait a couple hours until the dead hippo floats to the surface so you can make the retrieve.

The lake was shallow enough that drowning wasn't a big concern if the boat did happen to sink. Ticking off the wrong hippo was a different matter all together. The small, rocking boat moving through hippo-infested waters added a whole new dimension to the anxiety of the hunt.

I had an opportunity to shoot the first day.

"See the fifth one from the right?"

"The big one facing us?"

"Yes, that's the one. Shoot him when you're ready."

At the shot, all hell broke loose. Hippos dove, thrashed and rushed the water. When the splashing died down, I stared at the water.

"Did I hit him?"

"It was hard to tell. Let's climb up on that rock face over there and wait to see if he resurfaces."

By the time we climbed up the cliff and turned to look back at the water, he was already floating.

"There, Joe. Good shot. Go with Hussein in the boat to retrieve it."

Hussein and I hurried down to the boat and sped out into the smooth lake to collect the bull. As we approached, Hussein slowed down, studying the hippo with a puzzled look. He looked at me. I glanced back. Then he gave me an I don't know shrug before cutting the motor and grabbing an oar.

We drifted in slowly. Hussein was smiling, but something didn't seem right. Hussein stretched out with the oar to jab the hippo with the paddle.

The water erupted as the hippo thrashed.

"Sheet. Sunabeech."

Hussein began to lose his balance. When I grabbed him, he sat down, started the motor and thrust it into gear. His eyes were wide and my hands were shaking. I held tight to my seat as we sped away. After a few yards at high speed, we started to laugh one of those nervous Holy Shit laughs. Did that just happen?

Back at camp, Hussein told the story numerous times to the staff. At the end of the story, he would point at me, say something I couldn't understand and widen his eyes in mock fear. I would say "No, no," point at him and raise my hands above my head in exaggeration. Most of the natives would walk off laughing and we'd soon be approached by another wanting to hear the story. All in all, I think we told the tale at least a dozen times that evening.

I wasn't alone in missing a hippo. Both Mom and Dad had missed as well.

"Hitting those tiny little spots out in the water is harder than you would think," Mom said. "Looking through the scope at the rolling waves makes it feel like you're not steady. Obviously we weren't."

Just before heading off to bed, Mom switched gears from confident huntress to concerned mother.

"Now Joe, I don't want you leaving your tent tonight."

"I'll think about it."

"Joseph Anthony, I'm serious. If you get in a hippo's way, he will kill you."

"What do you want me to do? Wet the bed?"

"That's not funny. I'm telling you, don't leave the tent."

"Don't worry, Mom. I won't leave the tent unless I feel like it."

I turned to walk away and could hear Mom scolding Dad. "It's not funny, Dick. If he goes out in the dark, he could get trampled."

The next morning, I stopped by their tent on the way to breakfast. "Did you sleep well?" Mom asked.

"Yeah, until I got up to go to the bathroom. One of them damn hippos started chasing me."

"Oh, it did not. Stop fibbing. You know, your father went to the bathroom outside the tent last night even though I told him not to."

"So did I. There weren't any hippos around."

"You never know. That's why I held it until 5:00. I may be chicken, but if you were smart, you'd be too."

At breakfast, Nassos informed us we'd be hunting the river. The river was wide, slow and apparently not very deep. There were some dead trees out in the middle and we could see a few hippos out there as well. It was too far to shoot from shore, so Hussein went and rounded up two local natives with a fishing boat. The owners of the dilapidated contraption they called a boat insisted they must go with us to guide the boat for a price, of course.

One was tall, over six feet, and as thin as a pencil. He was bald and carried an eight-foot stick. The other fellow was much shorter, just as skinny and carried a coffee can. Both sported ear-to-ear smiles full of rotting teeth. I wondered what the hell Hussein had gotten us into. The so-called boat was nothing more than a few misshapen boards slapped together and bent to a point. You could see water through the cracks in the bottom.

Mom and Dad refused to test the waters in such a decrepit jumble of boards. I felt more daring and shook hands with the two happy owners. Hussein and I jumped in, followed by the two sailors. We quickly found out what the coffee can was for. Immediately after shoving off, the watercraft started filling with water.

The short guy with the coffee can went to work. His job was to continuously throw as much water out the boat as he could. I looked at Hussein with grave concern. He looked at me with a smile that was more apprehensive than happy. Then, trying to be the reassuring guide, he shook his head and patted me on the knee.

It wasn't convincing. As for our crew, they were as happy as could be. The tall, bald guy poled away with a big smile as if he were rowing a gondola in the canals of Venice, and the short guy pumped away with his coffee can, grinning like a kid digging a hole on the beach.

I waved nervously to my parents, who were sitting on the shore with puzzled looks on their faces. They wondered, no doubt, why that man was throwing water over the side. I wanted to go back to the bank. I forgot all about hunting hippo. It felt like we were sinking. The coffee can wasn't big enough and the man wasn't fast enough to keep up with the seeping water. I wanted to slap the smiles right off their faces, but I was afraid any shift in weight would cause the boat to crumble. I remained perfectly still. My eyes followed the rhythmic motion of the can dipping water as if I were hypnotized.

"Joe." Hussein pointed ahead of us at a group of hippos.

I only gave them a quick glance. I was too uneasy about the lack of progress our human bilge pump seemed to be making.

We eventually made it to a lone tree in the middle of the river where our tall captain started pushing us around in slow circles. Hussein motioned for me to hop out of the boat.

I laughed.

He nodded, smiled and said, "Yes".

I shook my head. "You're not serious, are you?"

The captain jabbed his long stick in the water to prove it wasn't too deep. All three of them began coaxing me out of the boat. Hussein was a constant jokester. It took me a few minutes to realize he was serious; it took another ten for them to convince me to get in the water. Finally, their assurances paid off. With an enormous amount of trepidation, I slipped off the boat, getting wet up to my ribs. Hussein handed me my rifle, indicating I should use the tree as a rest.

I couldn't see anything in the water. It was thick and brown, like chocolate milk. I looked back to the boat for guidance and was greeted with three smiling faces as they drifted away. I still wasn't exactly sure what the plan was, but I didn't like it. I held the gun above water, watching in increasing panic as the captain pushed them further and further away, leaving me all alone in the water. The comfort of having the boat nearby drifted away. At about fifty yards out, they stopped to stare at me with their evil little grins. The pump man continued to extract water, but they all looked at me as if they were waiting for something. Hussein would occasionally scan the water around me, but his eyes always returned to mine.

I held fast to the tree, the only stability in my life at the moment. I was trembling. Fear and cold had a grip on me that was cutting off circulation to my brain. I didn't know what to do. I wanted back in that sinking craft more than anything.

BLOOP

I jerked my head to the left, coming eye to eye with a hippo no more than ten or fifteen yards away.

BLOOP

BLOOP

Two more. Nine o'clock and twelve o'clock.

BLOOP
BLOOP
BLOOP

I was surrounded. They looked at me like I was a rival gang member who'd just invaded their turf. I finally understood the game plan. Use the stupid teenager as bait.

My eyes darted from head to head. All eyes were fixed on me. The one on the left had V-shaped ripples behind its head. It was moving. I turned around in search of an escape route, but I was surrounded. I turned back to the one that had been moving. It was gone. Soon, two more heads went under. I could feel them sneaking up on me. I couldn't take it any longer. Panic took hold of me. In desperation, I tried to climb the slick, limbless tree while attempting to keep my gun dry.

"Hussein! Hussein! Get the hell back here." I was screaming with an intensity I didn't know I had. "Hussein! They're coming in. Hussein!"

I couldn't get up the tree. More of the heads dropped below the surface. I thought I felt something touch my leg.

"Ahhh! Hurry!"

They were coming, but they seemed to be moving so slow. Baldy was pushing along like he was out for a Sunday drive. The Can Man was pumping away, happy he had something to do. Hussein was trying to hold back a giggle. That sunabeech.

Another hippo popped up between the boat and me. Hussein slapped the water in an attempt to push it out of the way. When it finally moved, it merely slipped back under water. I kept expecting it to come crashing up underneath the boat. They finally reached me. After I pried my grip from the tree, I climbed back in the boat. I was dripping wet, my stomach was in knots and I was a little perturbed.

Hussein was doing his best not to laugh, our two crewmen were still smiling as they pushed and pumped away and I...well, let's just say silence had overcome me.

There was little sympathy from the onlookers back on dry land. Dad and Nassos were laughing hysterically and Mom was doing a poor job of stifling her own chuckle.

Hussein slapped me on the back. "Fun, no?"

"No. I'm not getting in the water again."

"We hunt more. Good water there." Hussein pointed.

"I think I'll just stay here for a while."

"No, there," he pointed. "Many hippos. Easy, no get wet. Good boat."

I finally agreed, thinking he meant we'd be in a better watercraft, but I realized he was talking about Baldy and Can Man's boat when the two of them lifted it above their heads.

"No way," I said, waving my hands in front of me. "I'm not getting back in that."

"It okay," Hussein said.

Can Man looked back, held up his coffee can and smiled.

I finally convinced myself that if Hussein felt safe enough to get back in that boat, it would probably be okay. Nobody wants to be a coward. What was I thinking?

After a few minutes of walking, Nassos caught up with us and started a conversation with Hussein. When they were done, Hussein slapped my shoulder again and took off jogging back toward my parents.

"I will take you now Joe," Nassos said.

"Where's he going?"

"I sent him to bring your mom and dad so they can watch you shoot your hippo." He smiled. "There are many hippos in this pond. We will get one."

"You're not afraid to ride in that boat?"

"You can swim can't you?"

"Yeah, but that's not the point."

Nassos laughed. "You tested it for me. It stayed afloat. But just in case, if we do sink, try to swim quietly so you don't attract the crocodiles."

I prayed he was kidding.

We followed our two smiling buddies, Baldy and Can Man, to a small body of water covered with water lilies and other green vegetation. You couldn't see much, but there were plenty of hippos scattered throughout the lake. There seemed to be hippos everywhere we went.

Baldy and Can Man dropped the boat in the water and smiled. Nassos jumped in. It took me a few minutes to muster up the courage. So here I was again, Baldy pushing me around and Can Man pumping and smiling, pumping and smiling. I could hear Mom, Dad and Hussein back on the beach laughing at me.

"It's not funny," I said softly.

Nassos had his eye on the far end of the pond. I wasn't sure of the plan. It appeared as if we were going to work our way over to the other shore. A lone bull, half in the water, seemed to be contemplating moving up into the brush. We headed right into the heart of the herd. I wondered if we'd be hunting one of the others.

"What about that one?" I pointed.

"No."

"That one?"

"No."

We floated closer to the lone bull. He turned to face us.

"What about this one? He looks good."

"No, not quite big enough. Young male."

The bull had this nervous look in its eyes that said "don't come any closer." I couldn't stop staring at him. He seemed tense. I was trembling. I half lifted my rifle – just in case. I briefly glanced around at the other specimens, but we kept getting closer and closer to the one standing up – 20 yards – 15 – 10.

A furious rage broke the tension as the bull charged without warning.

Nassos was suddenly yelling. "Yes, this one! Yes! Yes! Shoot! This one! Shoot! Shoot!"

I was on my feet, firing before he could finish. At the bullet's impact, the hippo opened his jaws, revealing a mouthful of the most intimidating set of choppers I've ever seen. His mouth was a fleshy funnel full of sharp and blackened teeth that disappeared into a dark, endless hole. If I would've had time, I would've jacked another shell into the chamber and fired again. If I would've had an automatic, I'd still be pulling the trigger. Before I could reload, he crashed back down, spraying us with water and rocking the boat with an oceanic wave. It was all I had to keep from losing my balance and flipping into the water.

Only after the pond resettled to little more than an insignificant ripple did I realize how close the hippo had come. I didn't have to stretch when I reached out to poke it with the end of my rifle. When it didn't move, I finally let myself relax. Can Man was pumping frantically and Baldy was like a statue – neither of them were smiling.

Like it was an everyday occurrence, Nassos told Baldy to push us back to camp. "We need to get some rope so we can tow him back to shore."

I unloaded the rifle, but held tight to it. It was the only way to keep my hands from quivering. My knees were still shaking a little when we hit the beach. Mom and Dad were standing by the water, wide-eyed, but smiling. A band of natives were gathered behind them clapping and cheering.

"That was unbelievable," Dad said.

"It looked like the hippo was going to eat the boat," Mom said.

I smiled feebly. I couldn't have answered had I wanted to. I made my way to the shade to have a seat; many of the natives crowded around, smiled and congratulated me. I think they were more impressed with the fresh meat than by my hunting prowess.

Retrieval of the hippo was a whole other problem.

Nassos congratulated me and disappeared before I stepped away from the boat. When he returned, he had a length of rope draped around his shoulder. It looked old, but it was long, maybe 50 feet. He went to get Baldy and Can Man, who were smiling again. The three of them hopped in the boat and made their way to the hippo. I watched from the safety of the shore. I'd had enough floating around with hippos for one day.

When they pulled up next to the body, Nassos slipped from the boat and tied the rope around one of its legs. Just then the wind picked up in earnest. By the time Nassos had the rope secure and was back in the boat, the wind was howling. Now they had to struggle against the wind as well as the weight of Africa's second-heaviest animal. Baldy pushed with all his strength. Can Man pumped diligently. Nassos used another long stick to help Baldy tow the hippo back to shore. Progress was slow, appearing to be non-existent at first. Little by little, they inched closer, like a snow skier pushing himself up a gentle, but lengthy, incline.

A crowd gathered at the waters edge. As the boat slowly made its way closer, they began wading into the water. They eventually met and a concerted effort of manpower tugged the boat and hippo into shore. Nassos jumped from the boat, then waded past a few straggling onlookers. Once on dry land, he ran to retrieve the truck. He was able to bring it within 20 feet of the pond. He had anticipated the snag the villagers ran into; when the hippo began to drag on the bottom, manpower alone was no longer sufficient to finish the job.

He pulled with the truck only a few feet before the rope snapped.

Hussein ran over to grab the rope.

"Sheet. Sunabeech."

Soon, I was over with the rest of them, heaving and pulling until we had enough rope to reach the truck again. This time, Nassos was able to pull the carcass smoothly to shore. I tried to help with the cleaning, but there were so many bodies gathered around, I mostly just got in the way. I stayed close, however, to observe the process. When one of the villagers cut a piece of fat from the skin and popped it in his mouth, my jaw fell open. Pretty soon, the whole group was working and gnawing on raw hippo fat. Other bystanders began to gather around. Before long, pieces were being cut off and passed to anyone who wanted one.

Baldy brought it over. "No way," I said. Then I saw Mom heading my way. "Wait," I said. "Okay, I'll take it."

He handed it to me, his smile as big as ever.

I watched her from the corner of my eye. As soon as she said, "What are you doing, Joe," I pretended to take a bite.

"No. Oh my goodness. Joe don't eat that."

"Why not? It's not bad."

"You'll get sick. It'll give you parasites."

"Everyone else is eating it."

"Their systems are used to it. Oh my goodness. Dick, Joe was eating the fat."

When she turned to find Dad, Hussein came over snickering.

"Give me."

He reached for the piece of fat still in my hand. He dropped it on the ground and ran over to the hippo where he carved off a small piece of meat and rushed it over to the fire pit. He made it back with a cooked piece of meat just in time.

"Joseph, come over here." Mom said. "I want to talk to you."

"Just a minute," I said holding the meat in the air. I took a bite.

"Stop eating that, Joe. Oh my goodness. Dick, tell him to stop eating that. He's going to get sick."

"It's good," I said, walking over. "You want a piece?"

"It's not funny. Dick, go get Nassos. Maybe he'll listen to him."

"No, seriously, Mom. It's pretty tasty. Try a bite."

I could hear Hussein laughing behind me. When I extended it out to her she shook her head.

"I don't want a bite and..." She caught herself when she looked down at it.

"It's cooked meat, Mom. I didn't really eat any raw fat."

"That's not what you were eating before."

"I was just messing with you. I never really took a bite. Here, you should try it. It's pretty good."

"Are you sure it's cooked all the way through?"

It took Hussein and me a few minutes to convince her to have a bite, but she finally did. Though she didn't admit it, I could tell she liked it.

"So Nassos," Mom said later that evening around the campfire. "How come Joe is the only one shooting anything?"

"Beginner's luck, I guess."

"Luck has very little to do with it." I smiled slyly.

"Oh yes, you are the great white hunter," Nassos said. "Will you show me where to find a kudu tomorrow?"

"Sure, they're out there." I pointed into the darkness.

"They're in the lake?"

"Oh, I meant over there."

Nassos laughed. "He's one real cool kid," he said to my parents. "I think we should let the cool kid sleep in tomorrow. Let somebody else have a chance."

"That's very considerate of you," Dad said. "I don't think Joe will complain about having to sleep in."

We sat around the fire for another hour. I watched the faces glowing in the orange light. Tiny sparkles rose from the flame like fireflies. Above the fire's crackles and the bellowing of the hippos were the stories that were, before our very eyes, becoming integral pieces of who we were, of who we are destined to become.

We called it a night when the fire became a flicker. I caught up to Nassos on his way to his tent. "Thanks," I said and shook his hand. "This has been so much better than I imagined."

His mouth slightly curled up at the edges. "It has been a good day."

Then, with his hands on his hips, he turned, silently disappearing into the darkness.

The Leak: Mary

"It looks like Joe really is going to sleep in today."

"Looks like it."

"Well," I said. "I guess he's earned it. He's shot everything we're trying for. I wish they would've found his mountain nyala though."

"Nassos thinks they'll eventually find it. There won't be much left, but maybe they can salvage the horns. We pay for it either way. If they could at least find the horns, it would be some kind of physical reminder of the hunt."

"That would be something I suppose."

"I don't think they'll ever find it," Dick said. "But you never know. Nassos is a diligent fellow."

"Isn't there anything else for him to hunt here?"

"Nassos told me last night that after you and I get our hippos, we'd be moving to another camp for kudu, oribi, bushbuck and baboon, so I guess not. Here comes Nassos now."

"Are we going in the truck or the boat this morning?" I asked as he approached.

"Neither. Today I think we will walk. Did you sleep well?"

"As good as can be expected. I don't know which is worse, Dick's snoring or the hippos grunting and eating."

"Oh, I'm sure Dick is much worse."

"I do my best," Dick said.

"Are you ready?" Nassos said. "We will come back in a couple hours and have breakfast. Is this okay?"

"I'll grab the rifles," Dick said.

We stalked around the shore for a few hours, encountering many hippos, some too far out and others that were not quite what we were looking for. At one point, we all came to a quick stop. The tracker out front melted into the bush. From my position behind Hussein, I couldn't see what they were looking at, but the seemingly simple act of a tracker fading away usually meant we were in the company of game. The water was empty. They didn't seem to be looking out into the lake anyway. I strained my neck to peer around Hussein's shoulder, but all I saw were trees and a few scattered boulders on the shore.

Pretty soon, Nassos was steadying his binoculars against a small tree. I still couldn't figure out what the heck we were looking at. Nobody seemed to care. They were having their own little pow wow, pointing and whispering.

A moment later, we were stalking slowly and quietly. I couldn't understand why. There had to be something there. Where was it? What was it?

Nassos looked through his binoculars again, then shook his head back and forth. We all moved behind an acacia. I got snagged by a thorn and let out a muffled shriek.

Nassos turned and put his finger to his lips. I leaned down next to him. "There are hippos there," he said. "But no bull. A few cows and a baby calf. Very dangerous."

"Where?"

"There," he pointed. "By the trees."

The boulders.

I looked at them again. They still looked like big rocks, but I could only see the tops of their backs. They weren't moving. Maybe they were sunning themselves. Now what?

We were contemplating our next course of action when the wind changed, wafting our scent straight toward them. They were up and moving to the water with a speed and agility I didn't think an animal of that portly shape and size could possess. The tiny baby scampered along with them. It was so cute I could have hugged it like a teddy bear. In protection mode, one of the cows veered from the group, coming right for us.

"Oh my God," I said.

Nassos stood, gently pushed me behind him with his hand and then raised his rifle to his shoulder.

I felt an urge to run, but my feet wouldn't move. Besides, I would have stumbled right into Hussein or Dick. The cow swerved back to the water. I relaxed, but only for a second. She was coming for us again, not sure what kind of threat we posed to her calf.

"She's coming. She's coming." I was bouncing.

Hussein grabbed my arm. The look on his face said it will be okay. I didn't believe it.

Then, as quickly as before, she turned and splashed into the water, rejoining her calf. Thank goodness.

Half an hour later, we approached the shoreline. About 100 yards out, a small group of hippos were floating in a cluster. There was a big bull among them.

"The third one from the right," Nassos said softly. "When you are ready take him just behind the ear."

I tried to slow my heartbeat with deep breaths. When I felt steady, I squeezed one off. Hippos splashed in every direction. After a few minutes they calmed once again.

"Did I hit him?"

"I don't think so," Nassos said.

"Yes, good shot," Hussein said.

"Are you sure?" Nassos gave Hussein a skeptical look.

"Yes, good shot."

"Do you think you hit it?" Nassos said.

"I'm not sure. I doubt it, the way I've been shooting."

"Yes, good shot." Hussein said.

"What do you think, Dick?" Nassos said.

"I think she hit it well. But I'm not going to swim out there and check."

"Okay, we will wait. It usually takes at least an hour for them to float. Let's go have breakfast."

After breakfast, we all piled into the Zodiac.

"It looks pretty rough out there," I said. "Are you sure this little boat can handle it?"

The wind was blowing hard into shore. The waves on the lake were topped off by violent whitecaps.

"It looks a little too rough," I said quietly to Dick.

He either didn't hear me over the wind or was just ignoring me. I couldn't tell which. Either way it didn't matter. Nassos had the motor running and we were zipping into the crashing swells.

The little inflatable boat bucked in the water, its bow rising and slamming down over each successive wave. Holding on to my seat, I got drenched, but the rubber dinghy didn't sink. As we entered the modest cove where I shot at the hippo, the wind seemed non-existent, the water surprisingly calm.

"Madam, you got hippo." Hussein shouted as we approached.

Yes. I hadn't missed after all. I straightened my back to look over the bow. Like a tiny island, the rounded shape that was my hippo floated in the cove. Right where I'd shot him. I remembered when they thought Joe hit his and it came to life when they approached. Why did we zoom up to mine so hastily? Impetuous, I thought. But the bull was, thankfully, lifeless. I wiped the lake water from my face, accepting congratulations as graciously as I could while crammed, dripping wet, into a tiny boat.

"There is an island near the center of the lake where hippos often gather to sun themselves. I think we should have a look there since we have the boat. We will return for your hippo afterwards," Nassos said.

Twenty minutes later, Nassos pulled our little vessel into another calm cove, parking it next to a massive rock jutting from the water. He pulled out his binoculars and pointed to the island just off in the distance. It didn't look too big, but through the magnification of our optics we could see there was, in fact, a pod of hippos sunning themselves just out of the water.

Fighting the wind and waves, it took us another 45 minutes to reach the island. We circled around into a small bay so as not to alarm the hippos. Beginning our stalk, I thought of how the hippo Joe shot rushed the boat and how dangerous it was. Then I remembered how agile that cow had been out of the water. I decided the scenario I hunted my hippo in probably held the fewest hazards. I've been lucky that way. No charging elephants for me. I guess God knew I couldn't handle it.

We rounded the corner, slowing to a crawl. The hippos had moved back into the water, but not far.

"That is a good hippo," Nassos said softly.

Hussein nodded as Dick moved into position.

The bull was standing in water just deep enough to cover its stubby legs. His chin bobbed in and out of the water. Big droplets splashed back into the lake when it lifted its head. It was standing broadside, but it was a little too deep to attempt a heart shot.

Dick drilled it just below the ear. The hippo did a series of fantastic dives, thrashing and crashing, spewing blood, turning the water red. Finally, the bull rushed from the water, turning his head side-to-side, searching. It was met with two more shots in quick succession, one from Dick and one from Nassos. It splashed back into the lake and sunk.

"Now that's the hunter I remember from the elephant hunt last year," Nassos said. "Great shot." He shook Dick's hand.

"The big animals are easy to hit. Especially when we get this close," Dick said. "Should be fun pulling him back to camp."

"Do not worry, my friend. The boat will do all the work." Nassos put his hand up to his brow to reflect the sun. "It looks like the wind is getting worse. We better hurry to get Mary's hippo."

Nassos navigated the Zodiac right through the group of hippos which had moved further from shore.

That's when the motor quit.

Nassos yanked and pulled and jerked on the string as the wind pushed us ever closer to a nervous-looking hippo.

"We're getting closer," I said.

"It okay, Madam," Hussein said.

Nassos pulled the motor up to inspect it, a mixture of sweat and water dripping from his face. The wind slapped the waves against the rubber boat. The hippo glared at us from the corner of its eye.

"What if it tips us? We're getting too close."

Nassos slammed the motor back into the water. "Move over, Dick. I need to get the oars."

He slid them into the oar plates and started rowing. We barely gained a foot with each stroke. My jacket was whipping violently in the wind. Water exploded over the sides in furious crashes.

That's when the boat began leaking air.

Hussein's eyes widened. "Sheet. Sheet." He shuffled around under his legs, then pointed at Dick's feet. "Pump. Pump."

"Where?" Dick held up his hands. "Oh." He dug the pump from under a jumble of rope. "Here," he thrust it at Hussein.

Hussein took the nozzle and shoved it into the hole.

Dick immediately began pumping. Nassos never missed a stroke. This can't be happening, I thought. To get to my hippo, we had to fight against the wind. After a few minutes of rowing and pumping in a losing battle, we spun around and used the wind to help push us back toward camp. Soon we were making some progress. A quick glance behind confirmed we were putting distance between ourselves and the hippos, but not much. The shore was far off on the horizon – so beyond our reach. I wanted to scream. What if the boat sunk? What if a hippo decided to sink the boat? Nassos couldn't keep it up much longer, could he? I was the only passenger not doing anything to help. What could I do? Then something bumped into my soaked boots. It was an orange plastic bowl floating in the water filling the bottom of the boat. I began dipping and dumping. Whether I was preventing the Zodiac from sinking I can't say, but at least I no longer felt helpless. The boat never completely filled up with water, nor was I able to dump it all back into the lake.

The pace at which we labored along was excruciating. We never seemed to gain ground. Two hours later, I could hardly lift my arms. I couldn't imagine how Dick or Nassos kept going, but they did. They had no other choice. They both found a rhythm, though they couldn't disguise their fatigue. It was in the strained looks on their faces and the determined, yet dispirited stares. Dick was breathing heavily, near the point of collapse. At least there were no hippos around.

"Dick, you look like you're getting tired. Maybe you shouldn't have waited so long to shoot your hippo. Be like Joe and shoot it right away, close to the truck." Nassos said, smiling. Then he looked to me. "At least the wind is keeping the flies away. I know how you hate flies Mary."

We tried to laugh, but it wasn't honest.

Suddenly, there was a loud crack. Nassos lunged forward to catch one of the oars. The oar plate broke off.

We floated around at the whim of the wind and water as Nassos tried to pound the screws back in. Two of them plopped into the water, but he was able to secure the last one. There was no way it was going to hold. Dick grabbed it, trying to keep it steady while Nassos rowed. Every so often, we'd have to stop so Dick and Hussein could take turns pumping air back into the boat. I began shivering. We were all wet to the bones and didn't have time to notice the sun was turning our skin the color of beets. We're never going to make it. I felt like we were lost at sea.

Nassos tried to keep the mood light with jokes. It wasn't working. When the other oar plate started coming loose I wanted to pull out my hair. All I could do was try to hold the oar plate and pray it didn't give any further. No more, I thought. Please, no more.

A total of four hours after we started our row back to camp, Boletto waded out to his chest to pull us the rest of the way in to shore. Dick and I collapsed on the ground. We didn't move for several minutes. Nassos and Hussein, as beat as us, only rested a few moments before they started working on the motor. We couldn't have moved if we wanted to.

Finally, Dick pushed himself up into sitting position. "I need a beer," he said.

"I think I'll have one too."

"What? You never drink beer. You hate beer."

"I do. But I need a beer."

I somehow choked one down. Then I had another. When my body quit trembling and my muscles tightened with pain I would feel in the morning, I decided a shower was just what I needed.

"I can't believe Nassos rowed us all the way back," I said before walking away.

"He has to be one of the toughest men I've ever met," Dick said. "And he doesn't even know it."

Cliff-Jumping Kudu: Dick

"What's going on?" Mary asked.

Nassos, Kidane and Hussein were talking to two men in army green uniforms who had arrived in a matching green pickup.

"I'm not exactly sure," I said. "From what I can gather, it seems they captured four boys who they think stole our stuff. Unfortunately, they escaped."

"Do they want to talk to us?"

"I don't think so. We'll just have to wait and see."

A few minutes later, Nassos shook hands with the officers and Kidane climbed into the bed of the truck. He gave us a big wave with his hand way above his head as they sped away.

"What's going on Nassos?" Mary asked.

"The authorities are sure they will catch the thieves soon and need someone to help identify them. Kidane volunteered. He has family in the area."

"Did they find our things?"

"No. I'm sorry."

"It's okay. It isn't your fault."

"There is something else. I must go to Addis Ababa for a day or two. I cannot fix the motor here. Hussein and Boletto will take you to the next camp now. Susan and I will join you soon. Is this okay?"

"You got to do what you got to do. How far is the next camp?"

"Not far. Two hours. You will be there in time for dinner. You will stay at a hotel and drive to the hunting area each day."

"See you on Friday."

Hotel was much too kind a word for the accommodations. Roach motel was too kind. The hotel was surrounded on all sides by neighborhoods that made our city slums back home look like high-society living. We would've paid dearly for the cold, wind-flapping, rain-drenched tents of the mountains, but I guess you just roll with the punches – no matter how painful they are.

"It doesn't look like it's been cleaned in years. Look at those sheets." Mary shivered as she went to look at the bathroom. "Oh my God. I don't think the toilet has been flushed in years either." She retreated back into the bedroom. "Oh, oh, look at the size of that cockroach."

"What do you want me to do about it?"

"I don't know, but this is disgusting. It's got cockroaches, spiders and look at all the mosquitoes."

"It could be worse." Joe peeked his head into our room.

"How?"

"We could live here. This is probably the nicest place in town."

"It's probably the only place," I said.

"I feel like I need a shower just from being in here." Mary walked over to turn on the bathroom sink. "Look at this, even the water's dirty. The water's so brown I don't know what good it does to wash my hands." She did it anyway.

Joe disappeared, returning a moment later holding two cans of bug spray. "Everybody out."

Believe it or not, we all survived the night.

The next morning we drove away from the village. The area was flat and the grass was dead, but the mountains in the distance looked verdant. The further we distanced ourselves from the village, the fewer people we encountered and the landscape became wilder.

"You close windows in room, yes?" Hussein asked.

"We did."

"I didn't," Joe said. "Why?"

"Baboons come."

"What?"

"In window, baboons. Tear bed. Sheet on floor."

"They better not."

Hussein laughed. "It okay. No sheet every time."

We stopped at the base of the mountain and split up. Mary went with Boletto; Joe and I with Hussein. Halfway up the mountain, we spotted a nice kudu, but it spotted us too and was on the other side of the mountain before Joe could raise his rifle. We hiked up and down the hills until early afternoon when we met back up with Mary and Boletto at the truck.

"We go hotel, eat now." Boletto patted his stomach.

There may be starving people in Ethiopia, but Boletto wasn't one of them.

"No," Hussein said. "We hunt oribi. They come before hotel."

Boletto snorted and slumped into the back seat of the truck next to Joe. Fighting to stay awake, his head began bobbing within minutes of hitting the road. Hunger fatigue, no doubt.

Hussein would jerk the wheel on purpose and Joe would laugh at Boletto when he came to. He glared at Joe and tried to stay awake. He was fighting a losing battle. Before long, his head was jiggling like a bobble-head doll.

"Joseph, it's not nice to laugh at people," Mary said.

It only took a quick glance at his bobbing head before she began giggling herself. She hid it better than Joe and whenever Boletto jolted awake, it was Joe he glared at.

Like much plains game, oribi hunting was mainly a spot-and-stalk endeavor. The land was flat and, save for a few scattered thorn bushes and acacia trees, relatively open. Green grass was nonexistent, but oribi were pleasantly abundant. In short order, Joe and I each collected one – that is, of course, after I missed one first.

After a late lunch, we all split up to hunt kudu. We spent the remainder of the day scouring the thick, green foothills. Kudu have no problem hiding when vegetation is sparse. Locating the gray ghost in such dense cover sometimes felt futile. I was beat by the end of the day, barely able to take another step. Staring all day at shadows that turn out to be nothing more than shadows began to take a toll on my sanity.

"What happened to your legs?" I asked Mary back at the room.

"I don't know. Boletto says it's some sort of heat rash, but I think it's probably some kind of bug here in the room. Joe's fumigation seems to have helped, but I still spent the last 20 minutes killing cockroaches and spiders."

"Did you see any kudu?"

"Not one. We didn't stay out too long though," Mary said. "I've got terrible stomach cramps. I can't get out of the bathroom."

"That can't be any fun. Is there anything I can do?"

"No, thanks though. At least somebody turned on the water today and we can finally flush the toilet. Thank goodness – it was really starting to stink. The electricity's been off and on ever since I got back."

About that time, she put her hand on her stomach and hurried back into the bathroom.

Half the night was filled with the sound of flushing. I wish there was something I could've done. Other than digging the Pepto out of one of our bags, I felt helpless. By morning, Mary was tired, but feeling a little better.

"Would you like breakfast?" I asked.

"I am a little hungry, but I think I better wait. My stomach's still cramping up a bit."

"You want to stay in today?"

"No way. Feeling like crap out in the bush is way better than feeling like crap in this dump. I would much rather go hunting."

After an hour drive, we began a slow, quiet stalk up the mountain. We tried not to snap too many twigs with our bumbling human feet, but it was impossible. The ground was covered with twigs. One step – *snap*. Four steps – *snap*. Three steps – *snap-snap*. Every kudu on the mountain had to be aware of our presence, but we continued on, pretending we were stealthier than we were. For some reason, Boletto didn't seem to be as loud as we were. Then, through the intricate mesh of leaves, twigs and grass that could only be weaved by The Almighty's skillful hand, we spotted one of those shadows which turned out to be a kudu cow.

"Mary, come. Good bull. In bushes. Will come if patient."

Boletto gently pushed away a brush of grass. Like a hawk, he waited for the perfect moment.

I stayed back, crouching behind a bush just large enough to conceal my position, but not too massive that I couldn't enjoy the action. Boletto tried to point out the bull to Mary while I attempted to find it myself. It was in the deep shadows – somewhere. I saw nothing.

Then he moved – just a little, but enough to give away his position. There he was as plain as day, impossible to miss. I tried not to blink. If I lost him in the edges of gray again, I might not see the shot. In the hazy periphery of my vision, I noticed Mary raise her rifle. Boletto's fingers went into his ears. The kudu turned, sniffing the air, its muscles taut, but the swing of its neck fluid. The cow's head popped up alertly, her huge sonar ears turning our way. She took a step. It exposed the bulls shoulder.

Shoot.

Silence.

Come on, shoot.

The cows head jerked from side to side – danger was near, but where?

Shoot before they run. Shoot for goodness sake.

It was over in a split second. At the blast, they disappeared. The cow bolted to the right. The bull crumpled into the bushes.

"Great shot." Boletto sprinted toward the kudu. "Good bull. Very good. You shoot very good bull, Mary." He turned and ran back to her. "Come, we look."

Mary turned back to wave me forward before following after Boletto. "Come on Dick. Let's go look at him."

"Go ahead. I'll catch up."

It was her moment, after all. She should enjoy it before I interrupted. She was beaming when I finally worked my way over to them. After we skinned it and gathered the meat, she was still beaming. So was Boletto.

"We eat good." He held up the kudu liver and then the heart. "We eat very good."

We hauled the skin, horns and all the meat back down to the truck. It was more than an hour later when Joe and Hussein returned. Their feet were dragging. Neither of them were smiling.

"Did you see anything?" Mary asked.

"Yeah, I shot a kudu."

"Really, that's great."

"No it's not," he said. "We lost it."

"What happened?"

I got out of the truck, but Mary kept her seat.

"Well, we were walking down this heavily used game trail. You should have seen it, tracks were everywhere and it was real deep. Anyway, we were hiking along when a kudu crossed right in front of us. Hussein's all Shoot. Shoot. So I shot him as he was walking by. It was a quick shot, but I hit him well."

"How far?"

"Not too far. Maybe 75 or 80 yards. There was blood everywhere. It was easy to follow the trail."

"What time?"

"Right away this morning. We hadn't been walking for more than 15 minutes. We tracked the trail of blood everywhere – up and down the mountains, through creeks and everything. It was a really good blood trail. After an hour or two, Hussein started in with his "'sheet, sheet'."

Hussein seemed amused at Joe's animated imitation of him.

"It was so frustrating. Hours and hours on this blood trail and it didn't seem like we were getting any closer. We followed it up to the top of this mountain and all of the sudden it stops right at the edge of a 75-foot cliff. We looked for another hour all around there, but it had to go off that cliff. The way the blood kind of spilled over the rocks – it had to go over the cliff. It was really steep. There were a few tiny rocks it could've jumped down onto, but not many, and besides it was wounded. It'd been bleeding bad forever. I just don't see how it could've made it down there."

"It probably fell off."

"It had to. There's no other explanation. We looked through our binoculars for a long time and couldn't find anything. We could see the bottom clearly. We could see everything. We just couldn't get down there. So we're like, what the hell? We walked all around the edge of the cliff and could see real well on the bottom and everything."

"How can we get down there to have a look?"

"Hussein sent two trackers on a ten-mile hike around the mountain to see if they could find any sign of it. Hopefully they'll find it. They should. I don't see how it could've gone anywhere else."

That afternoon, the two trackers caught up with us just before we called it a day. The two slender young men had traveled on foot for a total of 20 miles up and down those mountains. Neither of them were breathing hard. The smiles on their faces and the animated rendition of how their afternoon had gone led us to believe they had indeed found Joe's kudu. But after a ten minute explanation, Boletto's translation was "no find, is gone."

Joe's shoulders slumped. On the way back to the hotel, he complained of a stomach ache, said he wouldn't be joining us for dinner on account of his not feeling well. We understood, but boy did he miss a succulent meal. Boletto had been right, the kudu fillets and liver were absolutely delicious. It was topped off with potatoes, carrots and a little red wine. We ate far too much and were paid back with full, tired bodies. Too tired to stay awake, too full to sleep.

Joe and Hussein went looking for the cliff-jumping kudu again the next morning. Mary stayed in camp since she'd already collected hers.

"It's better if there aren't so many people," she said. "Too hard to be quiet. Besides, my stomach is kind of crampy again today."

I couldn't wait to get back out. There were only a few days left before we had to return home. I'd been skunked by the mountain nyala and was determined not to go home without a kudu. Unfortunately, determination alone is not enough. There are many essential ingredients also required. Time for instance – its greedy hold on our lives limits more than we could ever imagine. And luck – we can never have enough good fortune. Sure, we can create a bit of luck out in the field through our determination, but even the best hunter on the most fertile land will need that last element for it all to come together. There are many more components to the hunt, but these three are absolutely vital for success.

So there we were again, on that long, tough climb up the mountain in search of kudu. As a young man, I could've made that hike at the same pace without breaking a sweat. I wasn't over-the-hill yet, but I struggled. I was glad to be with Boletto – he took it easier than Nassos or Hussein. His speed was better attuned to my own. The mountain wasn't overly steep, like in the mountain nyala area, but it was full of ankle-gripping grass and seemed an endless incline. We hiked and climbed for so long, Boletto finally decided we needed a break. Plains game – yeah right. Not always.

We plopped ourselves down on a couple boulders. I had to wipe the sweat out from underneath my glasses. Boletto leaned back for a moment, but apparently the jagged rock wasn't as comfortable as it looked. He pushed himself back up and grabbed my wrist.

"Kudu."

Sure enough, across the valley, several cows were standing in an open field. They moved at a leisurely pace, but would soon be in the trees.

"No bull," I said.

"Yes, good bull."

I looked through the binoculars again. One, two, three, four cows, but no bull.

"Where?" I asked.

"After cows."

I scoured the field behind the cows. Still nothing. Then something caught my eye at the edge of the brush line. The bull hadn't yet ventured into the field. I let the binoculars drop around my neck and raised my rifle. Around 300 yards – far, but not too far. I'd let him step into the open before taking the shot. I held on him and waited. He didn't move.

"Shoot," Boletto said. But there was too much brush covering the kudu.

I held. My arms began trembling, so I lowered the gun and glanced toward the cows. Two had already reached the brush, the others not far behind. He had to move. I put the crosshairs back on him and held.

Move your stubborn ass.

He didn't move.

I repositioned myself beside the boulder, gave myself a less stressful rest and held. Then he moved deeper into the brush. What the hell is he doing?

"Shoot," Boletto said.

I was tempted. Tempted to the point of applying a wee bit of pressure on the trigger, but the shot was through even more brush now. Then I lost him in the infinite shadows of the mountain.

"I wonder why he didn't come out." I said more to myself than to Boletto.

He just ignored me anyway.

"Shoot."

"What?"

"Kudu back." Boletto jabbed his finger toward the field.

No branches, twigs or bushes this time. He had fully exposed himself. I jerked the rifle butt to my shoulder and squeezed one off. The kudu switched directions nervously until he was facing the brush again. How could I have missed?

I rammed another bullet into the chamber and fired again. This time it had the desired effect. The kudu bucked, staggering downhill a few steps before crashing to the ground.

Boletto was clapping. "Good shot."

It turned out I hadn't missed the first time. There were two bullet holes in the bull, but the first had been too far forward, failing to hit a vital. Thank God the kudu hesitated before rushing into the trees or it would've been a long day and, perhaps, a depressing end to the hunt.

I don't know who was more pleased, Boletto or me. He clapped all the way there with a little spring in his step that, at times, made it look like he was skipping. When he cut out the liver and heart, held them up and said "We eat good," I knew, without a doubt, who was more pleased.

Nassos and Susan showed up at lunch to spend the last day and a half hunting with us. It was good to see them again. I'm sure Mary was overjoyed to have another woman in camp, if only for a short period. After all, regardless of society's attempt to make us all the same, men and women are different – always have been, always will be. Sure, Mary can shoot just as well as many men and, though outward appearances may not portray it, she can push herself just as hard as the rest of us. Those aren't the things that make her different though. She's more emotive, more responsive to the needs and wants of others and finds it exhaustingly more difficult to answer the call of nature in the bush. These and many other things are better received by another woman than a bunch of uncouth bulls. Sure, we try to be sympathetic, but being as different as we are, our empathy doesn't go too far.

Later that day, I was fortunate enough to take a bushbuck that had moseyed into a small clearing where we just happened to be waiting in the shadows. Mary was fortunate enough to have Susan, who knew her

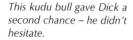

This kudu bull gave Dick a second chance – he didn't hesitate.

much less intimate than myself, but who could understand certain things far better than I could. And Boletto was fortunate enough to enjoy another couple of plates heaped with kudu liver, heart and steaks. All in all, I'd say it was a pretty fortunate day.

Last days always come with mixed emotions. We hunted in a strange silence. Not the anticipation-filled quiet of a stalk, but more of a hushed calm, unable or unwilling to express what we all felt. We hunted hard, no doubt, but the fervor of the first day had died away long ago. Anxiousness for home and a strong desire to stay snap at each other like two lions fighting for scraps. It was a long day and, at the same time, much too short.

It was the end, but, in many ways, only the beginning.

This, I think, was true for our youngest son, Joe, more than anyone else. He began this expedition glad to have time off from school. He knew next to nothing about shooting and less about big-game hunting. The last day, he dropped an oribi in its tracks and drilled a baboon between the eyes. But more important than that, his understanding of the hunt and all it entails had increased exponentially. The finality of squeezing the trigger, the intensity of the stalk, the awe, wonder and fear of the unknown, the intimacy of discovery, the camaraderie of the campfire, the insignificant barrier of language – the list is never-ending. Whether he realized it or not, these things would stay with him – become a part of him and evolve through him, as they have for Mary and me.

Dick topped off their Ethiopian hunt with this nice bushbuck. It was a good hunt.

Though none of us recognized it at the time, the gathering after dinner on our final evening held great significance.

I consider the tip at the end of the hunt one of my most important duties. The PH and his staff have worked hard to make our hunt not only enjoyable, but unforgettable. That kind of effort should be rewarded. And yet, we'd grown close to many of them. They'd become more than just the man who led us to game, the man who fetched us water, the tracker who found game we wounded and the hundreds of other tasks they perform – more than just that indeed. It's because of those things they deserve to be compensated a little something extra. You cannot put a price on memories they helped us create.

Joe knew this too – but what could he give? There were things in his possession that were easily replaceable in the U.S., but nearly impossible to come by in Ethiopia, so he began emptying his bag. The raingear he offered Hussein had the greatest effect. The small man with the eternal smile had some raingear, but it was old and leaky so he hardly ever wore it. Joe's simple gift meant more to him than anything our son could have pulled from his bag.

"Oh, thank you, thank you, ishi dishi, ishi dishi." He pumped Joe's hand before charging from the room.

He didn't return for several minutes. When he came back, he had a bouquet of flowers for Mary and a small offering for Joe – a small polished rock that obviously held some significance for him, though we never found out what.

"You come back, I be your scout – yes? If alive, I be your scout for Nassos."

We chuckled at this and said, "Ishi dishi," which had many meanings, one of which was okay. We chuckled and said ishi dishi, but we didn't know what Hussein knew.

He never made it to 1992.

"If alive, I be your scout."

The modern plague of Africa has created a continent of young faces. Our friend Hussein had not been immune to its unrelenting grip.

We were blessed to have known him.

A month later, we received a call from Nassos. He'd found Joe's nyala, just as he'd promised. They were able to salvage the horns; everything else had been devoured by scavengers.

After hanging up, I sat next to Mary on the couch. A few moments later, I turned to her.

"You know dear, I've always wanted to go to Tanzania."

Epilogue

Are we obsessed? We can't say for sure, but our love affair with Africa and our strong desire to see the world, having a little fun along the way before we leave it, is probably as close to an obsession as we've ever held. So, where did it start? Our best guess is these stories have shown that as well as we could. And though our early and humble introductions to hunting allow a glimpse into how and why we've led the lives we have, we believe it goes much deeper.

Those first desires, when we jumped at our first opportunities to head into the field or to the water, where did they come from? We believe they've always been there – a tiny seed of one of the infinite elements that make us individuals. It has grown, changed, evolved. We have shaped it, as it has shaped us. It's something we couldn't fight if we wanted to.

We look back where we started and wonder if we've really come as far as it seems. At times, we find ourselves wishing we could go back. To truly return is impossible, but that little girl and that little boy, they still exist. We encounter them sometimes – riding the swells of the ocean, climbing the heather-covered mountains of Ethiopia, tracking water buffalo in Australia, and in the eyes of our children, our grandchildren – an intimate peek at our own past and our future. If we could give the kids anything, it would be awe, wonder, innocence.

This is the beginning of a lifelong story in which two people from not-so-different, simple backgrounds, discovered together that dreams and desires are attainable and that the most complex of human emotions lie in life's simplicities.

This unquenchable thirst has led us to indescribable places of beauty and wildness found in so many places. We've found them all over the United States, in Canada, Spain, Argentina, Mexico, Mongolia, New Zealand, China, and every time we step foot in Africa. We've journeyed to Africa over 30 times, never failing to be inspired by her beauty and diversity. Our quest for mountain nyala, for instance, has taken us back to Ethiopia four times, only two of which were successful. But if we believed in giving up, Cabela's would have never made it past the first year. Who knows where we'd be now. If we let trepidation control our actions, we would've missed too much. To discover what's beyond the next hill, around the bend, across the river, below the surface and what it's really like to enter the jungle are journeys worth taking.

Yes, we've come a long way from the mountains of Wyoming and the plains of Nebraska. We often wonder how much further we could go.